*Number Five: The Centennial Series of*
*the Association of Former Students*
*Texas A&M University*

Judge Legett of Abilene

# Judge Legett
# of Abilene

## *A Texas Frontier Profile*

*By*

VERNON GLADDEN SPENCE

*Introduction by*

RUPERT NORVAL RICHARDSON

TEXAS A&M UNIVERSITY PRESS
*College Station and London*

Copyright © 1977 by Vernon Gladden Spence

Library of Congress Cataloging in Publication Data

Spence, Vernon Gladden, 1924–
    Judge Legett of Abilene.

    (The centennial series of the Association of Former
Students, Texas A & M University; no. 5)
    Bibliography: p.
    Includes index.
    1. Legett, Kirvin Kade, 1857–1926. 2. Judges—
Texas—Biography. I. Title. II. Series: Texas.
A & M University, College Station. Association of
Former Students. The centennial series of the Association
of Former Students, Texas A & M University; no. 5.
KF373.L43S66      347'.73'14' [B]      77-89508
ISBN 0-89096-041-0

*Manufactured in the United States of America*
FIRST EDITION

To the memory of
LORA BRYAN LEGETT,
her son,
KADE,
and for her daughters,
JULIA and RUTH

# Contents

# List of Illustrations

# Preface

ONE can assume that all frontier pioneers encountered some difficulty and danger in their struggles to survive, but generalizations based upon such collective experiences are timeless. Generalizations do not make history move forward, as Carl Becker has pointed out, until the historian returns in some fashion to the individual, to the "thin red line of heroes." On the other hand, a biography of Stephen F. Austin might emphasize many significant events in the early history of Texas yet scarcely mention the vast region called West Texas. A study of Judge Roy Bean might emphasize his unique experiences as a frontier magistrate but still ignore the day-to-day activities of other people who lived west of the Pecos.

Since a student of frontier history should not depend upon generalizations to show how West Texas developed, and since he should not attribute the thoughts and ideals of an Austin or a Judge Bean to all West Texans, perhaps he should seek a representative pioneer whose energies and talents epitomize the energies and talents of thousands of other pioneer settlers. Because Judge Kirvin Kade Leggett's characteristics and achievements represent a West Texas profile and because his surviving daughters, Ruth Legett Jones and Julia Legett Pickard, allowed me to research the Legett papers, I have undertaken to show through the experiences of a remarkable man the day-to-day development of a remarkable country.

The K. K. Legett papers contain an abundance of information about the judge's varied activities between 1879 and 1926, yet they reveal little about his contributions to his community, his county, or his section of Texas. As a consequence my search for other sources of information required six years and the assistance of a multitude of friends and acquaintances. During the process I accumulated obligations too numerous to express in full, but my deep gratitude requires that I should make the following brief statements.

My indebtedness to the Legett family spans three generations. K. K. Legett's granddaughter, Julia Jones Matthews, conducted a personal tour through the section of Texas which was especially familiar to Legett—from Abilene to Elmdale to Buffalo Gap and beyond—and provided other assistance as I attempted to reconstruct her grandfather's travels about the area. A great-granddaughter, Jill Matthews Wilkinson, and her husband, Stephen Wilkinson, located and reproduced several family photographs and original oil paintings which appear in the illustrations of this book.

Vernie E. Newman, professor emeritus of history at McMurry College, who for many years has been a faithful mentor and inspiration, provided help and encouragement in innumerable ways.

Katharyn Duff, author, newspaper editor, columnist, and indefatigable booster of West Texas, did everything in her power to make this project worthy of Legett and the Abilene country. She pointed directions to many good sources, and when she could not point, she took my hand and led me to such knowledgeable pioneers as Tommie and Bobbie Clack. Katharyn Duff read every chapter of the manuscript and rescued me from so many inaccuracies that I dare not make a public confession. Also in the Duff household I am indebted to Beth Duff, who caught spelling errors that Noah Webster might have overlooked.

Maude King, professor of English at Hardin-Simmons University, read every chapter (many of them more than once) and carefully scrutinized every sentence. Her selfless labor and helpful suggestions improved every page.

Rupert N. Richardson, Distinguished Professor of History, Hardin-Simmons University, guided me through the entire project and consented to write the introduction to the completed manuscript. His dedication to accuracy in theory as well as accuracy in fact kept me constantly alert to my responsibilities as a historian. Furthermore, Professor Richardson worked mightily to restructure my "Eastern style of thought and expression" into something more acceptable to West Texas readers.

A small group of West Texas pioneers who clearly remember Abilene's early years and recounted many of their personal experiences include Bobbie Blair Clack, Tommie Hazlewood Clack, Ruth Bradfield Gay, Florence and C. A. Creagh, and Clarence L. Hailey. Mr. Hailey also wrote lengthy letters that enlightened me on several of Legett's personal traits.

Henry J. Doscher, Jr., Abilene attorney and educator, helped to locate and then interpreted in layman's language various state and federal court records, and W. B. Trammell of Houston paved the way toward a speedy location of sources at Texas A&M.

Also at Texas A&M I am indebted to Robert G. Cherry, assistant to the president; Charles Schultz, university archivist; and Ernest Langford, former university archivist, for their courteous assistance while I researched the board minutes and other university records.

At Hardin-Simmons University, President Elwin L. Skiles permitted access to all records that pertained to Legett's long association with Simmons College, and Julia Jones provided efficient and friendly assistance as I hunted for materials in the rare book section. Also at Hardin-Simmons University, T. N. Carswell clarified several points related to the school's early history.

At other libraries and repositories many competent professionals assisted me in countless ways: Frances Vaughn and Ruth Hodges at the Jay-Rollins Library, McMurry College; Melvin W. Holt, Eugene M. Allen, Mrs. E. D. Fomby, Mrs. Fred Green, and Walter W. Ford, members of the Dodge-Jones Foundation staff, Abilene; Connie Chapman at the *Abilene Reporter-News*; Vincent L. Wiese in the general records section of the Federal Archives and Records Center, Fort Worth; and Shirley Glazener, Dahrl Moore, Carol Henderson, and Patrick F. McIntyre at the Fenwick Library, George Mason University, Fairfax, Virginia.

George Mason University also provided a summer research grant that enabled me to wander about Texas in 1973 and search for Legett records.

Mrs. Volney Farnsworth, Abilene, typed the original manuscript and eliminated numerous technical errors. May L. Thompson, Doris Suttlehan, and Sue Cooper provided the same efficient service on the revised manuscript at George Mason University.

At home, my mother, Ruth Gladden Spence, and my father, Vernon Lewis Spence (now deceased), offered encouragement. Kirk McKinnon, Bobbie Hull McKinnon, and Natalie White Doub lent aid and sustenance at every opportunity. My children, John Randolph, Deborah Anne, and Kevin Douglas, never complained about my constant absorption in the career of Judge Legett.

And finally my wife, Wanda Smith Spence, assisted me as always every step of the way. Without her moral support and assistance this book would not have been written.

*George Mason University*      VERNON GLADDEN SPENCE
*Fairfax, Virginia*

*From the standpoint of a West Texas lawyer,
no collection of stories of pioneer life would be
complete which omitted the rare and rich incidents connected with the part played by the
judges and lawyers in the formative period of
the country's history.*

K. K. Legett to Andy Adams
April 7, 1906

## *Introduction*

ENDING a horseback journey from Cleburne, one hundred and fifty
miles to the east, on a November day in 1879, Kirvin Kade Legett
entered the village of Buffalo Gap, then the county seat of newly
organized Taylor County. He was twenty-two years old, and his principal physical assets were a good horse and saddle and a license to
practice law earned through study and work in a lawyer's office. He
resided in the county the rest of his life, nearly half a century; if it be
said that he grew up with the country, it must be added that he helped
the country to grow up.

After a few months' law practice in Buffalo Gap, Legett realized
that Jay Gould's Texas and Pacific Railroad, building westward from
Fort Worth a mile or so a day, would miss Buffalo Gap by twelve
miles. The little county seat was doomed to remain a village, so Legett joined the railroad and cattlemen in building a new town called
Abilene. He married a ranchman's daughter, established a home in
Abilene, and for years lived in the most attractive residence in the
city.

Genial and sociable, talented at writing and speaking, K. K. Legett had the qualifications of a successful politician, but he never sought
public office. He served as presidential elector in 1884—voting for
Grover Cleveland—and he accepted an appointment as referee in
bankruptcy for the Abilene Federal District. The bankruptcy post,
which called for only a part of his time, did not pay well, but it gave
him the opportunity to aid people in trouble, the kind of work that
he loved most. To his fellow lawyers, to the public, and even to his
family he was always "Judge Legett," or "the Judge."

In addition to his law practice, Judge Legett operated a stock
farm and ranch. In this as in other vocations or avocations he found

time for public service. Through letters to newspapers, speeches and leadership in groups and organizations, he promoted farm diversification, the idea of farm and ranch people "living at home." It was a way of life that proved a boon to thousands of families during the Great Depression.

K. K. Legett was a founder of Simmons College (now Hardin-Simmons University). He wrote its charter and served on its board of trustees for a quarter-century. During much of that time he was president of the board and shared generously in carrying the burdens of the struggling school. His love of service was afforded even greater opportunity for realization when Governor S. W. T. Lanham appointed him to the Board of Directors of the Agricultural and Mechanical College of Texas. He was president of the board for four of the eight years he served, and he gave sound leadership, guidance, and aid to the institution during a critical period of its history.

Through the courtesy of his daughters who still reside in Abilene, Judge Legett's private papers were made available to Vernon Gladden Spence when he was writing the biography of another renowned West Texan, Colonel Morgan Jones, the railroad builder. Professor Spence was amazed and delighted with the depth and breadth of the collection. The methodical lawyer, businessman, and servant of others apparently had retained and preserved nearly every written item of consequence pertaining to himself and his family. By using this collection and others that were available, and with liberal use of official records and newspapers, Spence has related Legett's life story with a completeness that is truly gratifying.

Spence realized that Judge Legett was a pioneer and a man of stature, that his life story is to a great extent an epitome of the history of his section of Texas. Knowing, furthermore, that in order to have a full meaning an individual's experiences must be related to an adequate background, the biographer has supplied a great deal of interesting and significant history. This book is the story of a Texan of stature. It merits a wide audience.

*Hardin-Simmons University*                RUPERT NORVAL RICHARDSON
*Abilene, Texas*

Judge Legett of Abilene

*This is not a land of legend and story, nor is it a land of poetry and song, and yet its history is not sterile and barren.*

CHAPTER ONE

# Westward—to the Callahan Divide

THE Civil War did not directly touch the Kirvin Kade Legett family of Monticello, Arkansas, but like most southerners, they did not find the 1860s prosperous years. Plagued with chronic asthma, Legett had to support his family of ten with only the assistance of his three small sons as farm hands.[1] In 1869, Kirvin Kade, Sr. (his seventh child was eleven-year-old Kirvin Kade, Jr.), made an inspection trip through Texas to seek new and better farmland. With his wife, Mintie Berry Legett, and several of his oldest children, he traveled in a covered wagon and visited wide areas of North, East, and South Texas. Later that year the family moved to a farm near a small village named Red River City in Grayson County and just south of the Red River in North Texas.[2]

It was typical of the Legett family, and of migrants in general, that they moved in a westerly direction. John Legett, Kirvin Kade's father —and the first native-born American citizen in his branch of the Legett family—had moved in 1823 from the original home on the

[1] Information concerning the early generations of Legetts is from the Legett Family Records, held by Mrs. Ruth Legett Jones, Abilene, Texas. Kirvin Kade Legett's children and their birthdates were: Valencia Ann, October 4, 1843; Eliza Virginia, April 16, 1845; Mary Luisa, February 19, 1848; Susan Berryman, April 21, 1850; Nancy Elzara, April 7, 1852; Thomas Riley, December 12, 1854; Kirvin Kade, Junior, November 6, 1857; and John Berry, February 19, 1860. Genealogical compilation by K. B. Legett (in Legett Family Records, file 5, paper 3).

[2] Genealogical compilation entitled "Legett Family Record," author unknown, addressed to K. B. Legett, Hereford Lake, Legett Family Records, file 4, paper 1; undated newspaper article from the *Denison* (Texas) *Gazetteer*, in Julia Legett Pickard scrapbook, Legett Family Records, file 5, paper 6.

Cape Fear River in southeastern North Carolina to Hardeman County, Tennessee.[3] He moved again in 1832 to Choctaw County, Mississippi. In 1842 young Kirvin Kade and his bride moved from Mississippi to Monticello, Arkansas. When, in 1869, they decided to move again, it apparently did not occur to Kirvin Kade that they should migrate in any other direction but west.

Grayson County, Texas, had prospered for a decade, partly because of its location near the Texas route of the Butterfield Overland Stage Line that operated between St. Louis and San Francisco. Upon his arrival in 1869, Legett discovered that he had moved his family almost directly into the path of another transportation system—the Missouri, Kansas, and Texas Railroad. The Red River City folk eventually moved nearer to the proposed railroad route, and their cluster of homes developed into a terminal town for the MK&T. In 1873 they incorporated the town and named it Denison.

The little railroad center soon degenerated into a far more violent and disorderly place than Legett and his neighbors had anticipated. After the rails arrived, outlaws soon outnumbered the farmer-citizens and quickly placed their rowdy imprint on the town's image.[4] This crude environment disturbed the family men in town, but it provided much excitement for such young boys as Kirvin Kade, Jr. In time the teenager sought odd jobs to help his father support the family, and eventually "Governor" Owings hired him. In spite of his pretentious title, Owings was in fact mayor of the rambunctious little town.

For several years young Legett worked as a general handyman around Owings' stables, and he learned far more on that job than how to care for horses. As time passed the stables became the gathering place for the town's loiterers, job seekers, visitors, businessmen, and anyone else who had reason to see the mayor. Eventually Legett knew most of the citizens of the town. This was his first sustained contact with people of diverse social and economic backgrounds, and he learned to deal successfully with all of them. The "long-legged,

---

[3] Genealogical compilation entitled "Legett Family Record," Legett Family Records, file 4, paper 1.

[4] Rupert Norval Richardson and Carl Coke Rister, *The Greater Southwest*, p. 397.

white-haired" young man quickly won the respect and confidence of an assortment of men many years his senior.[5]

Young Legett's parents grew dissatisfied as their quiet country village turned into a raw, crude railroad town. In 1875, therefore, they decided to seek a more civilized environment for their family, and before the year ended they moved to a new farm near Alvarado in Johnson County. Their new home was, as usual, farther west—about fifty miles—and more than one hundred miles south of Denison.

Kirvin Kade at age seventeen had completed whatever public education Denison provided. Now, more than anything else, he wanted to study law, and, as soon as his family had settled in Johnson County, he investigated the possibilities. Before many weeks passed, he arranged to do the general office chores for a Cleburne attorney in exchange for the opportunity to study the attorney's law books. His natural intelligence and talents quickly emerged, and within four years he had schooled himself sufficiently in the law, without benefit of law school, to pass the bar examination, secure a license, and practice law in the state of Texas.[6] By harvest time in early November, he had decided to begin his practice in a little West Texas town named Buffalo Gap in Taylor County. Buffalo Gap was located approximately one hundred and fifty miles due west of Cleburne. It was, in 1879, frontier country.

Kirvin Kade Legett left no record to explain why he moved beyond the line of frontier settlement, but there were many good reasons why Buffalo Gap would seem attractive to him. Just the year before, in 1878, Taylor County was organized, and Buffalo Gap, the only town in the county, inherited the county seat. Legett probably drew upon his own experiences and observations in Cleburne and reasoned that opportunities for legal work in a new county seat should equalize his competition. The young lawyer also could have heard that the Texas and Pacific Railway Company was at that moment arranging to extend its tracks through West Texas. A careful study of the territory west of Fort Worth strongly indicated that the Texas and Pacific rails

5 Undated newspaper article from *Denison* (Texas) *Gazetter*, Julia Legett Pickard scrapbook, Legett Family Records, file 5, paper 6.

6 T. S. Rollins, comp., *Taylor County: An Early History of Pioneer Settlers.*

would pass through Buffalo Gap. As both a county seat and a railroad terminal, Buffalo Gap promised to grow as rapidly as Denison, but Legett was shrewd enough to surmise that competition from more experienced and more formally educated attorneys would not be as intense in the growing town as in the more settled areas of the state. So, like his father and grandfather, Legett looked only to the west when he sought a new home.

Whatever his reasons, Kirvin Kade Legett, Jr., with his meager savings, bought a good horse and a new suit, rolled his new license to practice with his other scant belongings, and headed for a new life at Buffalo Gap, Taylor County, Texas. He departed his parents' Alvarado home on November 7, 1879, just one day after his twenty-second birthday.[7] Perhaps to emphasize the conclusion of one era of his life and the beginning of another, he shortened his Christian names to initials, dropped the designate *Junior*, and from that day onward was K. K. Legett.

The young attorney stood exactly six feet tall, and he was handsome in the sense that his facial features were evenly proportioned and uniform. His eyes were blue and his hair, once "cotton white," was dark brown. Unlike most youths of that day, he was clean shaven. Also unlike them, he kept his straight, thick, unusually coarse hair cut in a short razor trim which fell into a natural part on the left side.

Those who knew him said that he was a good listener whose steady, direct gaze complimented the speaker and invited confidence; consequently, men much older than Legett confided in him and sought his advice. He had the self-confidence, without the arrogance, of a young man who had matured early and had accepted responsibility readily. Legett's intimate friends claimed that he had a quick sense of humor, a ready wit, and an ability to laugh at himself, although a quiet dignity usually concealed these personal qualities. In public, he rarely displayed traits of stress or strain. When he believed the occasion called for it, however, he could deliver a sharp reproof which was sometimes vexatious and sometimes humorous, depending upon the impression he sought at the moment.[8]

At twenty-two, K. K. Legett was proud, perceptive, ambitious, and resolute. In November, 1879, he expressed no embarrassment

[7] Ibid.
[8] C. L. Hailey to the author, n.d., mailed November 22, 1976.

because of his straitened economic circumstance, but his actions prove that he was unwilling to accept it as a permanent way of life. Years later, when these personality traits had molded into character and principle, an old friend portrayed him as a "clear-eyed dreamer" and a "thinker who drives things through."[9] His associates described him as a self-made man, which meant in the nineteenth century that he was self-trained and highly successful in his profession without benefit of significant formal education.

Buffalo Gap, an isolated frontier village with great potential as a cattle and railroad center, fitted Legett's desire to embark upon a new life style. He abandoned the slow and measured pace of his early childhood in antebellum Arkansas, he turned his back to the traumatic disruptions caused by the Civil War, and he ignored the confusion and recrimination of the postwar years. He responded instead to the excitement of the frontier environment, where railroads brought in their wake a strange, crude, boisterous people whose talents and ambitions fascinated him.

Texas belonged to two divergent worlds: the Old South, which Legett remembered from his childhood, and the New West, with which he had recently become familiar. Whether he should involve himself in the emotional residue of the war and Reconstruction periods or direct his energies toward more constructive goals evidently posed no problem for K. K. Legett. He would go west and "grow up with the country." His decision was not unusual in 1879. Since the end of the war, the West Texas frontier had attracted a large number of dissimilar people. As desolate as it seemed to many who passed that way, the treeless interior prairies appealed to such sundry people as Texas Rangers, federal soldiers, Comanches, Apaches, Kiowas, buffalo hunters, bone collectors, range cattlemen, railroad builders, rogues, and farmers.

Legett's trail to West Texas would take him near the old Butterfield Overland Mail Line (Southern Overland) north of Buffalo Gap. The famous transcontinental stage passed Legett's boyhood home in

[9] From an original poem, "The Thinker," written on February 4, 1916, by J. M. Radford and dedicated to K. K. Legett. Other personality and character sketches on this and other pages are selected from an aggregate of characterizations by newspapermen who seemed fascinated by his personality, by educators, politicians, and church leaders who introduced him to many audiences, by his daughters, and by such friends as Tommie and Bobbie Clack and Mr. and Mrs. C. L. Hailey.

Denison and then followed a southwesterly course to El Paso. That portion of the line made up the Texas section of the St. Louis–to–San Francisco mail and passenger service for which the United States government had contracted in 1858. The Texas route paralleled in a general way the old Marcy Trail that Captain Randolph B. Marcy blazed and logged in 1849 for the United States army. A series of forts built shortly thereafter provided some protection from the bands of Comanche marauders who wandered through all areas of West Texas.

The route of the Butterfield Trail between old (and abandoned) Fort Phantom Hill and Fort Chadbourne bisected Taylor County from its northeastern to its southwestern corner. As the trail crossed Taylor County, it meandered through a chain of small mountains which stretched east and west through the central and southern portions of Callahan, Taylor, and Nolan counties. Collectively, these low-lying mountains were called the Callahan Divide. In Taylor County, three principal gaps—Cedar Gap, Buffalo Gap, and Mountain Pass—intersected the Callahan Divide. Legett's destination was a small town located in the second of those gaps where for many years buffalo herds made their way through the mountains as they moved from the southern to the northern grasslands. The town emerged when the first buffalo hunters and bone collectors visited the area, built a small cluster of dugouts in the hills, and eventually prevailed upon Abe Hunter to bring in a stock of groceries from Fort Worth and open a store.

These were not the first permanent settlers to move beyond the ninety-eighth meridian, but they were part of the first wave that followed the Civil War. Before the war, immigrants had moved onto the lower western-plains region of West Texas in the wake of a string of army forts. When the government abandoned the forts, however, Comanche raids threatened to annihilate the westernmost settlements. The raids continued during the war and, to the great consternation of the settlers, increased in frequency and viciousness during the latter half of the 1860s. As a consequence, the line of frontier settlement in some areas of West Texas receded more than one hundred miles. In East Texas general economic conditions slowly improved during the 1870s, and ultimately that prosperity affected the frontier. Many cotton farmers in the eastern counties adopted the sharecrop system, and immigrants who came to farm learned that cotton would thrive on the rich uplands of North Texas. Simultaneously ranchers moved their Longhorn cattle onto the West Texas open range just as buffalo hunters extinguished the last of the southern herds.

Railroad construction, particularly in North and East Texas, also reflected the state's improved economic condition. Inevitably eastern prosperity helped to reverse the receding frontier line of settlement, and by the late 1870s ranchers and farmers challenged one another for land on both sides of the ninety-eighth meridian. They were a part of no organized movement of settlers, but all seemed obsessed by a common goal to "grow up with the country."

The West Texas area around Buffalo Gap was predominantly devoted to the cattle industry. A few ranchers operated in the immediate vicinity, while other cattlemen brought their Longhorns up from the southern ranges, guided them through several gaps in the Callahan Divide, crossed the northern ranges, and ultimately loaded the herds into railroad cars at the Kansas railheads. This era of the long drive would end when the tracks of other transcontinental railroads crossed the cattle trails south of Kansas. K. K. Legett apparently was convinced that the little town of Buffalo Gap would become a significant rail center for cattle shipments to northern markets just as soon as the Texas and Pacific rails stretched across West Texas.

Legett's westward journey commenced approximately one hundred and fifty miles due east of Buffalo Gap. The gently rolling hills of the Grand Prairie region offered few obstacles to a traveler on horseback, and the first short leg of his trip, from Alvarado to Cleburne, was familiar to him. He remained for two days at Cleburne, where he had studied law books for the past four years. During the brief visit he saw friends and business acquaintances, requested letters of recommendation from former law associates, and learned what he could from those who knew the routes to Buffalo Gap. On the morning of November 9 he departed Cleburne.[10]

Legett followed a trail that roughly paralleled the northern boundary of a line of counties that stretched due west to the Texas–New Mexico border. Immigrants before him had made the trail fairly distinct in that area, but as the trail moved westward its direction dimmed

[10] Rollins, *Taylor County*.

and the number of settlers' homes decreased. The Brazos River valley, near the center of Hood County, represented to East Texas immigrants a major dividing line between familiar and unfamiliar territory. Indians had not troubled travelers in that area for several years, but all along the West Texas frontier horse thieves, stage robbers, and other highwaymen were so numerous that Governor Oran M. Roberts had expressed his concern earlier that year in his annual report to the Texas legislators. Stage robberies were so frequent that lone travelers preferred not to follow such familiar routes as the old Butterfield Trail. Legett realized that no route was entirely safe, and tales gleaned from his Cleburne friends made him a cautious and alert traveler. He had sought to reduce the danger by investing virtually his last dollar in a "fine-blooded and speedy horse."[11]

West of the Brazos River, Legett's trail entered the Cross Timbers region, a huge grassland with contrasting areas of soils, shrubs, trees, and grasses. The trail then led to a belt of deep sandy loam where sturdy post oaks prevailed. Beyond lay a stretch of prairie, broken here and there by mesquite and live oak trees, its rich, black soil covered with a carpet of grama and mesquite grasses. Deer, antelope, jack rabbits, wolves, and coyotes occupied the country.

The valleys deepened in the direction of Erath County. Traces of the Chisholm Trail, which in its early years had contributed so significantly to the Texas cattle boom, still marked the area. Since the first year after Appomattox, when a Texas steer brought $38.40 in Kansas and $86.00 in Massachusetts, more and more cattle trails crossed Texas enroute to the northern railheads. Texas cowboys drove north a total of 260,000 cattle in 1866, and within four years they delivered a million and a half Longhorns to Abilene, Kansas. In 1879, as Legett rode toward Buffalo Gap, hundreds of thousands of Texas cattle still filled the stockpens at Dodge City, Caldwell, and Hunnewell, Kansas.

In Eastland County the trail reached the western edge of the Cross Timbers region. The trees diminished in size and the soil was increasingly sandy. The high hills and deep valleys in the eastern part of the county changed briefly to gently rolling plains but once again grew more rugged near the county's western boundary. Sandy-soil

[11] Mary Hampton Clack, *Early Days in West Texas*, p. 14; Rupert Norval Richardson, *Texas: The Lone Star State*, p. 233; Rollins, *Taylor County*.

cedars disappeared almost entirely and the oaks shrank to the size of shrubbery. Later Legett would learn to call this collection of stunted oaks "the shinnery." Grass grew abundantly in that area, but never as tall as in the eastern regions.

As the elevation rose toward Callahan County, the sun became brighter, the air drier, the colors more faded, and the wind more constant. Near the western limits of Callahan County, high, broad, sandy flats, covered by short grass and mesquite trees, dominated the area. Occasionally a gnarled and knotted live oak stood in isolation. One could look for a dozen miles in any direction without spotting a house or any type of human shelter.

In 1879 Taylor County did not appear particularly inviting to a stranger approaching from the east; it was nothing more than a broad, flat plateau almost entirely without trees. Someone back home had warned Legett that West Texas was fit for only the red man and the buffalo. He hoped his informant was wrong, but he could not challenge the claim that West Texas had plenty of room for everybody. There was nothing within his first view of Taylor County to suggest civilization—not "a living, breathing creature in sight."[12] To the left of Legett's trail and approximately twelve miles south appeared the first faint outline of low mountains. They were the Callahan Divide. Nestled at the entrance to one of the mountain gaps lay Legett's destination, Buffalo Gap.

[12] Rollins, *Taylor County.*

*I was advised by the sheriff that she was mak-
ing serious threats against me, and soon after
that she dropped into the office. . . . I saw what
I felt sure was the bulk of a six-shooter concealed in her bosom.*

CHAPTER TWO

# Buffalo Gap, West Texas

TREES along the creeks of the Callahan Divide seemed unusually large
to travelers who approached them from a north-by-northeast direction.
The tight, red-colored alluvial soil and the mountain streams nurtured
an abundance of mesquite trees and scattered clusters of live oak. The
chain of well-defined, flat-topped mountains provided a dramatic back-
drop for the level unbroken land to the north. From a distance, there
was no visible break in the Callahan Divide, but Cedar Creek flowed
northward from its headwaters in the hills, then through Cedar Gap,
and finally emptied into Big Elm Creek. Big Elm was a tributary of the
Clear Fork of the Brazos and flowed through the divide's second
major gap, where lay the town of Buffalo Gap.

The mountains rose four or five hundred feet above the level
plain. They had concave sides at most points and only occasionally
bulged outward to form lower foothills. From a distance, the moun-
tainsides seemed to rise almost perpendicularly to a distinctly formed
top ledge (which K. K. Legett soon learned to call cap rock). From
a closer view the mountains were rough-edged and made up principally of white, loose limestone and dotted with numerous scrub cedars and mountain oaks.

The gap Legett sought was a natural pass through which millions
of buffalo had instinctively made their way from the feeding grounds
of the Colorado River to the watershed of the Brazos and through
which, more recently, thousands of South Texas Longhorn cattle had
made their way to Kansas. The pass was a mile or more wide and was
bordered on either side by high, cedar-covered peaks. Along Big Elm
the live oak and mesquite trees were enormous.

The village was in the exact center of the pass, and Big Elm Creek flowed along the town's western edge. The huge trees along the banks cast deep shadows that contrasted sharply with the white glare of sunlight glancing off the limestone hills nearby. Unusually heavy and frequent rains since 1876 had kept Elm Creek—normally dry during the fall months—full of water for several miles beyond the town.[1] On such misleading evidence Legett decided that the country was suitable for farming, but he learned not to express such sentiments around local ranchers. The farmer was not always looked upon as the rancher's natural antagonist on the frontier, but, in the Taylor County area during the 1870s and 1880s, few cattlemen owned the land they used and thus did not welcome farmers to the area. The few farmers who had moved into the area from the east had greatly disturbed the cattlemen, who preached that the area was exclusively cattle country.[2] The unusual quantities of moisture over the past three years seemed to make liars of them. The farmers scoffed at the tales of droughts and scorching winds and tried to ignore the exaggerated stories of Indian massacres in which women and children were the favorite targets. No rancher in the area hesitated to tell in gory detail how a bunch of Indians down on Jim Ned Creek killed a Mrs. Williams, then took her seven-year-old daughter and left her to die hanging from a tree a hundred miles away in the Double Mountain Fork of the Brazos River. Cattlemen tried not to mention that this atrocity occurred in 1873 and that there had not been an Indian raid of any sort since 1875. Still the efforts of the cattlemen failed, for the pioneer farmers came on in their covered wagons, drawn by a horse or two, followed by children of all sizes, and inevitably accompanied by a milk cow and a nondescript yellow-orange dog.[3]

Nature was particularly generous during those first years of heavy

---

[1] William Slaughter to *Abilene Daily Reporter*, March 28, 1905. Precipitation diminished during 1879–1880, however, and Elm Creek went dry early in January 1880 and remained that way until spring. For a broader view of drought conditions at that time see W. C. Holden, "West Texas Droughts," *Southwestern Historical Quarterly* 32 (October, 1928): 103–123.

[2] See Wayne Gard, "The Fence-Cutters," *Southwestern Historical Quarterly* 51 (July, 1947): 1–15; and R. D. Holt, "The Introduction of Barbed Wire into Texas and the Fence Cutting War," *West Texas Historical Association Year Book* 6 (June, 1930): 65–79.

[3] See *Abilene Daily Reporter*, January 13, 1924; T. S. Rollins, comp., *Taylor County: An Early History of Pioneer Settlers*.

precipitation. William Dunn, the first farmer to arrive, came to Taylor County in 1876 and raised a good grade of corn that same year. In 1877 he raised a variety of other feed crops in spite of an unusually late frost on June 10, and John E. Seaton was equally successful that year near Lytle Gap. Dunn repeated his successes during 1878 and 1879 in spite of unfriendly warnings from irate cattlemen. Word continued to spread as S. E. Friend raised a good corn crop in 1879 and P. T. Hurt grew several acres of millet that he claimed was head high. His experimental patch of sorghum also flourished. All of the first Taylor County farmers successfully raised garden truck during 1876–1879. They were pleased by the rainfall, and there were very few bugs to "eat us up."[4]

The first settlers who made permanent homes in the area, however, were neither farmers nor cattlemen. They were buffalo hunters who made winter camp in the gaps of the Callahan Divide in the early 1870s and from there trekked with their hides into Fort Griffin, the nearest trading center.[5] Temporary homes in the area dated back into the late 1860s when C. W. Merchant, Sam Gholson, William E. Cureton, and others wintered their cattle at the headwaters of Big Elm Creek, just above the gap. But it was not until 1874 that ranch headquarters were established on a continuing basis near Buffalo Gap's eventual location. During that year M. C. Lambeth, with two stockmen identified as J. W. Carter and Dock Grounds, brought 3,700 head of cattle from Shackelford County and established the Y–Y (Y bar Y) Ranch in Mulberry Canyon northwest of Buffalo Gap.[6] Their "permanent" homes were trenches dug in the level plain, topped with cedar posts and covered with weeds. During 1875 other pioneers moved in and constructed dugouts and cabins. The following year cattlemen brought their herds through the gap enroute to Fort Griffin, which was on the main branch of the Western Trail to the railroad at Dodge City, Kansas.

The immense buffalo herds disappeared as rapidly as the cattle

[4] Slaughter to *Reporter*, March 28, 1905.

[5] An eye witness description appears in Tommie Clack, "Buffalo Gap College," *West Texas Historical Association Year Book* 35 (October, 1959): 133. For a definitive study of the buffalo hunter see Wayne Gard, *The Great Buffalo Hunt*.

[6] Rollins, *Taylor County*; see also Katharyn Duff, *Abilene . . . on Catclaw Creek*, p. 33.

herds increased. In 1877, when hunters slaughtered a herd of several hundred buffalo in the gap, the era of the buffalo hunt ended in central West Texas. A few of the hunters remained for several years as bone collectors. They gathered the sun-bleached bones, piled them into enormous stacks, and sold them to eastern fertilizer manufacturers at prices which ranged from $8 to $22 per ton.[7]

The year that marked the end of the buffalo hunt marked also the year of the first frame house built in Buffalo Gap. Lumber was brought from Fort Worth, more than one hundred and fifty miles to the east, and priced at $3.90 per hundred pounds.[8] With several permanent settlers at home in their dugouts, cabins, and frame homes, and with buffalo hunters, bone collectors, cattlemen, and farmers moving in or passing through the county, the settlement was well on its way toward development. Abe Hunter's small stack of retail groceries, which he sold from his one-room dugout called by his customers the Dead Fall, soon failed to meet local demands for household items. Consequently, two merchants named Wiley and Davis opened a general store and soon thereafter Rodney Knight opened a second one. The little cluster of stores and homes took the name of the gap in which it was located, and Buffalo Gap rapidly developed into "headquarters" for pioneers in Taylor and neighboring counties.

Approximately thirty men resided in the town early in 1877. Later that year the town secured a mail and passenger line and the state of Texas located a post office in a one-room frame house. By the end of 1877 the permanent population of the village numbered more than one hundred. Throughout 1878 Buffalo Gap suffered the traumas of constant change and growth. Gamblers, gunmen, and other unsavory frontier characters joined and mixed with the original settlers. To the consternation of some and the delight of others, Buffalo Gap developed into a typically raw frontier town with very few trappings of civilized law and order to restrain the newcomers. Local law was needed at once, but first local government had to be established.

An act of the Texas legislature on February 1, 1858, had separated Taylor County from the Bexar and Travis land districts, but

[7] Michael Bonine, "Buffalo Gap, the Living Ghost Town," *Junior Historian* 20 (September, 1959): 1. The article was written under my direction and based entirely upon early issues of the *Buffalo Gap News*. See also Gard, *Great Buffalo Hunt*.

[8] Bonine, "Buffalo Gap," p. 1.

for twenty years the county remained unorganized. For all legal purposes, Taylor County was attached to Eastland County. Its boundary lines embraced nine hundred square miles (576,000 acres), and the county shared boundary lines with Jones County on the north, with Callahan County on the east, with Coleman, Runnels, and Coke counties on the south, and with Nolan County on the West.[9]

In the spring of 1878 the scattered settlers in Taylor County called an election for organizational purposes and agreed to vote on July 3, 1878. They placed four voting boxes about the county: one at Buffalo Gap; one at a small settlement on Jim Ned Creek in the southeast corner of the county; another on Bluff Creek in the southwest corner; and a fourth at Altman's ranch, approximately eight miles north of Buffalo Gap. Men came on horseback from as far away as J. N. Simpson's ranch in the northeast corner of the county, from the Tobe Odon ranch and the Roberts ranch near Phantom Hill, and the Dunn ranch southward near Jim Ned. They cast eighty-seven votes to fill nineteen county offices.[10] Several weeks later the commissioners asked Governor Richard B. Hubbard to designate Buffalo Gap as the temporary county seat and to set an election date on which voters could determine the permanent site. On August 8 Governor Hubbard granted the request, but there is no official record that the special election was ever held. With no challenge to Buffalo Gap's initial selection, the scattered settlers in Taylor County probably did not bother to reassert an established fact.

When K. K. Legett reached Buffalo Gap on November 12, 1879, the town's legal history was less than two years old, its population ranged between four and five hundred, it had not suffered an Indian raid in almost four years, wire fences pushed its open range cattlemen farther west, and its ranchers and farmers eyed one another suspiciously while they pondered the future economic development around the Callahan Divide. As the population expanded and the society grew more complex, the need for legal aid increased. The farm-

[9] *Texas Almanac and State Industrial Guide for 1970–1971*, p. 339 (hereinafter referred to as *Texas Almanac 1970–1971*).

[10] The first officers of Taylor County included the following: J. W. Drury, county judge; W. C. Isaacs, district clerk; M. C. Lambeth, county clerk; J. W. Carter, sheriff and tax collector; A. Whitehurst, assessor; C. P. Gamble, county treasurer; A. M. Hunter, W. H. Lowell, and J. W. Holliday, county commissioners (from Rollins, *Taylor County*).

ers and ranchers sought "honest lawyers" at all hours of the day and night as they closed out land sales, tracked down cattle rustlers, and dealt with drunken cowboys. A favorite prank of the cowboys was to shoot out candles and lamps as more sober citizens tried to read.

As Legett neared the small frontier town, still half hidden in the gap, the bustle of activity reminded him of a beehive, and from that day he claimed that he heard Buffalo Gap before he saw it.[11] The village was built around a public square, and in the center of the square men's high-pitched voices mingled with the sounds of hammers and saws, wagon wheels, and horses' hooves. By the end of the year only three vacant lots remained on the entire square; all other lots were occupied either by finished buildings, buildings under construction, or piles of new lumber awaiting the hands of a frontier carpenter.[12] A few private homes were interspersed with business houses, and almost all were built in the same A-frame style. Only the rectangular false-fronts with their crudely lettered advertisements distinguished the business establishments from the homes.

The courthouse-jail, although only half completed when Legett arrived, dominated the square. The county commissioners had levied a courthouse and jail tax of twenty-five cents on the $100 property evaluation in order to pay for the structure. The square, sturdy-looking building was made of large red sandstone blocks mortared together with cannon balls. It replaced the original courthouse built of cedar logs, covered with boards, and located next door to the Alamo saloon. There were approximately twenty-five business firms, including dry goods stores, grocery stores, two banks, a blacksmith shop, two butcher shops, five saloons, an undertaking establishment, a livery stable, a hotel and several boarding houses.[13]

Legett spent his first night in Buffalo Gap at the Buffalo Gap Hotel—one of the few two-story business buildings in town. Although it was the largest frame building on the square, it contained only three rooms: a large front room on the ground floor which served as both lobby and dining room, a smaller back room which

[11] Rollins, *Taylor County.*
[12] Ibid.
[13] *Abilene Daily Reporter,* July 14, 1922; *Buffalo Gap News,* May 6, 1880, reprinted in *Abilene Daily Reporter,* May 10, 1904. See also Rollins, *Taylor County.* The original courthouse still stands as the Ernie Wilson Museum.

was the kitchen, and the dormitory-style bedroom above. The entire top floor was one long rectangular room with beds lined along the walls. Obviously, the female owner did not expect to accommodate female guests. At the far end were three wash stands, each with a water pitcher, a wash bowl, and a mirror. The hotel's owner and operator, Mrs. Fannie Hamrick, had moved from Warren County, Tennessee, to Buffalo Gap earlier that year. Her rates were twenty-five cents per meal and twenty-five cents per bed.[14] A handmade sign above the door announced the best meals of any hotel in West Texas, but there was little opportunity for comparison.

On the east side of the square was the establishment of D. W. Wristen, a jovial fellow from Parker County. He originally had dealt only in the purchase of buffalo hides but had added a line of mixed goods when the buffalo virtually vanished from the area. The Smith & Steffens Company was located next door to Wristen. From the outset the two partners had combined banking with store-keeping. They had moved from Brown County and stocked their general store with groceries, dry goods, and ranch supplies.

Near the northeast corner of the square, J. V. Cunningham operated a blacksmith and wood shop. Near the same corner, "under the tinkling music of the bell," the Holly & Collins saloon advertised that its owners were in business "to Keep the Spirits of Our People Up." Other businessmen on the square included M. W. Northington, who was in general merchandising, and J. C. Davis, who was both postmaster and groceryman. The Alamo was the oldest of Buffalo Gap's saloons.[15]

The county assessor, A. Whitehurst, announced a few months after Legett's arrival that Taylor County's population approached six hundred, that Buffalo Gap had almost five hundred inhabitants (a 500 percent increase over the previous year), that Buffalo Gap was located within three miles of the geographic center of the county, that town lots were selling at $75.00 to $100.00 each, and that lands in the county were selling at fifty cents to $3.00 per acre. The grocers

---

[14] Mrs. Hamrick enlarged the building, ran the same hotel for thirty years, and never raised her rates. She eventually earned her claim to serving the best meals in West Texas and upon her retirement owned substantial farm land in Taylor County (*Abilene Daily Reporter*, July 14, 1922).

[15] Rollins, *Taylor County*.

advertised Rio coffee at nineteen cents per pound, beans at seven cents per pound, kerosene oil at fifty cents per gallon, flour at $5.50 per sack, and hams at eight cents per pound.[16]

Every Buffalo Gap businessman wanted to "swap lies" about the Texas and Pacific Railroad. When new arrivals such as Legett admitted they knew little or nothing about the T&P plans to build west, they were obliged to listen to lengthy assurances that Buffalo Gap would indeed get a railroad. The latest word was always that the rails would come "right spat through town." If the T&P was going from Fort Worth to El Paso, then it couldn't miss Buffalo Gap! Another news item that interested local folks—apparently because it was a Taylor County first—was that N. N. Brown, down along Jim Ned Creek, "was putting several hundred acres of land under fence."[17]

Legett found the Buffalo Gap people friendly, and he always remembered their warm welcome, but his clearest recollection of his arrival concerned his first night at the Buffalo Gap Hotel. To his dismay, he found that the bedbugs were no less energetic than the people he had met. After much bloodletting, none of the guests could sleep. "So we sat up all night," he explained, "and made fun of one fellow over in the corner, who didn't seem disturbed by the tormentors which kept us awake. He just lay motionless all night and we had lots of fun at his expense." The next morning, shivering with cold, the men went downstairs and warmed themselves around the stove. Suddenly someone rushed down and announced that there was a dead man in one of the beds. "We had spent the night ridiculing a poor fellow who had passed beyond the petty annoyances of this world," Legett ruefully admitted.[18]

The newcomer sought other accommodations for his second night in Buffalo Gap, but there was not an empty bed in town. As a last resort, D. W. Wristen, the "jolly merchant," allowed him to make a pallet on the floor in the rear of his store. The pallet proved to be more comfortable, Legett later remembered, but the all-night poker game in the same room denied him a second night's sleep.[19]

[16] *Buffalo Gap News*, May 6, 1880, reprinted in *Abilene Daily Reporter*, May 10, 1904.

[17] Ibid.

[18] Rollins, *Taylor County*.

[19] *Abilene Daily Reporter*, September 23, 1909.

He engaged a semiprivate room at Mr. and Mrs. Wiley's board-
inghouse near the public square. The Wileys served meals to their
guests and to other men who used their own wagons as beds. Legett
secured the room through the assistance of G. A. Kirkland, a young
attorney who had moved to town a year earlier. Kirkland had previously shared the room with another lawyer, Don B. Corley, from
Eastland County, who had vacated his half of the room earlier that
same day. According to Kirkland's description, the quarters were
"comfortable . . . , convenient to the public square, clean . . . , and
of nice appearance." The room had a fireplace at one end, and on
either side each young lawyer had his own bed, a desk, a chair, and
a wash stand. "At night," according to Kirkland, "I can sit at my
desk & write or read & toast my shins all at the same time." The
house was built of "hewn logs (not pickets), painted and whitewashed." [20] Legett presumably enjoyed the same comparative comfort and appreciated it more after his sleepless nights on the square.

More than a dozen lawyers had arrived in Buffalo Gap ahead of
Legett. In addition to his new friend and benefactor, G. A. Kirkland, the others included Hal Fisher, Frank Hamilton, M. A. Spoonts,
J. S. Porter, Luke Matthews, John W. Murray, Burl Aycock, John A.
Nabors, and Don B. Corley. Because of the critical lack of space,
most of those enterprising lawyers converted their rented bedrooms
into daytime offices. But in spite of what seemed on first sight an
overabundance of lawyers, the bustling town generated enough legal
confrontations to require professional assistance from each of them.
During the town's early history, thefts and murders made up most of
the criminal cases, and land title disputes predominated the civil cases.

West Texas was a country so new that it had little real history of
its own, and Buffalo Gap's pioneer settlers rarely talked about such
relatively recent historical events as Goliad, San Jacinto, or the Alamo.
Most settlers talked, instead, about their own experiences—which
was the only history many of them knew. To such pioneers, Taylor
County's first Fourth of July celebration, in 1878, was an historic
event. There was no public speaker, but the announcement that there
would be a barbecue on Jim Ned Flat brought men, women, and

[20] G. A. Kirkland to Stribling, November 29, 1878, Katharyn Duff Collection,
Abilene Reporter-News Building, Abilene, Texas. Copy in Legett Family Records,
file 6, paper 11.

children on horseback and in wagons from a hundred miles away. Trouble flared between two cowboys before the first meal was served, and, like magic, guns and six-shooters appeared in the hands of every man present. Jim Carter, the newly elected sheriff, proved his mettle when he told the boys that he liked to fight as well as anybody, but since they did not come for that purpose, they must fight at another time and place.[21]

Even the Civil War was likely to be viewed by pioneers from the local standpoint. Thus, the first wave of settlers labeled an Indian incident in 1862 the "Battle of Buffalo Gap" only because it occurred during the war and involved a dozen soldiers. Under Captain Jack Wright, the small company from Camp Colorado spotted a band of Indians and followed them into the mountains at Cedar Gap. Before the day ended, the two parties engaged in three desperate struggles. In the first encounter, the Indians captured the soldiers' pack mules, and, during a lull in the fighting, the "copper-faced criminals" beat frying pans against rocks and thoroughly provoked the soldiers. The outraged men attacked a second time, but again both groups tired before victory was won. After another brief rest on opposite sides of Cedar Mountain, each made a third desperate charge against the other in hand-to-hand combat. Finally, exhaustion or painful injury immobilized every survivor. They lay only a few yards apart and awaited the cover of darkness. Neither challenged the other as each survivor went for water at the same nearby spring.[22]

When reinforcements arrived from Camp Colorado the following morning, the soldiers found that nine of the twelve Indians had been buried during the night and three survivors had escaped. They found evidence, also, that at least one of the survivors was injured. Among the soldiers, three were "gravely injured" and three others, including Captain Jack Wright, suffered "painful wounds." Although fought to the death, the Battle of Buffalo Gap, an isolated event in an isolated region, was without historical significance beyond the hills and valleys of Callahan Divide.[23]

The Indians who engaged in the Battle of Buffalo Gap were typical of the dozens of bands of wandering Apaches and Comanches

21 *Abilene Daily Reporter*, June 20, 1905.
22 Joseph Carroll McConnell, *The West Texas Frontier*, pp. 66–67.
23 Ibid.

who forced back the line of West Texas settlement during the sixties and seventies. Often they managed to avoid confrontations with the military outposts and attacked instead the pioneer settlers. Their victims complained bitterly to their Texas government that something should be done to make life and property more secure in West Texas. Their complaints were generally ignored during the war and Reconstruction eras, but by the time General E. O. C. Ord wrote, in 1878, that "all Indians penetrating the country have been so hotly pressed by the troops as to prevent their doing much damage," he wrote with considerable truth.[24]

Violence was so much a part of the local history of the frontier that murder attracted special attention only when it involved some unique feature. Thus, the first edition of the town's first newspaper, the *Buffalo Gap News*, reported a recent murder in the following disinterested manner: "On the morning of the 24 ult., Mr. Louis Collins was killed by some unknown parties in the back room of the Alamo saloon. The deceased was a cow-boy. He was buried in the town burying grounds."[25] A routine murder, following a routine argument, between two lowly cowboys was not bizarre enough to be newsworthy. Furthermore, it was not the type of activity the editor cared to spread abroad.

Stories of Indian encounters lived on for many years if they were far-fetched enough to make them worthy of fireside recollections. Andrew Mather's Indian story, for example, was a simple tale, but it was unconventional enough to rate frequent repetition. Down in Jim Ned Valley a grim cat-and-mouse maneuver between a band of Indians and a company of Texas Rangers was in progress when a huge bear got caught in the middle. As Sergeant Mather darted around a boulder for a better view of the enemy, the bear confronted him. From a higher ledge just above, Captain Maltby saw Mather's predicament and by hand signals warned Mather not to shoot the bear. The gunshot would expose their position to the Indians. Mather, in utter frustration, but in absolute silence, roped the bear, tied him to a nearby mesquite tree, and silently worried him down until Mather

<hr/>

[24] R. C. Crane, "Some Aspects of the History of West and Northwest Texas Since 1845," *Southwest Historical Quarterly* 26 (July, 1922): 41.

[25] Reprinted in *Abilene Daily Reporter*, June 13, 1908.

got close enough to the exhausted animal to kill him with a Bowie knife.[26]

K. K. Legett thoroughly enjoyed the accounts of Buffalo Gap's brief history as told by pioneers who had experienced it. He was a good listener, gave close attention to detailed descriptions, and rarely belittled any story. He soon won acceptance and popularity from men of all ages and occupations and an early reputation as one of the most prominent young lawyers in West Texas.[27] His reputation as an attorney did not prevent his being a gregarious young man who told his share of human interest stories. One of his favorites concerned the stage driver who complained to him one day about the frequent highway robberies he had suffered. "Why don't you get a gun to protect yourself?" Legett asked the driver. "Well, I've got a good pistol at home," he replied, "but I'm afraid to bring it with me. The robbers might take it."[28]

Another favorite story in later years, although at the time Legett feared he would be murdered during his first year on the frontier, concerned a case of mistaken identity. On a large and successful ranch a few miles out of Buffalo Gap lived an elderly woman with several unusually wayward sons. They ran afoul of Taylor County law so frequently that their mother hired young Legett to represent them "in cases without number." But finally, Legett explained,

they got too raw even for a lawyer, so I passed them up. It angered the aged mother very much. She was well in the 80's, but had a pretty rough reputation.

I was advised by the sheriff that she was making serious threats against me, and soon after that she dropped into the office. Expecting some trouble, I watched her closely, and pulled my chair near enough to see her and protect myself if any hostile demonstration was made.

I saw what I felt sure was the bulk of a six-shooter pretty well concealed in her bosom, and she kept fumbling at it, and I kept edging closer, expecting to jump and grab the gun as she drew it out. I was ready to spring like a cat on a mouse.

[26] *Abilene Daily Reporter*, September 15, 1911.

[27] Unidentified newspaper clipping, Julia Legett Pickard scrapbook, Legett Family Records, file 5, paper 6.

[28] Rollins, *Taylor County*.

Suddenly the fastening of her dress gave way, and there rolled out of her bosom, into her lap, and on the floor, a large, round, tin snuff box eight inches long.[29]

Such experiences helped to teach Legett how to accommodate himself to frontier life. He watched Buffalo Gap double its population during his first year in West Texas, and he apparently found the town so financially rewarding that he wrote to his father and brothers suggesting that they join him. The town was indeed growing at a spectacular rate, and every resident there readily predicted its "future renown." The Texas and Pacific Railway, as it moved west between Fort Worth and El Paso, had nowhere else to go but to Buffalo Gap.

Nevertheless, one worrisome rumor spread in 1880 that the western-bound rails would slant through Callahan County at a northwest angle, miss Taylor County entirely, and cross Shackelford and Jones counties. Another rumor claimed that the railroad company would follow the original government railroad survey, which projected a road through the Fort Phantom Hill area.[30] Around each of these potential routes, Fort Worth lawyers, West Texas ranchers, Belle Plain merchants, and speculators from far and near bought land—or attempted to. A group of Fort Worth lawyers bought land near Fort Phantom Hill, and John and C. W. Merchant bought ranches in Callahan County, claimed other land rights in Jones County, and tried unsuccessfully to buy out certain disputed land claims in the Buffalo Gap area.[31]

Meanwhile, Buffalo Gap folks looked upon such rushing around to buy land in the path of the Texas and Pacific with a bit of amusement.[32] "She's coming," they told one another knowingly. To miss their booming town with its predicted population of twelve hundred before the end of 1880 was unthinkable. What better way to get around the Callahan Divide than to go *through* it at Buffalo Gap, they asked one another. Simple logic convinced them, but they were encouraged by other straws in the wind. The March 6, 1880, issue of the *Buffalo Gap News* opined, "We are no prophets . . . but the

---

[29] Ibid.
[30] Duff, *Abilene*, pp. 52–53.
[31] *Abilene Daily Reporter*, May 31, 1907.
[32] Duff, *Abilene*, p. 53.

opinion prevails that we will get the T.&P.R.W. here. We believe it too. There are few towns this side of New York City that do not believe it."

Another barometer of the "truth" appeared in the same issue: "The managers of the T.&P.R.W. have selected Buffalo Gap as a supply depot and headquarters for the engineers on this end of the line. Already their stores and men are coming in. Straws show which way the wind blows, and if we are not badly fooled, the indications are all favorable for a road through Buffalo Gap at no distant day." Every man in Buffalo Gap tried to determine the exact route the Texas and Pacific would follow into town. If two men discovered that they agreed on the same route, then they debated the issue of first claim to the proposal. Meanwhile, land prices skyrocketed.

Legett did not engage in this flurry of speculation, but he benefitted in other ways during that boom year. New settlers moved to town in increasing numbers, and their demands for his legal services kept him busy. For the first time in his life he was able to establish a bank account, and, although he made no investments in 1879–1880, he was alert to every possibility.

Suddenly in mid-summer 1880, a rumor through town shocked every Buffalo Gap resident: word spread that N. C. Withers, a track and townsite locator for the Texas and Pacific, had purchased for himself a tract of land in an area then known as Tebo.[33] If true, Withers' purchase indicated that the railroad would cut across northern Taylor County and would miss Buffalo Gap by at least fifteen miles. The resulting trauma deepened among the residents as news of other north Taylor County land purchases suggested that something big was afoot up north.

It was, indeed. The Merchant brothers, S. L. Chalk, and John T. Berry had joined with John Simpson, owner of the Hashknife Ranch, and created an enormous block of land adjacent to Simpson's Hashknife headquarters near Cedar Creek. In August, railroad representatives and the recently formed land syndicate agreed that the railroad route should pass through the syndicated property in north Taylor County. At a later meeting in the fall, as the Texas and Pacific construction crews worked their way toward Taylor County, the same

33 Ibid., p. 54.

landowners met with J. Stoddard Johnston, the Texas and Pacific town locator and planner, and decided to locate the new railroad town — the "Future Great City of West Texas"—south-by-southwest of the Hashknife headquarters, between Cedar and Big Elm creeks and just to the east of Catclaw Creek.[34]

Suddenly, the residents of Buffalo Gap realized that Buffalo Gap, the "Uncrowned Queen of the Woolly West," would remain uncrowned. Without the magic of a major railroad, no land-locked West Texas town could ever become a great city. Convinced of that, Legett prepared to move fifteen miles to the north.

[34] Ibid., pp. 55, 56.

*Pine Street was a soggy mass of mud. One
wagon came through with thirty-two donkeys
hitched to it, and it stalled in the mud.*

# CHAPTER THREE

# *Abilene, on Catclaw Creek*

K. K. LEGETT quickly adjusted to the disappointing news that the
Texas and Pacific rails would by-pass Buffalo Gap, and he considered
the personal advantages that might result from a relocation of the
town. Almost everyone intended to move to the rails and, if possible,
take advantage of the new land market. Every man in town was a land
speculator at heart, and each looked forward to March 15, the date
announced by Texas and Pacific representatives for the public auction
of town lots. It was next to impossible to judge the best locations until
the rails could provide a central focus for the future towns. Meanwhile, roadbed and construction crews worked their way toward the
northeast corner of Taylor County as rapidly as the wet, cold weather
allowed. On December 17 the railhead was still twenty-five miles to
the east, in central Callahan County.[1]

The new townsite revealed no feature that distinguished it from
any other parcel of land on the West Texas prairie: a barren pasture
laced with dry, shallow creeks. No white man—not even the rancher
—had challenged the Indian for this remote territory until the wooded
and watered lands farther east were claimed. Nevertheless, as Legett's
boyhood days in Denison had taught him, a railroad through this
country could make a great difference in the value of the land.

While he awaited the railroad, more personal responsibilities
pressed upon him. His father, sixty-one years old, suffered from
chronic asthma and found it increasingly difficult to provide for his
family. As a consequence, he grew more and more dependent upon
his three sons for support. Under such circumstances, Legett persuaded his parents, his unmarried sister, Eliza Virginia, and his two

---

[1] Katharyn Duff, *Abilene . . . On Catclaw Creek*, p. 60.

bachelor brothers, T. R. and John, to move to West Texas.² He bought one of the many houses up for sale in Buffalo Gap and gave it to his father and brothers. Thus emerged a pattern of family dependence upon the middle son. The youthful attorney was the seventh of the eight Legett children, but natural qualities of leadership made him the family's stabilizing force.

At approximately the same time that K. K. moved from Buffalo Gap, local ranchers named the new town Abilene to honor the famous cattle town in Kansas with which all of them were familiar. Texas and Pacific officials immediately sponsored a campaign to attract settlers and speculators. J. Stoddard Johnston, who was locator and promoter for the railroad company, issued broadsides that were uncommonly honest and straightforward. One broadside, for example, cautioned prospective settlers that "the prairie grass is not long, but short . . . not green, but brown. Where there are trees they are not large, and trees will appear scarce. . . . So also as to water. The maps of Texas show many rivers but you will find that every creek is apt to be called a river and every hill a mountain."³ It was not a land where men should go to pick up quick fortunes. "Unless they go to work," Johnston warned, in the same broadside "they will become tramps or worse."

But Legett and all Taylor County pioneers believed, even more intimately than Johnston, that the Abilene country was not entirely barren of nature's bounties and that an industrious man could prosper in it. Cattle and sheep thrived on the short, nutritious prairie grasses just as the buffalo had before them. The rich soil, moreover, could produce grains as easily as grasses, and there were still enough deer, antelope, jackrabbits, and wild turkeys to feed indefinitely many more waves of immigrants. A railroad into such country could mark the difference between survival in Buffalo Gap and prosperity in Abilene. The older town had a better natural location along the Western Trail and a much more picturesque setting among the hills and under

² Lander Legett to Ruth Legett Jones, November 25, 1928. Copy in Legett Family Records, file 5, paper 3. The eldest daughter, Valencia Ann, married A. J. Hale and lived with her family at Lone Oak, Arkansas; Mary Luisa, wife of J. F. Pollard, died in 1874; Susan, wife of Joel Larkin, died in 1870; and Nancy Elzara, wife of G. W. Flemister, lived with her family at Keller, Texas. T. R. was three years older than K. K. and John was three years younger.
³ *Abilene Reporter-News*, October 3, 1971.

massive live oaks. The new town, on the other hand, would have the railroad to lift West Texans from the sand and mud whenever horseshoes and wagon wheels failed them. Wet weather sometimes made remote Buffalo Gap almost inaccessible. The town had received approximately twenty-four inches of rain during the fourteen months since Legett's arrival, but most of that precipitation fell from a half-dozen cloudbursts. At such times roads and riverbanks were almost indistinguishable, and the dusty streets of the town square turned into rivers of brown mud. The railroad, then, was essential to any town with dreams of becoming an important commercial center.

The roadbed crew, the rail crew, and, finally, the magic rail itself reached the townsite during the week of January 9–15, 1881, but the continued westward progression of the roadbed crew clearly indicated that Abilene would not enjoy the extra trade benefits of a railhead town.[4] Ordinarily the briefest delay in construction attracted settlers to the westernmost point of a railroad, and no matter what caused the delay—lack of money, lack of labor, blizzards—pioneer settlers from all directors beyond the rails flocked to the railhead for supplies. Rarely more than a few weeks passed before the nucleus of a town emerged: a few dusty streets, a depot, a lumber yard, a saloon, a hotel, and a dozen or so box houses.

Since construction continued past the townsite, Legett and his friends believed that Texas and Pacific officials would not rely on the usual railhead method of promoting the new town. The company had more to gain from government land subsidies than from town development as it raced across Texas to join the eastbound Southern Pacific Railroad out of San Francisco. The two rails met at Sierra Blanca, ninety-two miles east of El Paso, approximately a year later. Within a few days after construction passed Abilene, new broadsides from Johnston's promotional headquarters convinced everyone that the railroad company had more ambitious plans for the town. White canvas tents sprang up like giant mushrooms atop the grassy, windswept prairieland, as pioneer businessmen jockeyed for position along the railroad right of way. Those who owned no tents opened for business in canvas-covered wagons.

Other settlers rushed to the area in such numbers that older com-

[4] Duff, *Abilene*, p. 60.

munities near and far expressed surprise and envy. From Fort Griffin, fifty miles to the northeast, on February 3 the editor of the *Fort Griffin Echo* reported that the woods were full of immigrants. He hastened to add, however, that Fort Griffin folks were not among them. The *Fort Worth Democrat* ridiculed the "future great city" theme while other newspapers, though forced to report the newsworthy stampede to Abilene, managed to misspell the town's name.[5] Their label, "Tent City," emphasized the temporary nature of the boom town. Nearer home, the *Buffalo Gap News* editor called the upstart "Canvas Town."

Local men moved in advance of the public auction, and many of them raised tents or located their wagons on the exact lots they hoped to purchase on March 15, the auction date. George S. Browne, who represented Charles Goldberg of Fort Worth, operated a general store, which he located in early February in a covered wagon north of the tracks. On the other side of the tracks, Theodore Heyck built the first frame structure—a tiny storehouse—and planned to locate his freight and hide business in it.[6] A tent hotel, the Donnely, opened adjacent to the Texas and Pacific roadbed. A pioneer guest later described the Donnely as "just one big canvas room in which were forty or fifty cots." A second hotel, with canvas top, pineboard walls, and dirt floor (covered with a carpet to keep down the dust) opened a few weeks later. Its unique feature was a den of prairie dogs permanently entrenched in one corner of the room and near the front entrance. The frisky little prairie animals regularly came out of their hole and barked at any hotel guest who tried to stake a claim to that corner.[7]

K. K. Legett succumbed to the mounting pull of the rails and moved to Abilene in late February—presumably, to the luxurious Donnely. Local townsmen regretted the loss of such promising young men as the versatile lawyer from Cleburne. A humorous item in the *Buffalo Gap News* soon after Legett left failed to conceal the writer's chagrin:

[5] Duff, *Abilene*, pp. 60–61.
[6] Ibid., p. 62.
[7] P. H. Carter, in *Abilene Daily Reporter*, September 22, 1911; Tommie Clack, "Buffalo Gap College," *West Texas Historical Association Year Book* 35 (October, 1959): 74–75.

"TAKE HIM IN!
A young lawyer, K. K. Legett by name, a rising young prince in his profession, has strayed, been stolen, or washed away. . . . It is feared that he is lost. If you see him take him in."[8]

The ambitious youth was already infected by Abilene fever as he joined the hundreds of others who jammed into Canvas Town. Estimates of Abilene's permanent population in late February ranged from three to seven hundred, but the mass of men who milled around the railroad depot, the hotel, the canvas tents, the hide tents, the wagons, and the dugouts gave credence to the higher estimate.

Although all thoughts focused on March 15, Abilene's birthday, the precise date when the rail crew, with their steel rails and ties, reached the town went unrecorded. The roadbed crew had attracted attention as it ended all speculation about the road's exact location, and men made wagers among themselves about the time of arrival of the first train, but the arrival of the track itself was of no particular consequence.

For a town still unborn, Abilene accumulated some amazing statistics: it had a graveyard—with a few plots already occupied; it had a hotel with all four sides flapping in the breeze and the top threatening to become airborne at any moment; it had dusty streets and a noisy, rowdy citizenry; and, finally, it had a First Presbyterian Church organized and housed in a tent since February 27. W. A. Minter, whose entire family had accompanied him, organized Abilene's first church. It was a coincidence that February 27 was also the date that Abilene's first official train arrived. Many years later, however, Legett suggested the possibility that the two events were not coincidental: "Mr. Minter might have heard the rumor that 'all hell would break loose' when the first train pulled into Abilene."[9] Coincidence or not, it was indeed a red-letter day when the train arrived:

The town waited, eyes strained to see the first glimmer of the headlight over the rise on the prairie east of town. . . . Here it came, and behind the light the train with whistle squawking news of the arrival. Everybody yelled

[8] *Buffalo Gap News*, n.d., in Julia Legett Pickard scrapbook, Legett Family Records, file 4, paper 4.

[9] *Abilene Daily Reporter*, April 30, 1913. Copy in Legett Family Records, file 4, paper 18.

until the train screeched to a stop, whistle still blaring. The anvil was fired
with a mighty boom that shook the centerpoles of tents and set their sides
to flapping. Horses strained at their stakes and stray cows took off for the
country.[10]

During the following two weeks, J. Stoddard Johnston and other
railroad officials worked feverishly to plot the townsite ahead of the
March 15 deadline. Surveyors measured off townlots and mapped out
the official streets. There would not be a town square. Instead, streets
paralleled the railroad from east to west and were numbered so that
the two "Front" streets which faced the rails changed to North First
and South First. Other parallel streets advanced to higher names as
they moved away from the rails. The intersecting streets—north to
south—were named for trees, presumably on the promoter's theory
that future Abilenians should think trees even if they could not see
them. Northside streets were named Plum, Mesquite, Walnut, Pine,
Cypress, Cedar, Hickory, Orange, Mulberry, Grape, and Osage. Southside streets were named Willow, Cherry, Locust, Pecan, Oak, Chestnut, Sycamore, Elm, Butternut, Poplar, Palm, Peach, and—to complete the image—Vine.

Johnston's townlot plan proved that he was both a skilled promoter and a shrewd businessman. While men argued among themselves and placed bets on whether the north side or the south side of
the tracks would become more valuable, Johnston reserved public
school sites on both sides, at North Third and Cedar and at South
Fifth and Chestnut. As evidence of Abilene's "future greatness," he
reserved another site for a "future federal building." Most interesting
of all, however, to Legett and his law associates, Johnston ignored
Buffalo Gap's earlier claim as the county seat and reserved a site for
Taylor County's courthouse. The Texas and Pacific Company then
hired a draftsman to prepare a master plan, which Johnston posted
for the convenience of all who planned to bid at the public auction.[11]

A few days before the big event, Abilene's streets, townlots, and
tent floors melted into a sea of cold, thick, chocolate-colored mud.
During the evening of March 14, the weather threatened to turn into

[10] Duff, *Abilene*, p. 64.
[11] Ibid. See also T. S. Rollins, *Taylor County: An Early History of Pioneer Settlers.*

a typical plains blizzard. Sleet and freezing rain camouflaged the area under a blanket whiter than the canvas tents as two special T&P trains pulled slowly into Tent City. Each iron horse labored to a noisy halt amidst the raucous roar of hundreds of land speculators from Fort Worth, Dallas, and other points east.[12]

The unruly mob stepped, slipped, and sometimes fell into the ankle-deep slush of the West Texas prairie as they sought to drown their discomfort in red-eye whiskey at the White Elephant, the Delmonico, the Cattle Exchange, and the Arcade. A few more civilized East Texans preferred a poker game in a warm T&P train to the comforts of a frozen West Texas tent. Everyone readily agreed that Abilene offered only two items for sale: "a train ticket to git away, or a drink to make you willing to stay."[13]

Mercifully, the wind shifted to the southwest during the night and Abilene's birthday turned into a mild, sunny day. Although the mud remained underfoot, the warm dry breeze lifted the spirits. "Tents and covered wagons emptied as soon as breakfast was over. The men crowded close to the [auctioneer's] platform to see and to hear. Women kept their place in the background and kept an eye on the children, shooing them out of the way of such an important event. There was a great crowd. Visiting newsmen reported it in their papers as . . . 'more than two thousand.'"[14]

The platform and the huge townlot map were located at the intersection of South First and Chestnut streets. Legett and Kirkland selected a position directly in front of the auctioneer, J. H. Hasack, of Jefferson, Texas, who called for bids promptly at ten o'clock.[15] A Callahan City storekeeper, representing his son, W. T. Berry, offered $710 for the right to select the first lots.[16] He chose two adjacent lots on the northwest corner of North Second and Pine streets. All eyes shifted to Johnston's poster drawing of the townsite as Hasack marked them "sold."

William Cameron of the Cameron and Phillips Lumber Company —one of the largest lumber companies in the state—made the second

[12] Duff, *Abilene*, p. 65.
[13] *Abilene Reporter-News*, October 3, 1971.
[14] Duff, *Abilene*, p. 65.
[15] Alfred E. Menn, "The Abilene Story," p. 1. (unpublished manuscript, Katharyn Duff Collection, n.d.).
[16] Callahan City was renamed Belle Plain in 1888.

highest bid. He paid $335 each for two lots. A murmur arose from the crowd as Cameron also selected lots on the north side, between Mesquite and Walnut Streets and adjacent to the railroad right of way. Kirkland turned to Legett and commented: "That shows which direction the town is going. If a great firm like that chooses the north side, then that is . . . where the greatest business development will take place."[17] Accordingly, Legett gingerly manipulated the modest savings he had accumulated during the past seventeen months, waited for lulls in the bidding, and purchased several lots a few blocks from the rails but in the direction he hoped the town would grow.[18]

By the end of the second and final day of the auction, approximately two hundred local settlers and East Texas land speculators had paid $51,360.00 for 317 lots. The lowest priced townlots sold for $70.00. The Simpson-Merchant land syndicate, which had purchased the prairieland for $1.50 per acre, and the Texas and Pacific Railway Company, which had just recently received its free and equal share by building the rails to the townsite, sold their remaining lots through individual negotiations.[19]

Fortunately for Abilene, most purchasers intended to improve their property at once. Out-of-town speculators bought several lots adjacent to the rails, but purchasers such as Legett bought for speculation at lower rates and farther from the tracks. All shared with Legett the hope that Abilene's business district would expand toward their property. Local purchasers hoped to move out of their tents, wagons, and dugouts as quickly as possible. Blizzardlike weather returned shortly after the auction, however, and delayed construction. On April 1, icicles four feet long clung to the bottom of the T&P water tank and severe winds blew away several tents and tore others into shreds.[20]

No Abilenian could lay claim to building the first permanent structure in Tent City. Everyone built at once. Railroad cars laden with lumber from East Texas and Louisiana arrived every day, and settlers waited at the tracks for the morning's shipment. Often they completed transactions with Cameron and Phillips before lumbermen

[17] K. K. Legett, in Rollins, *Taylor County.*

[18] Legett eventually owned the lot where the auction was held, but his heirs gave it to the city (Ruth Legett Jones to the author, April 15, 1974).

[19] Duff, *Abilene*, pp. 66–67.

[20] John L. Stephenson, in *Abilene Daily Reporter*, April 1, 1908.

could remove lumber to the yard.[21] By some subtle and unspoken agreement, most businessmen managed to purchase the lots upon which they had raised their tents. Thus they bought their lumber, built their box-house businesses, moved their stock from their tents, and almost simultaneously opened for business. Everyone agreed that Cameron and Phillips opened the first lumber yard, that John Medaris opened the first livery stable, and that George S. Browne was probably the first groceryman. His store was a covered wagon, not a box house.

But in those hectic days, *first* was not as important as *ready* when some critical need arose. It was far more important, for example, that W. T. Berry's home was ready on June 15, 1881, than that it was the first built of rock. On that date, Colonel Berry's daughter, Ellen, married attorney John Bowyer, of Lexington, Virginia. With help from neighbors, the home was completed in time for the West Texas rancher's daughter to marry the recent graduate of the law school at Washington and Lee University.[22] Again, in July, Abilenians lent a helping hand so that a marriage ceremony could be performed in a church. In that instance, the town's first schoolhouse at North Third and Cedar served first as a Baptist Church, for the wedding of Miss Belle Dalmouth to W. H. Weatherstone.[23] Presbyterian and Christian congregations also shared the building with the Baptists, and on Sunday Abilene's first school became the Union Church.

Each completed building helped to give form and substance to the empty checkerboard pattern designed by J. Stoddard Johnston. Tents disappeared along North and South First streets as box houses replaced them. The settlers' preoccupation with lumber and water needs frequently reminded Legett of his early childhood complaint that his work was never done: "If it ain't wood, it's water!" he protested. With his brothers, he had kept wood in the kitchen and water in the barrel for as far back as he could recall.[24] Abilene's need for the same two indispensable items was always critical.

Both problems were especially acute during the town's first

[21] Menn, "Abilene Story," p. 11.
[22] Rollins, *Taylor County*.
[23] Menn, "Abilene Story," p. 12.
[24] Unidentified newspaper clipping from Julia Legett Pickard scrapbook, Legett Family Records, file 4, paper 20.

months. As spring passed into summer, the showers diminished and then stopped entirely. The winds increased and the sun burned hotter. Just as snow and sleet made Abilenians hurry to complete their frame buildings in March and April, the sun and dust made them no less eager to move into permanent dwellings during the summer months. The railroad company's artesian wells never satisfied the need for water, although several well-digging crews searched constantly for new underground springs.

The lack of water concerned every West Texan, and both farmers and ranchers wondered whether the area's annual rainfall would support the farmer. Taylor County's earliest settlers insisted that every effort to raise truck crops had succeeded. C. E. Gilbert quoted their claims in the *Abilene Reporter*'s first issue, and in succeeding issues he sought to attract farmers to the area.[25] He believed that the country was large enough, the soil rich enough, the grasses were nutritious enough, and the precipitation was plentiful enough for both farming and ranching. Many West Texans, including Legett, were not so convinced, and facts seemed to bear them out. Between the 99th and 100th degree longitude, rainfall ranged between fifteen and thirty inches per year, and, as a consequence, no one could argue convincingly that the area was suitable for farming. Since Legett had no personal investment in farming or ranching at that time, he made no comment that would intensify the local disagreement.

The town itself served one significant purpose: it enabled settlers who came to West Texas to live off the land. Abilenians might be lumber dealers, hardware men, real-estate men, building contractors, mechanics, or innkeepers, but their success depended upon the success of those who came to develop the country's natural resources. Eventually the hundreds of railroad cars that brought lumber, paint, and products of every description to the Abilene depot must depart with some useful product from West Texas.

Pioneer settlers such as Legett must have shared a genuine satisfaction when they shipped the first cattle to eastern markets. Thirty carloads of cattle left Abilene during the first week in July, 1881, and 146 additional carloads followed before the month ended. Other trains pulled away from the station with carloads of sun-bleached

[25] Duff, *Abilene*, pp. 112–114.

bones destined for some eastern fertilizer and lime company which had paid $10 or $11 per ton for the strange cargo. One Abilene collector, the town's second largest exporter in 1881, shipped more than a thousand tons of bones during Abilene's first summer.[26] The supply was soon exhausted, but bone collecting contributed significantly to Abilene's trade during those early years when cattle were the only other export product.

Local trade between Abilene and the surrounding country was brisk from the beginning. As a commercial center and as a social center, the railroad town was an instant success. After weeks of hard, lonely work farmers and ranchers loaded their families into wagons, drove to Abilene, replenished their supplies, caught up on local and outside news, and in general reacquainted themselves with life beyond their own settlements. Throughout the day mothers, fathers, and children filled their wagons with flour and sugar, saddles and harnesses, overalls and dresses. Sometimes they had problems concerning land titles, complaints of fence-cutting, or wills to probate, and sought out K. K. Legett or one of the other half-dozen lawyers. By late afternoon they headed back home for another month or so of hard work. On the open prairie, survival was the settlers' first concern.

Farmers returned to town for such special occasions as the Great Barbecue on the Fourth of July, 1881. The date marked Abilene's first celebration since the March 15–16 auction, and townfolk and railroad officials worked together to make it a successful event. It was not easy during that summer of 1881 to ignore the weather, but they disregarded the swirling sand and dust that began in April and stretched through May and June; they disregarded the swarms of grasshoppers, which were particularly bad that summer; and they disregarded the heat wave that sent thermometers soaring to 107 degrees in the shade on June 29. More than three thousand persons, doggedly determined to have a good time, gathered on a site designated by name, if not by appearance, as the City Picnic Grounds.[27]

In the heat and sand, they ate, they visited friends, they reassured one another that the surrounding area was a great country, and finally they gathered around a speaker's stand. There they listened carefully to speeches designed more to lift the pioneer spirit than to

26 Menn, "Abilene Story," pp. 12–14, 21.
27 Ibid., pp. 10–11.

boost national patriotism. Generally the old-timers spoke first. Each assumed a somber, self-conscious pose and gave solemn variations of the same advice: "Be of good cheer." By the time young Legett was invited to speak, his predecessors had inadvertently created a somber mood quite contrary to the purpose of the picnic. Legett apparently sensed the need to change the mood. He referred briefly to the numerous claims that every West Texas pioneer was more affluent than his eastern counterpart. Then he added, "after looking around at some of the people who are succeeding in West Texas, I've concluded that it takes a lot more brawn—and a lot less brains—than I used to think."[28] The crowd, caught off guard by his change of tone, pondered his brief statement and then burst into laughter and applause. Having thus broken the solemn mood, the astute young attorney jumped from the platform and rejoined the crowd. From that moment Legett enjoyed a reputation as a crowd-pleasing public speaker.

The new town had its share of unattractive features. As its frontier reputation spread, drummers warned one another that they should not stay too long nor return too frequently. Cowboys claimed it was the wildest cattletown in Texas, and their employers sometimes forbade them to stop there as they passed by. Strangers went back East and said that Abilene "set a pace that left the wayfarer purseless and breathless."[29] Abilene's population included fifteen men for every woman during its first year, and such law-abiding citizens as Legett failed to convince the rowdier ones that laws passed in Austin applied to Abilene as well.[30] Cowboys particularly objected to the local restriction against six-shooters, and they saw no humor in efforts to restrict their gambling. Until the odds were favorable for those who preferred law and order, discretion was a much more sensible course. Men accustomed to wild and reckless pursuits would not change overnight into respectable, law-abiding citizens. Therefore Legett and his peers restrained the unruly whenever possible and at all other times tried to see the humor in situations too spectacular to ignore.

Two such incidents, both grim and humorous, occurred in 1881.

[28] Unidentified newspaper clipping from Julia Legett Pickard scrapbook, Legett Family Records, file 4, paper 24.

[29] Andy Adams, *Log of a Cowboy*, quoted in *Abilene Reporter-News*, October 3, 1971.

[30] T. S. Rollins, in Rollins, *Taylor County*; John Bowyer, ibid.

On July 29 Buck Smith, a barkeeper, and Horace Pickett, a dance-hall employee, fell into an argument over a saloon girl. The men drew their guns simultaneously, emptied them simultaneously, and danced simultaneously to each other's ricocheting bullets. Since neither man was injured, Abilenians saw the humor in the incident and declared that both men had earned simultaneous reputations as the worst shots in town. A similar encounter between Joe Chambers and John Campbell at the Red Light Saloon on August 11 also would have ended with empty six-shooters and no injuries, but Chambers drew a knife and stabbed Campbell. For that bit of unsportsmanlike frontier conduct, the Sheriff required Chambers to post $500 bond.[31] Needless to say, such humorous references to very serious incidents were sometimes misunderstood by visiting easterners.

Humor often lightened the telling of frightening occurrences. Legett had such an experience soon after he moved to Abilene, but he never told it except in a humorous vein. A stage line operated between Abilene and San Angelo, and as the stage passed through the Callahan Divide it stopped at Buffalo Gap. Pioneers claimed that the stage averaged one hold-up every week. One day as Legett prepared to visit his Buffalo Gap relatives, Sheriff J. V. Cunningham asked him to take a large sum of money and deposit it in a bank at the county seat. Aware of the frequent banditry along the route, Legett protested, but finally agreed to the sheriff's request:

It was in August and I had on my [summer] clothes, and when the sheriff gave me a big roll of bills, I hadn't any place to put it. In my pockets it showed too plainly. Finally he suggested that I put it in my hat.

The plan looked all right, so I put the . . . currency on top of my head and set my hat over it. Feeling none too easy in my mind I thus started out with a horse.

A little way out of town I spied two men approaching me on horses that I knew were not ranch horses. I was frightened unto death. My confusion would have been noticed by anyone. They asked me some questions. . . .

Now I have a habit of lifting my hat and scratching my head whenever worked up about anything, and that was what I proceeded to do. The money which I was so anxious to conceal and protect began to tumble about my ears and shoulders. . . .

[31] Menn, "Abilene Story," pp. 14, 15.

The reason for my agitation being explained, the two men began to laugh uproariously . . . as I hurried on.[32]

While Legett was in Buffalo Gap, trouble of another sort occurred in Abilene. A fire broke out about midnight on August 27 in the T. S. Horn saloon on South First Street. The flames quickly spread west toward Chestnut Street and east toward Oak Street. There was no fire-fighting equipment except a bucket brigade, and the entire block—a major part of the business district—soon lay in ashes. The loss included J. G. Taylor's drug store, D. A. Olds's tent hotel, G. W. Featherstone's grocery store, the Woodward and Bennett barbershop, T. B. Robertson's feed store, P. M. Jackson's bakery, the *Abilene Reporter* newspaper building, J. C. Woodson's livery stable, Horn's saloon, and the O.K. saloon. In all, thirteen buildings and their sidewalks, valued at more than $20,000, burned.[33]

But in spite of fires, fights, droughts, and grasshoppers, Abilene continued to grow. Trains arrived daily with lumber, barbed wire, farm implements, building stone, bricks, and for Theodore H. Heyck a complete two-story house. The dwelling was built some years earlier in Lavaca, Texas, then dismantled when Heyck decided to go West. It was first shipped by schooner to Galveston and finally by rail to Abilene.[34] Considering the shortage of building materials and labor, Heyck insisted that his method was both cheaper and faster than waiting his turn to build in Abilene. Nursery stock of every description, but fruit trees in particular, arrived from East Texas. With each improvement, land prices skyrocketed. For example, John Touhey paid Dr. J. L. Gatrell $75 per acre for 113 acres just at the foot of Oak Street (probably at South Seventh and Oak). Dr. Gatrell had paid $15 per acre for the property five months earlier. Also in 1882, a one-half acre lot "beyond the business district" on Pine Street sold for $1,200.

Immigrants poured in from California, from Iowa, from Kentucky, and almost every state east of the Mississippi River. Abilenians enthusiastically claimed in mid-1882 that Taylor County's population

[32] Rollins, *Taylor County*.
[33] Duff, *Abilene*, p. 111.
[34] Menn, "Abilene Story," p. 36.

totaled "4,000 persons, 65,000 sheep, and 35,000 cattle."[35] Before Abilene's second birthday, citizens claimed 480 dwellings and 75 business houses, and 100 new houses were in various stages of construction. Building needs grew so critical that mechanics and carpenters demanded and received $4 per day for their labor. New hotels almost equaled saloons in number, and business transactions increased at such a rapid pace that businessmen found it almost impossible to send a telegram out of Abilene. Such spectacular growth led William Cameron, the town's first lumber dealer, to announce that he would erect a two-story brick building on a lot at North Second and Pine streets which would house Abilene's first bank. Shortly thereafter, more than one hundred members of the Colorado and Clear Fork Stockmen's Association met in Abilene. Unable to find lodging, the latecomers camped in unfinished dwellings scattered about town.[36]

Intoxicating progress stimulated dizzying new goals. New rumors spread around town every day that Abilene would soon become Taylor County's new seat of government. Encouraged by that rumor, several citizens initiated a movement to transfer the United States District Court from Graham, Young County, to Abilene. J. Stoddard Johnston's original townsite marked a site on Oak Street for a county courthouse "should that be moved from Buffalo Gap," and another site on the north side of the tracks for a federal building "should Abilenians persuade Uncle Sam to build one."[37]

No fantasy was too absurd where Abilene's future was concerned. Having progressed from pride in Abilene's growth to conceit and finally to braggadocio, rumors spread in the spring of 1882 that Governor Oran M. Roberts planned to escape Austin's smallpox epidemic by moving the state government to Abilene. The general attitude was one of annoyance because Governor Roberts had failed to notify local officials earlier. Suitable preparations for accommodating the different departments must be made, they complained, before Abilene could accept such responsibility. Other local citizens, however, recognized the absurdity of the rumor and constructed their own colorful descriptions of a capital city with a water system limited almost entirely to

[35] Menn, "Abilene Story," p. 55. An exaggeration of population perhaps, since the official count in 1880 was 1,736 persons (*Texas Almanac,* 1970–1971, p. 69).

[36] Menn, "Abilene Story," pp. 45, 50, 61.

[37] *Abilene Reporter-News,* October 3, 1971.

water barrels. They envisioned Dan Foley busily filling Governor Roberts' water barrel from the "Famous Dan Foley Well." They used the incident to encourage the town to get busy and incorporate itself.[38]

Efforts to incorporate the town had failed earlier that year by twenty-nine votes. Open-range cattlemen managed to outvote those who were determined to make Abilene a metropolis. Their victory, however, was short-lived. Before the year was out frustrated tradesmen called another election for January 2, 1883. On that date, by a vote of 104 to 75, they won the right to incorporate. Editor Gilbert, delighted by the victory, rushed into print to explain the light vote: January 2 was a wintery day and no one should assume from the small number who braved the weather and voted that Abilene had ceased to grow.[39]

Through extended periods of the early 1880s, farmers outnumbered ranchers as the area received better than average precipitation. As their numbers declined cowboys in the O. K. saloon proclaimed that they had rather commit suicide, or even shear sheep, than touch their hands to a hoe. Eventually ranchers abandoned their efforts to frighten nesters and sheepmen from the area. Some of them followed the lead of land speculators and sold their ranch land—at a good profit—to the farmers. Usually they invested in more cattle and more grazing lands farther west. Experience taught them that farmers followed the railroad, no matter how unpromising the land.[40]

Sheepmen, however, aroused cattlemen to full fury. Where restrictions on the use of grazing lands were not rigidly enforced, cattlemen and sheepmen vied for position. Ranchers insisted that sheep ruined the range and stripped it of any future usefulness by eating the grass too close. The roots were thus exposed and the nutritious grasslands vanished. Since the cattlemen arrived in Taylor County ahead of the sheepmen, they believed they had prior claim to the open range. The sheepmen maintained that the land was free and open to everyone.[41]

[38] Menn, "Abilene Story," p. 34.

[39] *Abilene Daily Reporter*, October 16, 1916.

[40] Walter B. Stevens, *Through Texas: A Series of Interesting Letters*, p. 59; R. H. Looney, "Reminiscences of Early Days," *Abilene Daily Reporter*, October 20, 1909.

[41] T. R. Havins, "Sheepmen-Cattlemen Antagonisms on the Texas Frontier," *West Texas Historical Association Year Book* 18 (October, 1942): 10–11.

Prairieland war threatened the Abilene area, but, with the exception of a few isolated incidents, the controversy ended without the bloodshed suffered along other frontiers. Cattlemen grudgingly made way for the woolgrowers who cautiously and quietly took their uneasy places among the West Texas ranchers and farmers. Their labors were almost instantly rewarded. Within months after the railroad arrived, they shipped 1,500,000 pounds of wool from the Abilene station. Woolgrowers from as far west as New Mexico and as far south as San Angelo drove their sheep into the area for shipping. Within two years Abilene developed into the largest wool market in the state.[42]

Legett watched, fascinated, as Mexican wagons loaded with wool and supported by wheels six feet high rolled into Abilene. Depending upon the size of the wagon and the condition of the road, the vehicles were pulled by twelve to thirty-two donkeys. Legett described in detail one such arrival: "Pine street was a soggy mass of mud. One wagon came through with thirty-two donkeys hitched to it, and it stalled in the mud. Another wagon came across the right-of-way with thirty-two donkeys hitched to it, and it took all of the sixty-four donkeys to pull the first wagon out. The wagons were monstrously large and heavy, carrying about 6,000 to 8,000 pounds."[43]

By the time Abilene reached its second birthday it was a thriving shipping center for cattle and sheep, and farmers produced enough homegrown crops to reduce considerably the first year's importation of food supplies from East Texas markets.[44] In spite of droughts and cloudbursts, scorching heat and bone-chilling blizzards, and in spite of its dual reputation as "a land of milk and honey" on one hand and a town "not fit even for cowboys" on the other, Abilene prospered.

Conversely, Buffalo Gap continued to decline. Inevitably the "Gappers" expressed alarm over the frequent suggestions in Abilene that the county seat should be relocated in the future great city. As the issue grew more and more heated, K. K. Legett was drawn into the very heart of the controversy.

[42] Menn, "Abilene Story," p. 55; K. K. Legett, in Rollins, *Taylor County.*
[43] K. K. Legett, in Rollins, *Taylor County.*
[44] Menn, "Abilene Story," p. 54.

> *The State received every dollar for her school
> lands that she asked. It was valued and ap-
> praised by her own officers . . . and if she has
> made a bad trade, she ought to be more scrupu-
> lous in the performance of her part of the con-
> tract.*

CHAPTER FOUR

# A Most Promising Young Lawyer

K. K. LEGETT'S decision to move his law practice from a thriving
county seat to a nonexistent railroad town seemed senseless to those
who were unable to foresee the impact that the Texas and Pacific rails
would have upon Taylor County. Such shortsighted men failed to
comprehend the information provided by J. Stoddard Johnston's
townsite map, nor did they grasp the significance of Johnston's designated plot on Oak Street for a county courthouse. More astute observers realized that the new town would inevitably challenge Buffalo
Gap's right to remain the seat of county government. As they ap-
praised the situation, a town located on a cattle trail could never successfully compete with another town located on a railroad line. In the
end the railroad would make the cattle trail obsolete. In such a contest for political or economic supremacy, the railroad town would
surely triumph. By the summer of 1883, Abilene was prepared to
make that challenge.

Legett, meanwhile, moved from the tent hotel and rented a room
at Mrs. E. H. Polk's boarding house, where he and such other young
men as attorney David Hill and Will Young undoubtedly discussed
at length the inevitable County Seat War. Legett supported the transfer for his own professional convenience, but at the beginning he
tried to avoid public entanglement in the controversy. His brother
T. R. had recently moved to Abilene and opened a drug store, but
Buffalo Gap was still home for his parents, his sister and his younger
brother, and he hoped not to cause his family unnecessary embarrassment. Other Abilenians were convinced that citizens in other parts of
Taylor County would eventually recognize Abilene's superior claims.
"They have to make frequent trips here on business anyway," the
editor of the *Abilene Reporter* rationalized on September 1, "[and]

they recognize the importance of concentrating all county interests in
. . . one good . . . town where they can always have a good market."

Such reasoning led one hundred Abilene freeholders to sign a
petition for a special election, and county judge John Watts Murray
duly announced that Taylor County residents should vote on the issue
on October 23. From that moment the County Seat War threatened
to become violent, and Legett's efforts to remain publicly neutral
ceased. Within days he was the recognized leader of the pro-Abilene
forces. One responsibility led to another, and on August 25 the Commissioners' Court appointed him presiding officer of the second precinct (Abilene). Legett rejected the appointment because he was
committed to attend court at Colorado City, in Mitchell County, on
that date and George Wilson was appointed to preside over the precinct.[1]

Legett's task until election day was nevertheless formidable. Buffalo Gap's most persuasive arguments—that it was already the official
county seat and that it was almost perfectly centered geographically—
could not be challenged. Legett and his Abilene allies countered with
the argument that Abilene was the commercial center of the county,
but still another challenge loomed: the law required that the transfer
of the county seat could not be sanctioned unless two-thirds of the
voters demanded it. A heavy Abilene vote, therefore, was absolutely
essential. In Abilene's most recent election, in November 1882, the
total vote was 295.[2] In October, 1883, Legett and a special committee, which included Will Young, David Hill, G. P. Widmer, Samuel
P. Hardwicke, and T. W. Daugherty, counted between eight and nine
hundred eligible voters in the second precinct (Abilene).[3] They must
get those voters to the polls. Legett organized rallies wherever there
were sufficient concentrations of settlers to justify the effort. Abilene's
new brass band performed at every rally, and, for those voters who
needed stronger incentives than good speeches or good music, the
Abilene bandwagon always traveled with a full barrel of red-eye
whiskey. As election day approached, charges and countercharges
embittered the contesting groups. Each accused the other of plans to

1 Katharyn Duff, *Abilene . . . On Catclaw Creek*, p. 96; K. K. Legett, in *Abilene Daily Reporter*, May 6, 1913.
2 *Abilene Reporter*, September 1, 1883.
3 K. K. Legett, in *Abilene Daily Reporter*, May 6, 1913.

flout the state's ambiguous voting laws, and each claimed that the other would not enforce residency requirements. Lax enforcement of voting laws was a frontier tradition not unknown to either group. Editor Gilbert estimated that there were at least 450 men twenty-one or older who could not prove how long they had resided in Texas or in Taylor County.[4]

To Legett's chagrin, some of his former Buffalo Gap friends accused him of secret and anonymous political activity which, they said, was unethical if not downright dishonest. The editor of the Buffalo Gap *Index* referred to him as "the paid lawyer in Abilene" who wrote letters favorable to Abilene's bid and mailed them from other Taylor County settlements. Stung by such charges of clandestine operations, Legett wrote a denial to the editor of the *Abilene Reporter*.

Abilene, October 9th, 1883

Editor Reporter:

Dear Sir: I discovered from the last issue of the Buffalo Gap *Index* that the authorship of the Merkle [*sic*] letter to the *Reporter* is credited to "Legett." I hope I will not be considered presumptious [*sic*] for supposing myself the party to whom reference is made. . . . *I am not the author* of the Merkle [*sic*] letter, nor of any other communication relative to the removal of the county-site, which has appeared in any newspaper published in Taylor county.

It is also intimated by a correspondent of the *Index* that other communications to the *Reporter* were the productions of "a paid lawyer in Abilene." If reference is here made to the undersigned, I desire to give it an unqualified denial. For my feeble efforts in behalf of Abilene, I have never, nor would I receive one dollar remuneration. . . .

All honest and honorable efforts in behalf of the town have my undivided support. . . . I am for the removal of the county-seat from Buffalo Gap to Abilene, "first, last and all the time."[5]

By election day Taylor County residents were in such bad humor that Legett only half-jokingly claimed he would have invented an excuse to get out of town if a client's case in Colorado City had not made his absence necessary.[6] Those who remained in town marched

---

[4] *Abilene Reporter*, September 1, 1883.
[5] K. K. Legett to the editor, *Abilene Reporter*, October 12, 1883.
[6] K. K. Legett, in *Abilene Daily Reporter*, May 6, 1913.

to the polls in record-breaking numbers and gave Abilene a landslide victory of 905 to 269. The future great city lost four of the five precincts, but it carried its own precinct (the second) by 864 to 11.[7]

Buffalo Gap voters charged fraud, naked steal, deceit, and crooked deal. They hurried to the Commissioners' Court and demanded that it throw out the ballots in the Abilene box. The commissioners refused. The irate Gappers then petitioned District Judge T. B. Wheeler to place an injunction against Abilene efforts to remove the county records. Judge Wheeler declared that he had no jurisdiction in the matter. The petitioners returned to the Commissioners' Court and repeated their original demands. The four commissioners subsequently deadlocked at two votes for each town and thus County Judge John Watts Murray cast the deciding vote to accept the Abilene ballots:

With the announcement, Abilenians hustled him out of the courtroom and over to his house where he collected his family into a hack. Under escort of the Abilene horsemen the Murrays rode back to the newly designated county seat. Legend has it that during that night a group of Buffalo Gap men went to call on the judge. When they could not find him they built a fire in his yard, caught and ate all his chickens.[8]

Buffalo Gap voters still refused to accept defeat. They impounded the county records and declared that they would never give them up. The commissioners, nevertheless, ordered Sheriff Kinch V. Northington to transfer the records to a rented box house in Abilene; instead, the unhappy sheriff rode to Sweetwater thirty miles to the west and explained his plight to Judge Wheeler. The judge urged the sheriff to carry out the court order. Northington protested that Buffalo Gap would resist and that "would surely cause bloodshed."[9] He decided, therefore, to explain the situation to higher authorities in the state capital at Austin.

A week later Sheriff Northington returned to Abilene with papers from the attorney general and Governor John Ireland. Both state officials declared that Abilene was Taylor County's legal seat of government, that the courts would be held there, and that the retention of

[7] Duff, *Abilene*, p. 98.

[8] Ibid., p. 99.

[9] Alfred E. Menn, "The Abilene Story," p. 74 (unpublished manuscript, Katharyn Duff Collection, n.d.).

the county archives at Buffalo Gap would not alter the fact that it was no longer the county seat. Governor Ireland further stated that Sheriff Northington should carry out the commissioners' orders.[10]

Still, the sheriff did not hurry to complete the hazardous assignment. When Judge Wheeler arrived in Abilene to hold the 12th District Court, some of the records were under lock and key at Buffalo Gap. His patience exhausted, Wheeler thereupon rode alone to Buffalo Gap, verbally chastised its stubborn citizens, demanded the records, and threatened to accept Governor Ireland's offer to send up Texas Rangers if they continued to obstruct the law. Intimidated by the judge's tantrum, Buffalo Gap surrendered the records. Wheeler loaded the boxes in his hack and delivered them to the temporary headquarters on Oak Street in Abilene.[11] The jubilant victors boasted that they would build a $100,000 courthouse.[12]

Recriminations continued and old-timers debated the County Seat War for many years.[13] Legett somehow managed to disengage himself from the residue of hard feelings, and his law practice, his civic responsibilities, and his social contacts expanded as rapidly as Abilene grew in size and regional influence. Local news reporters attributed to him such flattering characterizations as "a leading member of the bar," "the most promising young lawyer in West Texas," and "one of Abilene's leading Beau Brummels." [14] The descriptions were not necessarily exaggerated. Legett frequently escorted about town several of Abilene's most eligible young women, including Lora Bryan, daughter of Colonel Washington Carroll Bryan, a leading West Texas rancher. Legett was one of Abilene's busiest lawyers, and he could claim the title of the most promising young lawyer in West Texas as legitimately as any other attorney in the vast region. His credentials were particularly impressive after the summer of 1883 when he

[10] Ibid., p. 76.

[11] Duff, *Abilene*, p. 99.

[12] Construction commenced on a more modest brick and rock structure on February 8, 1884 (Menn, "Abilene Story," p. 81).

[13] The Santa Fe railroad built through Buffalo Gap in 1911 and brought in its wake a mild boom. Thus the town felt sufficiently strong to challenge Abilene, and open hostility flared anew in 1913 when Buffalo Gap attempted to regain the county seat (see issues of the *Abilene Daily Reporter* for May, 1913).

[14] *Abilene Reporter*, February 2, 1882 and August 8, 1883; unidentified newspaper clipping in Legett Family Records, file 5; Duff, *Abilene*, p. 131.

stepped forward and publicly ridiculed the Texas legislature for "general bungling and careless legislation."[15] The attack drew statewide attention and made the brash Abilenian an instant hero among West Texans.

Causes for the outburst dated back to the Texas Constitution of 1876 and the conservative legislation that soon followed its adoption. The framers of the new constitution, in their efforts to reduce Civil War and Reconstruction-era debts, abandoned the state-supported immigration bureau. West Texans believed that the bureau had helped to attract settlers to the country west of Fort Worth, and thus they protested the bureau's demise. Nevertheless, in keeping with the retrenchment policy, Governors Richard Coke (1874–1876), Richard B. Hubbard (1876–1879), and Oran M. Roberts (1879–1883) practiced the most rigid economy. They operated under "a system of public poverty" and reduced expenditures in virtually every governmental department. As state agencies expanded, however, there were new and greater demands upon the legislature for increased expenditures.

Among the schemes to raise the government's revenues passed by the harassed legislators was the Land Act of 1879, which offered to sell the public domain in any quantity at fifty cents an acre. The legisislative act instantly created a wild spree of local speculation. This pleased those who hoped it would bring more settlers to West Texas, but it worried others who realized the new possibilities for increased absentee land ownership. Two years later the Land Act of 1881 also liberalized the sale of school lands in certain sections of the state. The resulting runaway sale of the public domain and the school lands brought severe criticism from Governor John Ireland in June, 1883. In their efforts to evade the governor's charges, the legislators claimed that land purchasers were guilty of widespread fraud—particularly in North and West Texas. They appointed a special Land Fraud Commission to investigate the alleged frauds.[16]

To fulfill its charge, the commission sought public testimony from

[15] Unidentified newspaper clippings in Julia Legett Pickard scrapbook, Legett Family Records, file 5. In some instances Mrs. Pickard recorded the dates of the newspapers but rarely identified the newspaper.

[16] For a brief summary of this problem, see Rupert Norval Richardson, *Texas: The Lone Star State*, pp. 229–232, 296–300. See also A. S. Lang, "Financial History of the Public Lands in Texas," *Baylor University Bulletin*, vol. 25 (Waco, 1932); R. D. Holt, "School Land Rushes in West Texas," *West Texas Historical Associa-*

volunteers who wished to speak under oath. K. K. Legett, who was
as angered as any other West Texan by the legislators' efforts to hide
their own ineptitude, agreed to testify before the investigating commission. The interrogatory included the key question: "Do you know
of any case or cases where the law, for the sale of school land, has
been evaded or violated in any county of the State, in any manner, to
the prejudice of the State or school fund? If so, by whom, where,
and how . . .?[17] Young Legett, who had patiently responded to sixteen preliminary questions so that he might answer the seventeenth,
replied:

> I am inclined to think that the strict letter of the "law for the sale of
> school lands" has been evaded in numberless instances, but I cannot under-
> stand that it was in any manner "prejudice of the State or school fund."
> The State received every dollar for her school lands that she asked. It was
> valued and appraised by her own officers, with the consent and permis-
> sion of the Commissioner of the General Land Office, and if she has made
> a bad trade, she ought to be more scrupulous in the performance of her
> part of the contract.
>
> After the State had declared to her citizens, through the Legislature,
> that these lands were for sale, and on terms specified in the acts of 1879
> and 1881, and after the citizens had purchased these lands under the terms
> imposed by the State, I do think that an effort on the part of the State to
> avoid the terms of a contract proposed and submitted by herself comes
> with exceeding bad grace.
>
> Under the land system, as it has heretofore, this portion of the State has
> grown in population and material wealth, but if the lands are advanced in
> price, you virtually take the lands off the market, and will very effectually
> retard the progress and development of the country, without benefiting
> any section or anybody.[18]

Legett's candid remarks expressed the sentiments of many West
Texans, and perhaps for the first time in its brief history, Abilene
attracted the careful attention of the Texas legislature. Legett's influ-

tion Year Book 10 (1934): 42–57; and W. C. Walsh, "Memories of a Land Commissioner," Southwestern Historical Quarterly 44 (April, 1941): 481–497.
    [17] Unidentified newspaper clipping, dated July ? 1883, in Julia Legett Pickard
scrapbook, Legett Family Records, file 5.
    [18] Ibid.

ence, if any, upon the legislators cannot be measured in this instance, but within a few weeks after his appearance before the commission the legislature passed new land laws.

The Texas Land Act of 1883 increased the sale price of school lands to a minimum of two dollars per acre (three dollars in some areas) and the competitive leasing price of grasslands to a minimum of four cents per acre. Ranchers whose cattle were already on the land, however, followed the old law of the range and refused to bid against each other for use of the grasslands. Each placed the minimum bid for use of the acres his cattle already grazed, and no one else competed against him. As a consequence, the state board of control began to reject the ranchers' minimum bids and demanded eight cents per acre. This arbitrary action by the board was eventually rescinded.

Meanwhile, West Texas ranchers did not forget the young Abilene lawyer who spoke so forcefully in their behalf, nor were his remarks lost on the state's Democratic party leadership. The following year, as the dates of the state and national elections approached, the state convention delegates from the eleventh congressional district caucused in August and named K. K. Legett as their candidate for presidential elector. The following month in Houston the convention officially approved their choice.[19]

The Abilenian was the youngest of the thirteen-man slate of Democratic electors. Although the office was both temporary and honorary, it brought with it a great many immediate responsibilities. Not only were Legett and his electoral colleagues committed to support Grover Cleveland and his vice-presidential running mate, Thomas Hendricks; the party also expected them to campaign long and hard for the nominees.

The position of elector was indeed an honored one for the twenty-six-year-old attorney. He was the first Abilenian in the town's three-year history to gain statewide political office and one of the first persons from Denison to receive such recognition. The editor of the *Denison Gazetteer* reminded his readers that "the K. K. Legett, Esq. who was among the electors chosen by the Democratic Convention in

---

[19] Public announcement from the office of the secretary of state entitled "Electors for President and Vice President of the United States," dated December 4, 1884 (copy in Legett Family Records, file 2, paper 1).

Houston . . . to cast the vote of Texas for Cleveland and Hendricks"
was, in fact, "Billy" Legett who had worked in Mayor "Governor"
Owings' stables only a dozen years earlier. The editor remembered
that Billy was a genius who grew so fast his legs were always too long
for his pants. Now, said the editor, Legett had "developed into a fine
appearance physically, and the fact that he was the choice of the Eleventh District as the one among all others best fitted for the honorable
position . . . bears testimony to his standing." The editor concluded
that Legett's rise to prominence resulted from his own industry and
merit.[20]

Abilene's editors heaped even greater praise upon him, and one
wrote that "no young man in Texas gives brighter promise of distinction."[21] An out-of-town newsman, after listening to the Abilenian's "brilliant speech," informed his readers that there was "nothing
bow-Legett about this gentleman."[22] In Alexander Hall at Cisco on
October 8, Legett shared the platform with the Democrats' nominee
for lieutenant governor, State Senator Barnett Gibbs. To an audience
which the Cisco editor described as large and quite intelligent, Legett
and Gibbs confined their remarks to national issues that, in their opinion, directly related to the Texas economy. Gibbs spoke first and
supported the lease-law plank in the Democratic party platform, and
then Legett "in an eloquent and masterly style" castigated the Republicans for their corruption and misdeeds. For his efforts the Cisco
newsman called the Abilenian "one of the best stump speakers in
the state."[23] Another newsman in the eleventh district somewhat
carelessly assumed that Legett was "an-all-wool-yard-wide free grass
man."[24]

On election day in November, Texas voters supported the
Cleveland-Hendricks electoral slate, and in December the thirteen
Democrats gathered in Austin to perform their electoral duty. An-
other unidentified newspaper reporter, apparently from Abilene, de-

[20] *Denison Gazetteer*, undated clipping, Legett Family Records, file 5. "Billy"
was a childhood nickname.

[21] Unidentified newspaper clipping, Legett Family Records, file 4.

[22] Unidentified newspaper clipping, datelined Cisco, October 9, Legett Family
Records, file 4.

[23] Ibid.

[24] Unidentified newspaper clipping in Julia Legett Pickard scrapbook, Legett
Family Records, file 5.

scribed the "Meeting of the Electoral College" for the voters back in
the eleventh district and observed that "it was an uncommonly youthful collection of men. K. K. Legett, a talented young lawyer from
Abilene, is barely 26—he is the youngest."[25] Henceforth, K. K. Legett's name rarely appeared in the newspapers without some form of
honorary title. Most of the time he was "Hon. K. K. Legett," and
occasionally he was "K. K. Legett, Esq." One newsman, particularly
impressed, wrote "Hon. K. K. Legett, Esq." The honored young man
returned to Abilene unquestionably proud of his prominent role in
leading his state solidly into the victorious Cleveland-Hendrick political camp in 1884. In the process he had met many political leaders
of Texas who continued their association with Legett beyond election
day.

Sometime during the fall of 1884, Legett formed a law partnership with M. A. Spoonts, another Abilene attorney who had moved
from Buffalo Gap. Spoonts was a native East Texan. They rented an
office on Oak Street, and from that southside location the two ambitious young men plunged into professional and civic affairs of every
description. Their parnership enabled them to accept clients whose
interests required one partner to travel out of town while the other
attended to clients' business at home.

Legett made frequent out-of-town business trips in the spring and
summer of 1885 in an unsuccessful bid to bring into Abilene the
Gulf, Colorado, and Santa Fe rails. That company had announced an
early extension of its line from Brownwood to the northwest High
Plains and beyond. In April and again in June, Legett accompanied
J. T. Berry, C. W. Merchant, and J. W. Red to Brownwood, and
later in June he traveled alone and met with railroad officials in Chicago and New York. The Santa Fe did not build out of Brownwood,
however, until 1909, and to Abilene's amazement the rails missed
Abilene entirely. The Santa Fe built through Buffalo Gap, but too
late for the town to compete with Abilene as the area's trading
center.[26]

---

[25] Ibid. The 1884 Texas electors were Silas Hare, J. H. McLeary, J. E. Mc-
Comb, P. F. Edwards, N. W. Finley, H. C. Hynson, A. L. Matlock, W. F. Ramsey,
J. B. Wells, R. H. Phelps, G. W. Tyler, J. T. Brackinridge, and K. K. Legett.

[26] The *Taylor County News*, April 24, 1885 and June 5, 1885, passim. See
Duff, *Abilene*, pp. 191, 192, 196, 197 for other railroad interests in West Texas.

Throughout 1885 the local news reporter noted Legett's arrivals and departures at the train depot. The busy attorney attended court for clients in Corsicana (Navarro County), Sweetwater (Nolan County), Whitney (Hill County), Anson (Jones County), and Colorado City (Mitchell County), according to the reporter's news items. At times, however, the reporter could only record the more obvious fact that "Hon. K. K. Legett is attending court out West" or "K. K. Legett, Esq. is attending court back East," the locality depending upon the direction the T&P engine pointed at the time the news-hungry reporter saw Legett climb aboard. With so many clients, the Spoonts and Legett law firm needed larger office space only six months after the partnership moved to the Oak Street location. Consequently, in May, 1886, they moved to the north side of town and rented the entire second floor above the Maverick Saloon on Pine Street.[27]

Busy as he was, Legett also added to his civic responsibilities. The Independent Order of Odd Fellows, a fraternal benefit society which built homes for the aged, indigent, widowed, and orphaned throughout the United States, elected him Noble Grand (presiding officer) in 1883. Later he joined the 25,000 Club (the forerunner of Abilene's Chamber of Commerce) whose goal it was to attract twenty-five thousand citizens to Abilene. Still later the 25,000 Club elected Legett to its railroad committee. In July, 1885, he was appointed notary public, and the following spring the Board of Aldermen elected him mayor pro tem of Abilene.[28]

Just before the aldermen's action in 1886, Legett made another business trip to New York City. His clients were two Abilene youths who had fallen victim to a pair of New York swindlers. One of the swindlers in turn had fallen victim to an Abilene pistol. Locked in one of New York's infamous prisons, the Tombs, Tom Hill and Jim Holland finally concluded that they could not handle their problem without help from home. Their families persuaded Legett to go to their aid, raised $2,500 for bail, and sent Legett to New York. The West Texas lawyer eventually bailed out Hill and brought him home, but Holland, who had pulled the trigger against the swindler, remained in the Tombs six months longer to await trial. With assistance from

27 *Taylor County News*, May 21, 1886.
28 Menn, "Abilene Story," p. 66; *Taylor County News*, May 7, 1886.

former Civil War general Roger A. Pryor and B. B. Paddock, a Fort Worth editor and railroad promoter, Holland successfully argued his claim of self-defense and returned to Abilene.[29] The case attracted considerable local attention and added to Legett's stature in both business and social circles in West Texas. Although still in his twenties, the young man was already one of Abilene's founding fathers and a pillar of its fledgling society.

Suddenly, Legett's love for the town and for its people took on a new dimension. In 1885 he met and fell in love with Lora Bryan. From that moment he was never again the single-minded, self-interested frontier Beau Brummell.

[29] Naomi Hatton Kincaid, "The Abilene Reporter-News and Its Contribution to the Development of the Abilene Country" (M.A. thesis, Hardin-Simmons University, 1945), pp. 18–21.

*Nine-tenths of the happiness I have ever ex-*
*perienced was predicated upon "Futures." "Pres-*
*ent" happiness is a state or condition to which*
*I am almost a stranger.*

CHAPTER FIVE

## Colonel Wash Bryan's Daughter

IN many respects the Bryan family—father and mother, their two daughters, and their son and his wife—were not unlike the dozens of pioneer families who moved into Taylor County every week. Nevertheless, their arrival in the spring of 1885 aroused a flurry of comment. Only a few Abilene men knew Washington Carroll Bryan, but many had admired for some years his fine cutting horses and his T-Diamond brand cattle. Now and then an Abilenian would insist that Colonel Wash Bryan's cutting horses were the best in Texas.[1]

Colonel Bryan was born in Tennessee, spent his early years in Mississippi, and later moved to Galveston, where he remained for several years. He later established a cattle and horse ranch on Keechi Creek, near Marlin, in Falls County, East Texas.[2] In Falls County, Bryan married Sophia Wyers, whose ancestors had followed the moving frontier from Pennsylvania to Virginia (in Augusta County, where the tiny village Weyers Cave still exists), thence to Alabama, and finally to Falls County, Texas. The Wyerses, like the Bryans, had farmed for many generations and, like most Abilenians, were the first generation to try to support themselves by some other means. Although all Wyers men had followed the plow, records suggest that some of them promoted frontier education. One of Sophia Wyers Bryan's grandfathers, for example, laid the cornerstone for Wesleyan Female Institute at Staunton, Augusta County, Virginia. On a later frontier her father, Robert Wyers, helped to establish Waco Female College in McLennan County, Texas.[3] Mrs. Bryan's children con-

---

[1] Naomi H. Kincaid in *Abilene Reporter-News*, April 8, 1956.

[2] "Statement of Washington Carroll Bryan," n.d., in Bryan Family Records, file 4, paper 2, in the possession of Mrs. Percy Jones, Abilene, Texas.

[3] Unidentified statement, dated October 14, 1909, in Bryan Family Records, file 1, paper 14.

tinued the traditional family interest in education; by the time they arrived in Abilene, her son John held degrees from Texas Agricultural and Mechanical College and the Cumberland Law School of Tennessee, and her daughter Lora had attended both Wesleyan Female Institute and Waco Female College.

The Bryans joined an uncommonly large number of Abilene pioneer settlers who were college-trained. While local cattlemen welcomed Colonel Wash Bryan to West Texas, those Abilenians interested in broadening the cultural base of their frontier society welcomed the other Bryans into their circle. Their discovery that Colonel Bryan's title was not honorary but was in fact his rank in the Confederate army and that he was a Texas Ranger back in the 1850s increased their respect for him.[4]

As the T-Diamond Ranch outgrew its Falls County acreage during the late 1870s, Colonel Bryan purchased extensive ranch lands in Jones, Fisher, and Stonewall counties which, with later additions, eventually totaled 20,000 acres. Bryan had a standard answer in later years when anyone asked him how he managed to accumulate such vast acreage. With tongue in cheek he replied that he bought a buffalo dugout in Jones County for $40 cash, and, in appreciation for the cash payment, the owner threw in "all the lands within a twenty-mile radius of the dugout."[5]

When the Bryans reached Abilene, they moved directly into a new home on the western edge of town. The two-story frame house on South First Street faced north toward the Texas and Pacific tracks and was located approximately one mile west of the railroad depot. The Bryan women were introduced to local society with all of the traditional formality one might expect in a community two or three centuries older. Among the women, Victorian custom flourished in Abilene from its earliest days and perhaps accounted for the instant fellowship among all respected females in the town. As in any frontier town, the imbalance in the number of males and females created an intense rivalry among the local Beau Brummels. They conspired in devious ways, therefore, to meet the colonel's young daughters.

[4] Charles Schreiner, III, to W. B. Trammell, March 29, 1971 (Mr. Schreiner is president of the Texas Rangers Historical Arms, Inc.), Bryan Family Records, file 5, paper 4.

[5] Naomi H. Kincaid in the *Abilene Reporter-News*, April 8, 1956.

In due time, twenty-eight-year-old K. K. Legett managed to meet
eighteen-year-old Lora Bryan. From the beginning they were almost
inseparable, and within weeks the Legett-Bryan twosome was a common pairing at social gatherings. Each had spent the childhood years in
East Texas, but beyond that their early years had few parallels. As the
daughter of a successful rancher, Lora knew no other life styles than
those at the ranch and at the two colleges where she had studied
music and art. She would have remained at the Virginia school when
her family moved from East Texas had not an epidemic of diphtheria
temporarily closed the school and forced her to spend several months
at the Washington, D.C., home of Texas Congressman Roger Q.
Mills. When the school reopened Lora chose not to enroll until the
fall. She returned to Texas during her family's final preparations for
their move to West Texas. Later they prevailed upon her to abandon
her plans to return to Virginia and to accompany them instead to
Abilene.

Legett had never experienced Lora's opulent world—indeed, he
had little chance to know that it existed—and viewing its richness
through her eyes and from her perspective undoubtedly added to her
allurement. He plotted endless ways to monopolize her social hours
and soon discovered that Abilene entertainment suffered the limitations of all frontier towns. Such restrictions, combined with Abilene's
traditional Victorian morality, severely taxed his ingenuity. The traveling opera and dramatic companies, which appeared regularly at the
Maltby Opera House on Pine Street, provided their favorite entertainment. The opera house contained three hundred seats on the second
floor of the Maltby Building. George Walsh's grocery store occupied
the first floor.[6]

As the summer of 1885 passed into fall, the couple discovered
one another's likes and dislikes, their similarities and dissimilarities,
their fears and their dreams. Among the trivialities, they learned that
he loved cabbage and she loathed it, she knew the name of every
flower and he knew none of them, he liked lamb and she protested
that the Virginia school had fed her lamb until she despised it, she
loved to dance and he tolerated it, and he enjoyed penny-ante poker,

[6] Lora Bryan to K. K. Legett, November 6, 1885, Legett Family Records, paper
507; Irene Stewart, "James A. Lowery and the Taylor County News" (M.A. thesis,
Hardin-Simmons University, August, 1951), p. 134.

but she could not abide card games.[7] More significantly, they shared a life-long interest in literature. Lora read Sir Walter Scott and, to a lesser degree, Balzac and William Makepeace Thackeray; she tolerated Dickens, but her "love in life" was William Cullen Bryant, the American poet and newspaper editor whom she would quote at the slightest excuse. Legett preferred political philosophy, and, although he never expressed any particular favorites, he frequently quoted John Stuart Mill, the English economist, philosopher, and political theorist. He eagerly read any article about political philosophy that was based on Biblical themes.[8]

By October the romance had progressed to an "understanding," but Lora, younger by a decade and apparently unsure that the relationship would culminate in marriage, hit upon an age-old scheme to make her fiance's heart grow fonder: she would leave Abilene for awhile. She accepted an invitation to serve as a bridesmaid in Longview and then extended the trip indefinitely while she visited friends and relatives throughout East Texas. Her astute young lawyer suspected her strategy but played the game according to her rules. Consequently, when Lora reached Longview there was a letter from Abilene. After what appears to be a week's deliberate delay, she "hastened to respond, regardless of the difficulty (I have an engagement presently)."[9]

She then described at great length a recent wedding and, with an eighteen-year-old's subtlety, expressed the "thrill of marching up the altar by the lovely strains of Mendelssohn's wedding march." She described in similar detail the wedding reception but refused Legett's earlier request for a slice of the wedding cake because he "would never indulge in anything so silly as dreaming on it." Having exhausted the subject of the wedding party, she continued:

> We were awakened during the early hours of the morning by delightful music furnished by the Marshall [Texas] band. The boys are getting up a dance for Monday night and expect to have this same band. . . .

> Your friend,
> Obstinate[10]

[7] Mrs. Percy Jones to the author, March 24, 1972.
[8] Ibid.
[9] Lora Bryan to K. K. Legett, October 24, 1885, Legett Family Records, paper 506.
[10] Ibid.

By November 6 Legett apparently had decided that his earlier requests for her return only convinced her that prolonged absence indeed made the heart grow fonder, so he delayed his replies to her frequent and lengthy letters. Her reaction proved that she was playing a coquette's game:

Longview, Texas
November 6, '85

Mr. Legett:

My dear friend,

Must confess I deserve the reprimand [of silence], but I should have appreciated it much more had you corrected me [in writing] for so far forgetting the rules of etiquette as to write a second time. . . . Having had several letters lost on their way to Abilene, I thought it highly possible yours had met the same fate. I should never have written had I known it was nothing but negligence on your part, for I assure you, though it may seem obtuse, I can conceive no other reason for your long silence.

I leave Sunday night at eleven o'clock for Marlin. . . .

I will close by signing myself by the name (if I remember correctly) you so kindly gave me.

"Obstinacy" [11]

Legett's silent treatment had defeated his intended purpose, and Lora traveled to Marlin to visit friends and relatives. Her attempt to disguise her disappointment that no letter awaited her there probably prompted the vexatious opening paragraph in her letter of November 12:

Marlin, Texas
Nov. 12th '85

My dear friend,

I would use a more endearing term than this, but you are as apt to be married as not so I will spare my blushes and not offend your wife. I am right provoked about this letter anyway.

Her next paragraphs were clearly designed to install pangs of jealousy:

[11] Lora Bryan to K. K. Legett, November 6, 1885, Legett Family Records, paper 507.

Met such an entertaining drummer on the train . . . who was going to Austin. I was giving a glowing description of my western home and, in fact, trying to make an impression when, low and behold, he jumped up and said he had to send a telegram to his wife to meet him at the train. Well!! I don't know whether you can ever imagine my feelings or not.

By the fifth page Lora had abandoned her lover's game and was intent only in communicating her thought to the handsome West Texan whom she clearly wanted to see:

If you see me in Abilene in a week don't be very much surprised.

I am reading a perfectly splendid book now, David Copperfield. Did you ever read it. I like it much better than any I ever read of Dickens. It is considered his best anyway, I believe. . . .

I have two invitations to stop in Fort Worth as I go through, but don't know yet if I will or not.

I do think that after this you might give me a better non-de-plume than
Obstinacy[12]

On a mountain bluff near Buffalo Gap one Sunday afternoon in April, 1886, Lora accepted the young lawyer's proposal of marriage. They would marry sometime in June. Quietly, they selected a home site in southeast Abilene, and Legett engaged a contractor to build a house similar to several already occupied in the area by their close friends. Lora journeyed to Austin shortly thereafter to visit friends and to purchase certain items for her new home. With her marriage only weeks away, it was no longer necessary for her to play the lover's game.

Legett's letters were both long and frequent, and they provided his future bride with many new insights into his character and personality. He confessed in a letter written at the St. George Hotel in Dallas on April 24 that he had lost interest in earlier plans to celebrate his "last days of independence" and that their separation had produced instead a mood "where pressure is great and the anxious

---

[12] Lora Bryan to K. K. Legett, November 12, 1885, Legett Family Records, paper 505.

mind is burdened." He readily admitted that he was "a conquered victim," and that he was prepared to "enter into a new life."

Two weeks later, Legett's letter to Lora clearly revealed the effect of their protracted separation:

Friday night, May 7th 1886

Miss Lora—

Precious Girl:

I am seated alone in our new home "wrapt in the solitude of my own originality." . . .

It would simply be intolerable for me to remain out here alone if I were not supported by the reflection that it will not "always be thus."

It has never been my fortune to possess more than a share . . . of the happiness incident to human life. Often thought I didn't even get a share. But . . . I do know that nine-tenths of the happiness I have ever experienced was predicated upon "Futures." "Present" happiness is a state or condition to which I am almost a stranger. The phantoms of peace and contentment have always been in sight just ahead of me, seemingly "so near yet so far," I have followed these delusions with earnestness and with eagerness, only to realize how uncertain a thing is human happiness. . . .

But thank God it does seem as if the goal would be reached at last. . . . A few more short (long?) weeks would land me full and fair on the golden shores of perpetual happiness.

I am very sorry there is prevailing such an epidemic around the city, and I shall be *very, very* anxious and uneasy about you. . . . And then the weather is getting warm and you have gone down into a warmer climate, and I just won't have any peace of mind until you get home. . . .

Miss Julia and Miss Fay [Lora's sister and niece] and myself went to the exhibition last night and had a good time. It was the biggest crowd we have ever had in Abilene. Half of them couldn't get in the Opera House. . . .

I have a bed, water bucket, wash pan, and a broom out here. This composes my household goods. Yes, a lamp, but the oil is out & I have to close. It is so near out that I could hardly see the lines the last two pages, & I have nothing nearer than a mile with which I can replenish. So I must close. . . .

Tenderly yours,
K. K. Legett [13]

[13] K. K. Legett to Lora Bryan, May 7, 1886, Legett Family Records, file 3, paper 16.

Within a week Lora returned to Abilene, and together they made plans for a June wedding to coincide with the completion of their home. As household furniture from Dallas and Austin arrived in Legett's name, the grapevine telegraph rapidly spread the word that the wedding date was not far away. As late as June 4 there was still no public announcement, but an alert reporter inserted an item on that date in the *Taylor County News*: "Rumor has it that Mr. K. K. Legett will marry soon. It must be true, else why would he fit up such a fine residence?" The sensitive newsman held rigidly to Victorian custom for the time and avoided any mention of the bride's name prior to an official announcement from her family. In this instance, however, the Bryans never made a formal announcement, but instead employed local messenger boys to deliver personal invitations to the ceremony.

The entire town was alerted to the approaching event as numerous relatives, friends, and wedding attendants arrived on the westbound trains. All speculation ended during the day of June 10 as the hum and stir of activity around the Presbyterian church intensified with each passing hour. By nine o'clock in the evening it was obvious to everyone that the Legett-Bryan wedding was no longer a private affair, but had instead grown into a public celebration. By 9:15 P.M., as the bridal party carriages drew up at the west door of the church and formed a single line, every pew was filled, and the spectators who arrived late moved their vehicles below the open windows "and gazed through the casement upon the animating scene within." [14]

Frontier entertainment—the "respectable" kind—was rarely available to those who frowned on the opera house and condemned the saloon. As a consequence, a formal ceremony which united in marriage one of the town's best-known lawyers and the comely daughter of a prominent cattleman was more than a wedding ceremony; it was an entertainment. Ladies whispered to each other that Miss Lora's wedding gown was made in Louisville, Kentucky, and that the colonel had paid more than one hundred dollars for it. If true, their listeners responded, it was without doubt the most expensive wedding dress in Abilene's five-year history.[15] The editors of both local news-

[14] *Abilene Reporter*, n.d., in Julia Legett Pickard scrapbook, Legett Family Records, file 5, paper 8.
[15] Interview with Ruth Bradfield Gay, Abilene, Texas, July 15, 1973.

papers devoted most of their front pages to details of the ceremony, whereas the story of President Cleveland's recent marriage to Frances Folsom was relegated to an inside page.[16]

The newlyweds embarked on no grand honeymoon. They moved instead to their new home in southeast Abilene. It was a measure of their maturity, and symbolic of many future decisions, that they chose to invest their honeymoon money in extra furnishings for their home. They also had another reason to economize: a dry spell had turned into a protracted drought that stunted the grasses and turned the plowed land into dust clouds. It affected the economic security of all Abilenians as it threatened to drive every cattleman and farmer from the land. The Spoonts-Legett law partnership continued to attract a large clientele, but an increasing proportion of them delayed payment for their legal services. Coincidentally, Legett withdrew his land holdings from the market as sales diminished, prices fell, and storm clouds brought dust instead of moisture to his doorstep.

The bride realized that those who demanded so much of her husband's time ignored his changed marital status. Social and business organizations requested his appearance for public addresses, and his clients kept him scurrying about West Texas as if he were still a footloose bachelor. A murder trial in Scurry County might require a week's absence and a sixty-mile train and buggy trip to Snyder, the county seat, and the following week a habeas corpus trial in Baylor County would include a seventy-five-mile ride to Seymour.[17] A typical day in Abilene would include a busy daytime schedule with clients and a speaking engagement in the evening before one of the civic organizations. A holiday celebration invariably meant an appearance for Legett on some speaker's platform.

Thus, less than a month following his wedding, the groom shared the platform with General John Sayles at the Fourth of July festivities at Cooper Grove. A local newsman reported that the picnic dinner was abundant and excellent, the parade concert came up to the expectations of all, and the orations delivered by General Sayles and the Honorable Legett were eloquent and well received.[18] A grand ball

[16] Katharyn Duff, *Abilene . . . on Catclaw Creek*, p. 147.
[17] *Taylor County News*, September 2, 1886.
[18] Ibid., July 8, 1886.

at the opera house completed that year's national birthday celebration in dry and dusty—but still optimistic—Abilene, Texas.

A brief reference in his Fourth of July speech to "that old demon rum," which was not a part of Legett's written notes, inadvertently instigated a flood of invitations from prohibition groups throughout Central and West Texas to speak at their numerous rallies. Since the early 1870s the United Friends of Temperance had campaigned against liquor sales in Texas. A decade later, the Women's Christian Temperance Union strengthened and popularized the movement. Church and civic leaders in many frontier towns joined the crusade to reduce the number of murders and mutilations committed so regularly in their many saloons. All foes of liquor sales in Texas, dissatisfied with the half-way measures of the state's 1876 local option law, demanded statewide prohibition. A state law, they reasoned, could be more effectively enforced than a local ordinance. Efforts by Texas legislators to avoid the issue succeeded only in contributing to the movement's emotional momentum. Throughout 1886 and into 1887 prohibition groups increased their pressure upon the political representatives in Austin.

K. K. Legett agreed with his Baptist friends that demon rum accounted for most of the hardships suffered by Abilene's destitute families. Although he accepted fewer than half of his speaking invitations, his public appearances between July, 1886, and July, 1887, outnumbered those of any other Abilenian.[19] Privately, he did not consider himself a fanatic on the subject, but his audiences assumed that he was a confirmed—or "hard-shell"—prohibitionist. His prohibition speeches increased in number early in 1887 after the legislators weakened under intense pressure and submitted to the public a statewide prohibition amendment. They announced that voters should declare their opinions on August 4. On May 27 Legett addressed a large gathering of prohibitionists on the courthouse lawn in Abilene and, by popular demand, repeated the address at the same location on June 11. On June 17 he addressed the Merkel Prohibition Club. The following week the *Taylor County News* reported that Legett had delivered another able address on June 22 to a very large crowd assembled on the courthouse lawn in Abilene.

19 *Abilene Reporter* and *Taylor County News*, passim.

Early in July the Texas Prohibition Central Committee met to appoint delegates to a mass meeting of prohibitionists scheduled for July 30 at Fort Worth. Legett and his law partner, M. A. Spoonts, were among the twenty West Texas delegates appointed to attend the rally.[20] Other delegates from around the state included the Reverend G. W. Briggs, editor of the *Texas Christian Advocate*, the Reverend S. A. Hayden, editor of the *Texas Baptist and Herald*, United States Senators John H. Reagan and Sam Bell Maxey, and Congressman D. B. Culberson.

The prohibitionists were not without organized opposition, however. Legett believed that the opposing forces were about equally divided, and among his opponents was Congressman Roger Q. Mills. A close personal friend of Legett's father-in-law, Mills, only a few years earlier, had been Lora Legett's Washington host.[21]

On August 4 most West Texas voters learned to their dismay that they had lost to the opponents of statewide prohibition by a decisive margin. The total vote in Texas was 220,627 against the amendment and 129,270 for it. Perhaps the most shocking statistic was that which showed only 23 counties voted for the prohibition of liquor sales, while 119 counties had majorities against the proposal. Legett could take some comfort, however, in the West Texas vote, where 11 counties, including Taylor, won majorities for prohibition. In Abilene the prohibitionists won by 311 to 188, and in two nearby towns where Legett often spoke, Buffalo Gap and Merkel, the prohibitionists were in the majority by votes of 63 to 23 and 62 to 19 respectively.[22]

The West Texas vote was something of a personal victory for Legett and his allies, although by election day they worried about another problem far more threatening than demon rum: West Texas, they had to admit, was drying up and blowing away. Just as Abilene's economic stability seemed almost assured with cattle, sheep, and cotton, and the Texas and Pacific Railroad promoting greater diversity

---

[20] *Taylor County News*, July 1, 1887.

[21] Congressman Mills won national recognition in his efforts for tariff reform and was subsequently elected to the Senate. He later lost favor with Texas voters when he supported Cleveland's sound-money policies and opposed the free coinage of silver (Mrs. Percy Jones to the author, March 24, 1972).

[22] Ibid., August 29, 1887.

every year, the blazing sun relentlessly baked the earth. Even local thunderstorms that teased West Texans through 1885 and 1886 seemed to disappear in 1887. Some area ranchers, including Colonel Bryan, moved their herds east and south wherever greener grazing lands were within reach, but the few bales of cotton produced failed to cover expenses and the grain farmers' crops died in the fields for the third successive year.[23] Some of the men and their families returned to their earlier homes back east, and others moved into town to seek other means of employment.

Legett and the other city aldermen in Abilene, in emergency sessions, created a public work program to relieve the suffering and to arrest the rapidly diminishing number of those who tried to remain in West Texas. As a consequence, farmers constructed new plank sidewalks throughout the downtown area. Later, as the unskilled workers learned their new trades, they advanced to the construction of roads and bridges around Taylor County.[24]

For a time Abilenians tried to laugh away their worries. Presbyterians pointed to the practical advantages of sprinkling and clucked their tongues at the wastefulness of baptisms. A "prominent prohibitionist" (possibly Legett, since it was his type of humor) threatened to order a case of beer from Decatur so that he might shave with its lather. But the humor could not survive the endless days of cloudless skies when the temperatures, day after day, reached 100 degrees and at times climbed to 110. Hard-earned savings dwindled, then disappeared entirely as grocer George W. Clayton's customers accumulated debts which eventually totaled more than $115,000.[25]

The pinch of economic depression was especially galling to such a proud, ambitious, and sensitive man as K. K. Legett. He left no record of his personal trauma during those grim months, but he talked openly about opportunities elsewhere. Finally on August 19, the *Taylor County News* reported that K. K. Legett contemplated making a trip to California in the fall. With that difficult decision made, Legett hurriedly completed his plans and headed west alone within a week. In late September his bride joined him in Los Ange-

[23] William C. Holden, "West Texas Droughts," *Southwestern Historical Quarterly* 32 (October, 1928): 103–105.

[24] Duff, *Abilene*, pp. 104–105.

[25] Ibid.

les, where he had opened a law office. Later that fall he asked the Abilene city officials to accept his resignation as a city alderman. Within a few weeks, however, Mrs. Legett returned to Abilene and her husband made a business trip to Dallas. He stopped briefly in Abilene the following week and then departed alone for San Diego. Mrs. Legett joined him there in February, returned to Abilene again on April 27, and on June 8 she informed a news reporter that Mr. Legett would return to Texas within a few weeks. In mid-August, obviously disenchanted with opportunities in California, Legett announced that he would form a law partnership with his brother-in-law, W. J. Bryan, and that they would open an office in Dallas.[26]

In December, however, another local news item mentioned that Legett was back in town and shaking the hands of his many friends.[27] Rumors spread quickly that Legett would rejoin his old law partner, M. A. Spoonts. In mid-January, 1889, the *Abilene Reporter* announced that Legett had purchased the M. A. Spoonts law office, but the former partners had in fact exchanged offices; a week later the Spoonts family moved to Dallas, and Legett opened his office on Pine Street.[28] Dallas offered many opportunities which attracted Spoonts, but there was no place in the nation more attractive to Legett than his adopted West Texas home, now that the rains had returned.

The Legetts happily resumed their old Abilene life-style. They returned to the Baptist church and joined the church choir, and after the spring elections Legett was named president of his Sunday school class. Meanwhile he joined the Abilene Progressive Committee, which dedicated its efforts to attracting new immigrants to West Texas. Mrs. Legett also was active, for she entered one of her oil paintings in the Taylor County Fair and was named the first-place winner.

Their greatest happiness, however, sprang from a more personal source: sometime in early June, at about the time of their third wedding anniversary, the Legetts expected the birth of their first child. They had moved temporarily into a house directly across the street

[26] *Taylor County News*, November 18, December 9 and 16, 1887; August 17, 1888.

[27] Ibid., December 7, 1888.

[28] *Abilene Reporter*, January 18 and 25, 1889. The brief news items fail to explain the Legetts' frequent travels between August, 1887, and January, 1889. Obviously they were not satisfied with their locations at Los Angeles, San Diego, or Dallas.

from the Bryan home and there they awaited the child's arrival. Almost precisely on schedule—June 4—Kade Bryan was born, and both local newspaper editors duly reported K. K. Legett's happiness on the arrival of the "bouncing boy." [29]

Before Kade was one month old, his father gave the principal oration in the ceremony at which the cornerstone was laid for the new high-school building on South First Street. Partly as an expression of their confidence in Abilene's future economic stability following the drought, Abilenians had loaned the town $10,000 from their own pockets to cover construction costs of the town's first "permanent" (brick) school building.[30] To pledge their faith, and to lay the cornerstone, they arranged to hold Masonic ceremonies.

On Tuesday, June 25, at twilight, the Masonic fraternity at Abilene, led by J. H. Parramore, formed a procession on the north side of the T&P tracks and marched down to the school site where a large crowd awaited. Following the symbolic dedication with corn, oil, and wine, Parramore placed a Bible and a copy of the United States Constitution in the cornerstone. The attentive crowd then settled back to hear the main address. Legett based his theme on the contents of the cornerstone and entitled the address "The Bible and the Federal Constitution." His carefully constructed remarks included the following points:

The more we know of each [the Bible and the federal constitution] the more we approach the purpose of an intelligent creature. . . . They are the grandest productions of the ancient and modern world.

Individual and national greatness alike spring from the same source, and the two together exist in proportion to the individual knowledge of these two great productions.

The *sculptor* may . . . perpetuate the noble and the exalted; the *artist* may . . . commemorate the virtues of the true and the brave. The *poet* and the *historian* may eulogize . . . that which deserves to stand in perpetuity, but they all combined do not furnish the cloak of immortality to the creations of man. . . .

However useful these agencies may be . . . in preserving the past, they do not furnish sufficient light . . . for the future . . . without the Bible in one hand and the federal constitution in the other.

[29] *Abilene Reporter*, June 7, 1889; *Taylor County News*, June 7, 1889.
[30] Stewart, "Lowery and the Taylor County News," p. 122.

The wise man said: "With all thy gettings get understanding." John Stuart Mill, the great political economist, says that each generation owes it to the next to educate the masses. . . .

The framers of the Texas declaration of independence declared: "That unless a people are educated and enlightened, it is idle to expect the continuance of public liberty or the capacity of self-government."

The *children* of our time must soon become the "architects of the living temple of the Republic," and if we expect them to discharge this trust with efficiency and fidelity, they must be educated and enlightened.[31]

Although construction was completed before the end of the calendar year, the school was too small before the first student entered it, and plans were already underway for a second brick structure. For many years thereafter Legett used the growth of the school system as a barometer for Abilene's growth. Coincidentally, as Kade's birth marked the beginning of one school building in 1889, the births of the Legetts' two daughters, in 1891 and in 1892, closely paralleled the construction of other school structures. Julia was born on June 4 (her brother's second birthday) at about the time when the second permanent school was completed, and Ruth arrived on December 28, 1892, shortly after Abilene's new Baptist school, Simmons College, was formally opened.

As he approached his mid-thirties, K. K. Legett was a devoted husband, a father of three West Texas natives, a successful attorney, and a major force in bringing to Abilene a strong public school system and a college to which he would devote many more years of his energies and talents. There was nothing pretentious in his sometimes lofty expressions concerning an educated and enlightened citizenry. Self-taught, he never doubted that "schools and universities designed the keys to individual and national omnipotence."[32] With a small son and two infant daughters at home, Legett apparently decided in the early 1890s to dedicate a part of his spare time to the pursuit of educational opportunities for others. Typically his efforts began at home, but eventually he touched the lives of young men and young women throughout the Southwest.

[31] "Abilene's New School House," *Abilene Reporter*, June 25, 1889.

[32] A favorite Legett expression that appeared frequently in his addresses at Simmons College and the Agricultural and Mechanical College of Texas.

*Fortunately, nature has limited . . . the influence
of one generation upon its successors. It is precisely because youth is incapable of fully absorbing the wisdom of age, and trusts to its own
daring impulses, that progress is assured.*

CHAPTER SIX

# Many Years Ago . . .
# Some Ten or Twelve

AN unidentified Abilene newsman declared, in the 1890s, that an
Englishman in the 1880s probably would have stigmatized Abilene
as a beastly hole and that a Frenchman probably would have con-
temptuously used the word bourgeoisie to describe Abilene's inhabitants. The newsman opined that such descriptions might have been
accurate "many years ago, some ten or twelve," but in the mid-1890s,
the reporter assured his readers, West Texas was no longer a wilder-
ness and its citizens were no longer uncivilized or uncouth.[1]

It was characteristic of that West Texas town, at that point in its
history, to allow its local reporters such freedom to belittle Abilene's
pioneer settlers if the purpose was only to emphasize the town's progress in recent years. Conversely, reporters never hesitated to assume
their right to make such comparisons, since the present was always an
improvement over the past. They constantly sought ways to counter-
balance many of the frontier's less admirable traits by directing attention to some specific accomplishment. Thus, on this occasion in the
mid-nineties, the reporter hastened to remind his mythical Englishman and Frenchman that Abilene's womenfolk had organized the
first Shakespeare Club in the state of Texas.

To every responsible Abilenian, progress was a goal only slightly
less desirable than Godliness. There were perhaps no other frontiersmen west of the Mississippi who believed more firmly that God pros-
pers the righteous, and K. K. Legett was not the least among those
who held to this conviction. To him it was only natural that he become a charter member of Abilene's First Baptist Church and of the

[1] *Abilene Reporter*, May 10, 1895.

Progressive Committee. He was proud of his membership in each and looked upon such memberships as a civic duty. For other Abilenians, however, the idea of progress had other manifestations. For them, cows, loose and unattended, wandering about the downtown streets, were symbols of economic well-being and prosperity. Merchants and some businessmen protested that they could dispense with this kind of progress. They had suffered enough from "the depredations of said cows," and they demanded local action to outlaw the critters. The city council, eager to find a fair and democratic solution to the problem, asked local newsmen to check the sentiment of all Abilenians about the cows. Legett joined other members of the Progressive Committee and campaigned against the nuisance. To Legett's great disgust, the campaign lost by a small margin, and the *Abilene Reporter* announced on March 11, 1892, that local sentiment was "a little favorable" to the town cows' right to use the public streets.

This defeat did not discourage the Progressive Committee's efforts in behalf of other improvements. The same May 11 edition of the paper announced, for example, that the committee's chief efforts would be directed toward town improvements that might attract new settlers. Among immediate goals were listed the building of a grain elevator and a cottonseed-oil mill, and attracting another railroad. The basic targets seldom varied from year to year. With typical frontier optimism, and in spite of high winds and frequent droughts along the 98th meridian, committee members proclaimed with straight faces and clear consciences that "nature has done all in its power to favor this location upon which should be built the great city of central Texas."[2] Having long ago convinced themselves that nature was more often an ally than an enemy, they followed such pronouncements with reminders that there was much to be done by those already in residence.

Legett lent his name to all appeals for public cooperation. Whenever he could afford to do so, he offered financial support as well. On March 18, 1892, for example, he bought shares in a joint stock company that was organized for building a grain elevator. The company was authorized to commence operations as soon as capital stock reached a total of $25,000.[3] Civic activities consumed many hours of

[2] Ibid., April 17, 1891.
[3] Ibid., March 18, 1892.

Legett's time. He made speeches to build public support for an extension of the Gulf, Colorado, and Santa Fe Railroad from Coleman to Abilene; he helped to finance a second artesian well as the town's need for water increased; he cosponsored a plan to build a dam across Lytle Creek to provide an additional water supply; and he participated in such undertakings as the businessmen's campaign to build permanent sidewalks in the business district. He supported with particular enthusiasm the decision to celebrate Abilene's tenth birthday anniversary by installing electric lights in the downtown area. When he stood among his friends and neighbors on April 10, 1891, and marveled at the bright, steady light, entirely free of flickering and sputtering, he congratulated the Abilene Electric Light and Power Company for having the good sense to install wood arc lights, which were exactly the same as those used in St. Louis.[4]

Throughout the year Abilene's pioneer citizens congratulated one another on the town's progress during its first decade. When it was announced in early 1892 that the taxable property of Taylor County in 1891 was $5,057,969—which every businessman knew represented an increase of $819,706 above the previous year—their ambitions for the town and the county intensified. They concluded, however, that large numbers of immigrants—enough to satisfy local ambitions—were not likely to settle in the area unless Abilene advertised its varied and unique qualities. For variety they emphasized those geographic and environmental features which contributed to the area's prosperous economy; for uniqueness, they added such special enticements as they could devise or contrive for those potential immigrants with such physical disabilities as consumption, asthma, and nervous debility.

At times their consciences rebelled against overzealous advertising, so they counterbalanced their claims with a clearer definition of the type of persons they sought to attract to Abilene: "Persons who are skilled in mechanical, industrial, and manufacturing pursuits, persons wishing to build themselves into big business from small beginnings," and even those penniless persons "who have brain alone, but [are] resolved to conquer success."[5] All these would have no trouble reaching their goals in Taylor County.

[4] Letter to the editor, *Abilene Reporter*, April 17, 1891.
[5] *Abilene Reporter*, August 2, 1895.

At other times the pioneer citizens sought to counteract Abilene's image as a frontier saloon town by emphasizing its conspicuous devoutness. Parents eager to help their children escape the "dangers and evil tendencies in the North and East" should move to Abilene's healthful, productive locality. Legett and other civic leaders encouraged, although they did not always subscribe to, the Christian guidelines formulated and publicly promoted by the Abilene Alliance of Ministers of the Gospel. The guidelines were stated as follows: "1. That we do not approve of Christians engaging in the dance. 2. That we disapprove card-playing in general, and card parties in particular. 3. That, while we do not wish to seem puritanical in our views, we believe theatre going has an evil tendency. 4. That Sunday is a day of public worship. 5. That we regard the whiskey traffic as one of the greatest evils of the day. 6. That all other practices that have any tendency to lead people away from Christ are hereby condemned."[6]

Nevertheless, in Abilene as in all other parts of the frontier, the works of the Lord and those of the Devil succeeded simultaneously. As the town marked the close of its first decade of existence, therefore, hundreds of pioneers watched with stupefying attention on November 19, 1891, as Sheriff J. V. Cunningham mounted the hangman's scaffold at 2:20 P.M. and announced: "Ladies and gentlemen, it becomes my painful duty to execute one of my fellow men." The condemned man, W. H. Frizzell, who had emptied the contents of a .38 caliber six-shooter into his wife's body, showed no remorse. He puffed on a cigar and obviously enjoyed his key role in the hour-long ceremony that preceded his execution.[7]

This was Abilene's first hanging, an incident in the town's history that Legett preferred to forget. He often complained that Texans in other areas of the state showed far too much interest in such West Texas occurrences as the Frizzell murder but far too little interest when Abilene accomplished something constructive and less spectacular. For many years thereafter, whenever Legett needed an example of bad publicity negating good publicity, he returned to that early-day hanging and noted that in the same year the Abilene Baptist College opened its doors with no statewide notice in the press.

From the beginning of the movement for a Baptist college in

---

[6] Ibid., March 31, 1893.
[7] Ibid., November 20, 1893.

Abilene, Legett took an active part. The idea for such an institution developed into a favorite topic of conversation when he and other leaders in the Sweetwater Baptist Association got together. Eventually a group including Legett, the Reverend J. C. Wingo, Henry Sayles, Sr., Elder G. W. Smith, and William Young met regularly during the winter of 1889–1900 around the wood stove at the rear of Young's Dry Goods Store.[8] They looked with jaundiced eyes at the Methodist college at Belle Plain and the Presbyterian college at Buffalo Gap. The final spur to their college interests resulted, however, from competition within the Baptist denomination. In the summer of 1889, the Pecan Valley Baptist Association—just south of the Sweetwater Baptist Association—announced that it would locate a Baptist college in Brownwood. The Abilene group's challenge was thus twofold: they must not allow their Baptist brothers in the Pecan Valley district to overshadow them, and in a secular vein they could not allow Abilene to suffer in any comparison with its arch-rival, Brownwood. That competitor to the south was a Santa Fe Railroad town just as Abilene was a Texas and Pacific town, and they had been natural competitors since each had learned of the other's existence. Whenever Legett and his friends reminded one another that Abilene must be "as good as the best, and better than the rest" they usually had Brownwood in mind.[9]

Inevitably, the informal group around William Young's stove devised a series of resolutions to present at the August meeting of the Sweetwater Baptist Association. That organization served a large but sparsely settled region in West Texas. Its eastern boundary commenced at Baird (twenty miles east of Abilene) and its western boundary ended at El Paso, some four hundred miles away. The area was approximately the size of the state of Kentucky, but it contained only twenty-seven Baptist churches with an aggregate membership of slightly fewer than three hundred.

The Abilene Baptist churches appointed Legett, J. W. Steele, J. B.

[8] R. C. Crane, "The Beginning of Hardin-Simmons University," *West Texas Historical Association Year Book* 16 (October, 1940): 64; for a brief sketch of the formation of the plan, see also *The First Annual Catalogue of Simmons College, 1892–93* (Sidney A. Smith, printer, Abilene, Texas); for more complete details of the university's history, see Rupert N. Richardson, *Famous Are Thy Halls: Hardin-Simmons University as I Have Known It.*

[9] Crane, "Beginning of Hardin-Simmons University," p. 65.

Webb, Mr. and Mrs. W. B. Moss, William Young, and Elders J. C.
Wingo and George W. Smith to represent them at the Sweetwater
meeting.[10] By prior agreement the delegation discreetly lobbied for
the election of the Reverend Wingo as moderator of the convention.
Their successful maneuver assured an early reading of the resolutions.
Wingo eventually set the Abilene delegation's time allotment on the
agenda for 8:30 P.M. on Friday, August 1, which was the first day of
the meeting. Other business delayed the reading of the resolution,
however, until the following morning.

As soon as Saturday's session convened, Legett, Smith, and J. S.
Williams made "ringing report[s] in behalf of Christian education"
and then presented their resolutions:

Resolved 1st. That it is the sense of the Association that a Baptist high
school within the bounds of our Association is necessary;

Resolved 2nd. That a moderator appoint a committee of seven, consisting of K. K. Legett of Abilene, G. W. Smith of Abilene, J. M. Hanna of
Anson, J. F. Fergeson of Anson, H. C. Hord of Sweetwater, C. R. Breedlove of Fisher, and R. W. Smith of Colorado City. That said committee
have plenary power to accept bids for the location of the school. . . .

Resolved 3rd. That said Committee, when the school is located, shall
jointly with the church where said school shall be located have plenary
power to appoint a board of trustees and do all things necessary to the
establishment of said school;

Resolved 4th. That the locating committee shall report in full and in
detail to the . . . next session of the Association.[11]

Dr. R. C. Burleson, who was president of Baylor University and
who had come to the association specifically to oppose the resolutions,
immediately requested and received permission to speak. He argued
vigorously that there were too few people in West Texas to support
such a school, that it was doomed to failure, and that all other Baptist
schools in Texas—with the exception of Baylor—had already failed.
Even Baylor could not pay off its heavy debts, he explained, although
every Baptist congregation in Texas had promised to support it.[12]

Legett and his allies could not challenge Dr. Burleson's accuracy

10 Ibid., p. 62.
11 Ibid., pp. 65–66.
12 Ibid., p. 67.

so they questioned, instead, his logic. They protested that Burleson based his arguments upon past experience, whereas the Abilene delegation based its resolutions upon the future growth and prosperity of a new country. Legett argued that his audience included men filled with optimism and faith or they would not have moved to West Texas in the first place. The vote, at the conclusion of the debate, proved that Legett was right. The delegates voted overwhelmingly in favor of the Abilene resolutions.[13]

On October 17, 1890, the locating committee duly met in Abilene and its chairman, Dr. G. W. Smith, opened the various bids from those towns that sought the school's location. At length the committee accepted an offer from George P. Phillips, a local hardware dealer, and his two associates, Theodore O. Vogel and E. T. Ambler, to donate sixteen acres of land in north Abilene and $5,000 in cash if other Abilenians would match their cash donation.[14]

Before the locating committee disbanded, it announced that the new school should include a college division as well as a high-school department. The committee then completed its charge from the Sweetwater Baptist Association by appointing the school's first board of trustees: George W. Smith, president; K. K. Legett, vice-president; Dr. J. T. Harrington, secretary and treasurer; J. H. Parramore, C. W. Merchant, Thomas Trammell, A. J. Long, H. C. Hord, J. A. Walker, J. F. Fergeson, J. M. Hanna, A. W. Hilliard, W. D. Johnson, and A. M. Walthall.[15] All the officers and two additional members of the board were Abilenians, and the remaining members represented Sweetwater, Colorado City, Anson, Midland, and Pecos.

The school's architect, a Mr. Archer, delivered to the trustees on November 29, 1890, his drawings for the first building, and the trustees in turn announced that construction would begin sometime in the spring. Before construction got underway, the board of trustees met again, on February 18, in the Reverend Smith's Abilene office, and Legett read to them his first draft of the college charter.[16] The

---

13 Ibid.; see also Richardson, *Famous Are Thy Halls*, p. 18.

14 Crane, "Beginning of Hardin-Simmons University," p. 68.

15 Ibid., p. 70.

16 Simmons College, *Minutes of Board of Trustees*, 1:10, February 18, 1891; Richardson, *Famous Are Thy Halls*, p. 18; Crane, "Beginning of Hardin-Simmons University," pp. 68–70. Crane, who credits Judge C. R. Breedlove—an old friend of Smith's and a former trustee of Baylor College—with authorship of the charter, is

trustees duly adopted the charter and at the same meeting accepted
the architect's building plan.

Acute financial problems arose almost at once. The first two weeks
of construction exhausted the school's cash reserves, and "there were
no rich people in the country, . . . few were well-to-do people, and
no philanthropists at all."[17] To the board's embarrassment, their ambitious project threatened to collapse even earlier than President Burleson had predicted. It was saved, however, by a source that was both
roundabout and unexpected. Board president Smith, when he mentioned the school's troubles in a letter to his old friend Dr. Owen C.
Pope, commenced the chain of events that produced the funds. Dr.
Pope, who was a former superintendent of missions for the Baptist
churches in Texas and who had organized the Baptist church in Abilene, was, in 1891, working in New York City as a member of the
American Baptist Missionary Board. He in turn appealed to the Reverend Doctor James B. Simmons, a wealthy New York Baptist minis-
ter noted for his numerous gifts to Baptist causes in the East. Intrigued by the "impossible" task undertaken by the Sweetwater Baptist
Association, Dr. Simmons journeyed to West Texas, talked with the
college trustees and, without ceremony, presented them a check for
five thousand dollars. With it the contractor completed the first college building in Abilene.

Before the first semester commenced, Dr. Simmons gave to the
college another gift of one thousand dollars. He wrote first to Legett
and asked how the money might be used. By return mail Legett recommended that the money should be loaned at 10 percent interest,
paid annually, for a period of five years and that the income should
be reserved as emergency financial aid to deserving students. Simmons
agreed to Legett's suggestion and immediately forwarded the money
for that purpose.[18]

----

the only known source who names someone other than Legett as the author of the
original charter. Unfortunately, Crane did not provide his own source of information. It seems unlikely, considering Baylor president R. C. Burleson's opposition to
the new college, that one of his own trustees would in turn write the Abilene
school's charter. Another fact that weakens Crane's claim is that Judge Breedlove
was not a member of the college's original board of trustees.

[17] Richardson, *Famous Are Thy Halls*, p. 19.

[18] K. K. Legett to Dr. J. B. Simmons, July 22, 1892, Legett Family Records,
file 15, p. 4; *First Annual Catalogue of Simmons College*, p. 16.

At that point the appreciative trustees notified the college's New York benefactor that they would name the school Simmons College. Dr. Simmons suggested that Christlieb College was a more appropriate name for the Baptist institution. The trustees persisted, however, and shortly thereafter Abilene Baptist College became Simmons College. On December 4, 1891, the editor of the *Taylor County News* displayed on its front page a picture of the college's first building. In his haste he incorrectly captioned the picture "Simpson Baptist College."[19]

The first term opened as scheduled on September 15, 1892, with forty-eight males and forty-one females attending. President W. C. Friley contributed substantially to the total enrollment when he registered his three sons and two daughters. The school was a family project for all the Frileys, for Mrs. Friley was governess in the home department and a third daughter taught in the music department. Other departments offered Greek, Latin, French, German, mathematics, commercial science, shorthand, typewriting, drawing, and painting. Most of the students were Abilenians, but seven other Texas towns sent at least one student, and two nearby states, New Mexico and Louisiana, sent one student each.[20]

The purpose of Simmons College, according to its first catalogue, was to promote Christian education, and its officials pledged themselves to "keep Christ before our students first, last, and always." For those unfamiliar with West Texas, the catalogue located the campus one hundred and sixty-five miles west of Fort Worth. The catalogue also informed its readers that every student would attend daily devotional exercises and would worship each Sunday at a church of his choice. Swearing, obscene language, scuffling, and boisterous talking would not be tolerated. The first catalogue limited its welcome to Christians of any denomination, but Dr. Simmons soon rewrote the Foundation Agreement so that "no religious test shall ever hinder any person, even though he be an idol worshiping Hindoo or a heathen Chinaman, from entering and receiving instruction in said Simmons College."[21]

Within the first year K. K. Legett, the board's relatively youthful

[19] *Taylor County News*, December 4, 1891.
[20] *First Annual Catalogue of Simmons College*, passim.
[21] Richardson, *Famous Are Thy Halls*, p. 20.

vice-president, was a familiar figure on campus and perhaps the students' favorite guest speaker. As that year drew to an end, the combined literary societies invited him to deliver the first commencement address.[22] At eleven o'clock in the morning on that red-letter day, before an overflowing audience of students, faculty, parents, and interested friends, the popular trustee delivered the following message:

The imagination and ambition of youth . . . is a measure of the kindness and mercy of God. . . . To you the thing we call life is a beautiful dream. . . . This happy delusion I would not disturb. I could not if I would. . . .
Fortunately, nature has limited . . . the influence of one generation upon its successors. If each succeeding generation slipped into the same groove, progress would end. It is precisely because youth is incapable of fully absorbing the wisdom of age, and trusts to its own daring impulses, that progress is assured. . . .
The great practical question with each of you should be: what shall I do to be useful in this life?
If I were to be called upon to write a signboard indicating the road to success and prosperity, I would inscribe but four words: Christianity, Application, Industry, Economy. . . .
I am now engaged in writing a book which will never be published, nor is it intended for publication. It is not intended that any but one shall see it—my four-year-old boy who sits over there with his mother. . . . As I learn from experience, from time to time I shall attempt to give him the benefit of what I am forced to acquire, sometimes at a heavy cost. The book is private, but I shall let you know how it runs:
—Be a Christian. . . .
—Genius without application avails but little, but application without genius may accomplish much. . . .
—Add to this *industry*. It is not rank, family, or estate, but downright git-up-and-git that makes men great. . . . There is no place in modern civilization or in the service of God for a lazy man or woman.
—Supplement all these with prudent *economy* . . . and you will then be an honor and a blessing to humanity, happy while you live and happy in the great beyond.[23]

The editor of the *Abilene Reporter* quoted liberally from the commencement address and commented that it was "as usual, full of

[22] *Taylor County News*, June 9, 1893.
[23] Original copy in Legett Family Records, file 14, paper 1.

good sense."[24] Thus K. K. Legett, still a youthful man of thirty-five years, gained the respect and admiration of young and old alike. Hardly a week passed that he was not called upon to address local groups at service clubs, charity benefits, political rallies, memorial services, Baptist conventions, Democratic party conventions, Fourth-of-July celebrations, civic and professional banquets, cattlemen's association banquets, or college literary societies. A local news reporter paid Legett the highest compliment on June 29, 1894, when he apologized to his readers for his inability to report verbatim Legett's address to the state convention of Baptist Sunday school teachers because, he explained, the speaker was "so inspirational this reporter forgot all about taking notes."[25]

His popularity as a speaker coincided with his growing reputation as a capable, level-headed, and astute lawyer. Whether the case involved murder, embezzlement, or complex property litigations, clients eagerly sought his services. Two professional guidelines, which he ceaselessly sought to refine, helped him to win far more of his cases than he lost. First, he polished his natural oratorical skills until he became an extremely persuasive courtroom lawyer. His endless number of public addresses undoubtedly polished an innate ability. Second, he prepared his cases far more thoroughly than most of his courtroom opponents. Such conscientious effort probably resulted from his tendency to overestimate the abilities of those opposing attorneys who had learned their professions at eastern law schools. He never doubted the mystic powers of formal education, and thus he sought to compensate by working harder and longer than those with formal training.

Legett's skillful handling of three legal cases during the mid-nineties further enhanced his stature. Of the three, he won greater respect for the case he eventually lost than for the two which he won. The first concerned a particularly cold-blooded murder in Merkel, the second involved a charge of embezzlement against a close friend, and the third involved another personal friend, Sheriff J. V. Cunningham.

The Merkel murder occurred at the conclusion of a Christmas Ball on Monday night, December 26, 1892. Two local men, Elzey Easterwood and Sam Hamblen, met John Baker in a saloon late that night and, a few moments later, shot him, stabbed him, and left him with

[24] *Abilene Reporter*, June 16, 1893.
[25] Ibid., June 29, 1894.

wounds from which Baker eventually died. The brutal act so enraged
the small community that district attorney F. S. Bell asked Legett and
his law partner, S. P. Hardwicke, and attorneys Wash Jones and J. M.
Wagstaff to assist him in prosecuting the case. The defendants engaged attorneys J. E. Cockrell and Fred Cockrell from Abilene, Sweetwater attorney George Thurman, and B. A. Cox of Merkel.

Each of the accused was tried separately, and Easterwood was the
first to appear before the court. Two days of testimony revealed that
the two attackers confronted Baker in a Merkel saloon and that they
cursed him and accused him of swearing before a Sweetwater grand
jury to lies against one of their friends. Easterwood then drew his
gun, forced Baker to place both hands on the bar, made him treat the
crowd to drinks, and finally forced him out of the front door of the
saloon. A minute or two later those inside heard the sharp report of
two pistol shots. They rushed outside and found Baker lying fatally
wounded. Before his death on January 7, Baker claimed that the first
defendant shot him two times, and when the victim asked Hamblen
for help, the second defendant drew a knife instead and repeatedly
stabbed Baker.

On the third day of the trial a crowd packed the courtroom to
hear the final arguments by two of the best trial lawyers in Texas. An
Abilene newsman reported that J. E. Cockrell's silvery voice presented
two hours of closing arguments for the defense. Later that day, Colonel Wash Jones—in his seventies, noted for his great skill in swaying
juries, and considered the Dean of West Texas lawyers—argued for
the prosecution. The newsman was clearly disappointed. Wash Jones
"spoke in a low voice, . . . attempted no oratory, . . . harrowed up no
scenes of misery," and, in the reporter's view, had lost much of his
eloquence.[26] Old Wash, however, was unaware of his poor performance. Accustomed to winning his cases, the overconfident old man
left Merkel before the jury brought in its verdict.

Legett and his associates shared the news reporter's concern.
When Judge T. H. Connor called the case against the second defendant, Hamblen, the following morning (still without a verdict from
the first jury), Legett presented the arguments for the prosecution.

[26] Ibid., March 31, 1893.

He had hardly begun, however, when the judge interrupted Legett and announced that the Easterwood jury could not agree on a verdict. The announcement seriously damaged any chance for a guilty verdict in the second case, so Legett decided to appeal to his jury in a manner somewhat different from that of Wash Jones: the old man had lowered his voice, and so Legett raised his; Jones had painted no word pictures to describe the "scene of misery and wickedness," and so Legett painted vivid pictures of the nineteen-year-old victim's foul murder by two older men; Jones had lost his eloquence, and so Legett offered the jury a generous portion; Jones had appealed to reason and lost, and so Legett played upon the emotions in an effort to win.

As part of Legett's emotional appeal, he called upon Dr. J. T. Hensely to show the "very bullet that killed poor John Baker." The shrewd prosecuting attorney pointed to the victim's family: the father, James Baker; the two brothers, George W. and W. B.; the sister, Mrs. Mary Antry. As they sat quietly in the courtroom, Legett traced the family's movements in 1880 from Hill County to a farm in Taylor County only eight miles west of the scene of the murder. He described the mother's death in 1883 when her murdered son was only a youth of ten years. He reminded the attentive jurors that every person in Merkel knew John Baker and that no word against the victim's character had ever been spoken. In fact, the innocent youth was "kind and gentle in disposition; quiet and inoffensive; fond of music and dancing; sober, industrious, and frugal as became the son of an honest farmer, a worthy citizen and peaceful neighbor."[27]

The ploy succeeded, and the news reporter who expressed such dissatisfaction with the handling and outcome of the first case indicated that justice was done in the second:

Tuesday morning shortly after nine o'clock the jury in the Hamblen case announced that they had agreed upon a verdict. A few minutes later the prisoner was brought in and took his seat, the jury filed in, the judge arose, and the clerk read to the hushed audience their verdict, announcing that "we the jury find the prisoner guilty of murder in the first degree, and assess his punishment at imprisonment for life in the penitentiary."[28]

[27] Ibid.
[28] *Taylor County News*, April 7, 1893; *Abilene Reporter*, April 7, 1893.

It was a prime example of Legett's ability to assess his jury and adjust his appeal accordingly.

He had hardly returned to Abilene when another case, entirely different in nature, totally absorbed his attention. The new lawsuit involved charges of embezzlement against one of his close friends, G. A. Pearce. The accused man and his family had arrived in Abilene four years earlier and had appreciated the warm welcome that had already become the hallmark of pioneer settlers. Every member of the family displayed the self-assurance and social graces of those who are accustomed to social and civic responsibilities. Pearce gained immediate employment as a bookkeeper, school teacher, and insurance agent. Legett knew him more intimately, however, as an able leader in the Baptist church and as an enthusiastic participant in various community enterprises.

Legett was incredulous, therefore, when he learned on the afternoon of April 20, 1893, that Sheriff J. V. Cunningham had arrested his friend on an indictment found by a grand jury in Mobile, Alabama. Pearce immediately requested Legett's assistance. A local reporter commented that "the arrest was the sole topic of conversation on the streets yesterday evening," and word spread that the sheriff of Mobile was enroute with the necessary extradition papers. According to the rumor, the papers already contained the signatures of Texas Governor James S. Hogg and Alabama Governor Thomas G. Jones. A local paper reported that Pearce was accused of embezzling $80,000 during his years as secretary of the Planters and Merchants Insurance Company of Mobile.[29] Instances of eastern fugitives seeking anonymity in remote frontier towns rarely surprised pioneer settlers, but in this case they told one another that there must be some mistake.

Legett agreed to represent Pearce (he later explained that he had never been busier in his life) only because of their friendship and because of his faith in the man. He insisted, however, that he must have the complete story, and by daybreak the following morning he believed that he knew every detail. Pearce readily admitted that he had "got behind with the company" while he worked in Mobile, but he insisted that he had settled the matter to the company's satisfaction before he left Alabama. He told Legett that he had turned over every-

[29] *Abilene Reporter*, April 21, 1893.

thing he owned.[30] Convinced that his friend told the truth, Legett moved to block the extradition process. He left immediately for Austin where he met with Governor Hogg and explained that he needed more time to study his client's case. He asked the governor to rescind his earlier approval to extradite the accused to Alabama. When the governor hesitated, Legett explained that he had good reason to believe that the state of Alabama had no charge against Pearce and that, instead, the Mobile sheriff, Phelan B. Dorlan, and the insurance company sought to return Pearce as a debtor prisoner. Governor Hogg then agreed to a week's delay.

By the end of the week the insurance company had assured Hogg that it had not instigated the arrest for purposes of collecting an old debt, and James H. Webb, the prosecuting attorney in the city court of Mobile, had assured Hogg that the state of Alabama, not Pearce's creditors, wanted Pearce returned. Hogg thereby ordered Sheriff Cunningham to release the accused to Sheriff Dorlan.

Meanwhile, news reporters in other parts of the state grew interested in the case, and public sentiment seemed to turn against Legett's client. Those who knew Pearce believed that he was the injured party, but others stated publicly that the accused should return to Mobile to clear his name. Continued efforts to fight extradition suggested guilt. A few suspicious individuals began to whisper that the accused, his lawyer, and perhaps an unnamed judge were engaged in a conspiracy to obstruct justice. The *Dallas News* editorialized that Legett's client "may not be guilty of the crime for which he has been indicted back in Alabama. If he is not guilty he should be willing to embrace an opportunity to establish his innocence."[31]

Legett then decided that he must release to the public certain information that he had hoped to use in the courts at a more appropriate time. This key information had convinced him that he must remain on the case even though Pearce had admitted his misuse of company funds. Pearce had told Legett the following story: Many years ago, in Mobile, one Phelan B. Dorlan was arrested and charged with illegally operating a lottery wheel. Upon his conviction, Dorlan escaped imprisonment only by paying a heavy fine. Soon thereafter, Pearce gave the Alabaman a long moral lecture and concluded that Dorlan should

[30] Ibid.
[31] *Abilene Reporter*, May 5 and 12, 1893.

be ashamed to show his face in public. The two men were henceforth bitter enemies. Several years later Mobile voters forgot Dorlan's earlier difficulties and elected him their sheriff. Insanely vindictive, Dorlan immediately studied the public records for instances of unsolved or dormant cases involving his enemies. He tracked down and brought back to Mobile several minor law offenders before he spotted the Pearce case. Legett agreed with his client that, given that background, Dorlan was far more interested in seeking revenge than in seeing justice done.

Almost overnight these details regained public support for Pearce; he was the underdog—the victim of a vicious vendetta. Simultaneously, Legett's vigorous fight against extradition won him new laurels throughout Texas. Conversely, Sheriff Dorlan was suddenly the villain. His earlier expectations of a brief trip to Abilene during which he would pick up Pearce and return to Mobile stretched into days and then into weeks. As public hostility increased, he insisted that he was "actuated by no other motive than that of doing my duty." [32]

Legett used every possible argument against extradition. He claimed that the statute of limitations should protect his client against an indictment issued back in 1889. The maneuver forced another delay in proceedings while Dorlan telegraphed his chief deputy to secure a statement of denial from Judge Semmes in Mobile. Even while Dorlan awaited a reply, Legett prepared the next obstacle to removal of his client. As each litigant responded to the maneuverings of the other, it was inevitable that newsmen would begin to refer to the case as "Legett's game of chess."

On Monday, May 9, Legett appeared before District Judge Connor and argued before a packed countroom that both the indictment and the requisition from Alabama were insufficient in form and explicitness to warrant his client's removal or even his further detention. [33] Since he based his argument upon the statute of limitations, however, the timely receipt of Judge Semmes's telegraphed denial influenced Connor to rule against Legett. He ordered Sheriff Cunningham to place the accused in Sheriff Dorlan's custody. Dorlan hurriedly prepared to catch the next eastbound train, but, before he could claim

[32] Ibid., May 19, 1893.
[33] Ibid., May 12, 1893.

his prisoner, Legett appealed Connor's ruling to the state court of criminal appeals. His client remained in the Taylor County jail.

Sheriff Dorlan bitterly complained that he kept winning the battles but losing the war. With no end to the struggle in sight, he returned alone to Mobile, both embarrassed by his long and costly absence and agitated by his failure to return his old enemy. The editor of the *Mobile Register* pointedly observed that Dorlan had been away from the city for three weeks but had returned without his quarry. The editor wondered whether Dorlan was fighting "a lost—and perhaps foolish—cause." He further observed that, while interest in the case was unabated, "quite a revulsion in opinion" had occurred and "some believe [Pearce] innocent and think him the victim of other men's schemes."[34]

In mid-June Legett returned to Austin and on a Monday morning pleaded before the court of criminal appeals for a reversal of Judge Connor's ruling. The following Friday, Judge Simkins delivered the higher court's opinion, and again Legett lost. Since Pearce did not deny the actions charged against him and since those actions were illegal in Alabama, the judge said the state of Texas should deliver the accused to any authorized Alabama agent.[35] Instead, Legett kept Pearce out of the reach of his Alabama accusers by announcing that he would appeal the case to the Supreme Court of the United States. Pearce was released on bail. Legett submitted his arguments to the Supreme Court on November 19, 1894, and the following month, on December 10, the judges ruled in support of the earlier decision by the Texas Court of Criminal Appeals. Legett finally admitted defeat and released his friend and client to the Alabama authorities.[36]

A third case attracted statewide attention a few years later. Again another close friend, deputy United States Marshal J. V. Cunningham, needed Legett's skillful assistance. Just as Legett closed his office

[34] *Mobile Register*, May 13, 1893, quoted in *Abilene Reporter* May 19, 1893.
[35] *Southwestern Reporter*, vol. 23, first series, pp. 15–17 (23 SW 15), as provided by attorney J. Henry Doscher, Jr., in a letter to the author, October 3, 1974; see also *Abilene Reporter*, June 30, 1893.
[36] *United States Reporter*, vol. 155, p. 311; also *Lawyers Edition*, vol. 39, p. 164, as provided by attorney J. Henry Doscher, Jr., in a letter to the author, October 3, 1974. Eventually Pearce returned to Abilene, where he spent the remainder of his life as a highly respected citizen and church leader (Rupert N. Richardson to author, November 15, 1974).

on April 2, 1897, J. M. Cunningham rushed in with a telegram
clutched in his hand. The winded man hurriedly explained to Legett
that J. V. Cunningham, his brother, had shot a man named Joseph B.
McMahon only an hour and a half earlier in Wichita, Kansas. His
brother had voluntarily surrendered to Sheriff Cone in that city.[37]

During the course of the evening Legett agreed to accompany
J. M. Cunningham to Wichita. They left on the early morning eastbound train. Enroute they reviewed again all the information available to them. The sheriff had convincing evidence that a man named
Purdy had a few weeks earlier set fire to the Windsor Hotel in Abilene, that Cunningham had traced the accused to Wichita, where he
was employed by the McMahon Brothers' Circus, and that the same
circus had appeared in Abilene as the Bond Brothers' Circus.

When the two Abilene men arrived in Wichita, they learned that
the victim had died of his wounds and that the Wichita sheriff had
successfully intercepted a group of McMahon's friends who had attempted to break into the jail where Cunningham was held. As Legett
learned more about the victim, he grew more apprehensive that Cunningham's life was endangered. McMahon was a highly respected
citizen who had many influential friends. He and other members of
his family owned several successful local businesses in addition to the
recently purchased circus. McMahon held a law degree from the University of Michigan law school, although he did not practice that
profession; he was thirty-four years old, a family man with two children, and he was a thirty-second degree Mason. It seemed to Legett
that McMahon was one of the most popular men in town while Cunningham was its public enemy. Legett was relieved, therefore, when
someone told him that the influential editor of the *Wichita Eagle* had
called for the local "hot heads" to calm down: "Mr. Cunningham is
in the hands of the law of Kansas, and if he is guilty of offense
against that law, there is no reason to feel alarmed about his punishment, especially in a community like this where Mr. McMahon has
so many friends."[38]

The astute Abilene lawyer had to convince all Kansans that his
client was a highly respected law enforcement officer down in Texas.
He informed local reporters in Sheriff Cone's presence that Cunning-

[37] *Abilene Reporter*, April 9, 1897.
[38] *Wichita Eagle*, April 9, 1897.

ham also was a thirty-second degree Mason, that he had seen active service against the Indians, that he was a former Texas Ranger, that he had served as Taylor County sheriff for twelve years without physical injury to a single man, that he was known throughout Texas for his coolness and presence of mind, and that he was held in high esteem all over Texas. The impressive claims disspelled any lingering suspicion among Wichita reporters that Cunningham might be nothing better than a bloodthirsty Texas gunman.[39]

Legett then went to the telegraph office and sent messages to Texans scattered throughout the state, explained the situation, and requested them to send testimonials to his client's good character. On April 5 the *St. Louis Republic* commented upon his success: "The whole State of Texas seems to be intensely interested in the outcome of the pending murder trial in which J. V. Cunningham is the defendant. Telegrams by the hundreds are pouring in, signed by men of prominence and influence in the State."

Legett next sent telegrams to other Texans who could post Cunningham's bond, and before they responded he tried to piece together the series of events which led to the shooting. He learned that Sheriff Cunningham arrived in Wichita on April 1 and went directly to Sheriff Cone's office. He identified himself and explained that he had with him the necessary papers for extraditing Purdy to Texas. Sheriff Cone responded that he, too, had received orders from Kansas Governor John W. Leedy to comply with the Texas governor's request. Purdy was, in fact, already in custody. Relieved that there would be no complications, Cunningham arranged to spend the night at the Manhattan Hotel and to depart by train the following morning with his prisoner.

Almost immediately upon reaching his hotel, the Texas sheriff was confronted by McMahon, who identified himself as Purdy's employer. McMahon boasted that he had a local reputation for standing by his men. He demanded to know why Cunningham had come to take Purdy back to Texas. Cunningham replied that he had reason to believe that Purdy had set fire to the Windsor Hotel in Abilene. Legett found many witnesses who substantially agreed to the facts up to that point. The same men, however, gave contradictory statements on all succeeding events.

[39] *Abilene Reporter*, April 9, 1897.

McMahon claimed, in a deathbed statement, that he had called Cunningham a liar and that Cunningham immediately pulled a gun and shot him. The victim further stated that he had made no threat and had not reached for his gun. He claimed also that Cunningham shot him a second time while he lay wounded on the floor. Legett could locate no eyewitness to support the dying man's version of the incident and therefore reconstructed for himself the following series of events: Cunningham went straight to his room upon arriving at the hotel; a short while later McMahon appeared in the lobby and sent a messenger named Clark to Cunningham's upstairs room; the two men returned to the lobby; after a few preliminary remarks (which no one overheard), McMahon raised his voice and shouted, "It's a damned lie!"; simultaneously each man pulled his gun and shot; McMahon missed his target, but Cunningham's shot entered McMahon's side, penetrated his intestines, and lodged against a vertebra.

By the time Legett had satisfied himself that he had accurately reconstructed the story, he received a message from Captain Bickett with assurance that "all sheriffs in Texas stand ready to give [Cunningham] any assistance he might need."[40] A few days later, United States Marshal Love arrived from Dallas with authority from bankers in Dallas, Dublin, Comanche, San Angelo, and Abilene to make bond in any amount. At the preliminary hearing in Wichita on Friday, April 9, bail was set at $10,000. Legett, on first reflection, thought the amount was excessive, considering the evidence in the case, but he did not protest. The judge was aware of the many offers of help from Texas bankers and had set a heavy bail only to smooth the feelings of some of McMahon's close friends. According to the editor of the *Taylor County News*, Legett could have posted a $100,000 bond just as easily.[41]

Legett and the two Cunningham men returned to Abilene at once. A noisy group of hometown supporters greeted them at the depot to welcome home the popular lawman. Many of them congratulated his able attorney who, at thirty-nine, had convinced them that he was one of the most skillful lawyers in all of Texas. His peers in courthouses throughout West Texas marveled at his ingenuity in using public support and sympathy as an effective tool in his clients' behalf.

[40] Ibid., April 9, 1897.
[41] *Taylor County News*, April 16, 1897.

Legett returned to Wichita a half-dozen times during the intervening months to gather evidence for Cunningham's defense, and
finally, on September 17, he accompanied his client, Mrs. Cunningham, and several character witnesses to Wichita for the trial. Instead
of a trial, however, the judge announced on September 20 that the
state of Kansas had no evidence to refute the defendant's claim that
he had shot in self-defense, and thus the judge dismissed the case.
The editor of the *Abilene Reporter* congratulated Cunningham on his
complete vindication but reserved his highest praise for the defense
attorney: "Judge Legett, the leading lawyer for the defense in this
case, has worked earnestly and successfully, and has added new laurels
as an attorney of ability and conscientiousness." [42] Apparently the
editor used the title *Judge* as both a recognition of outstanding ac-
complishments in legal affairs and as an acknowledgment of a partially accomplished fact. Legett frequently presided over Judge T. H.
Connor's 42nd District Court whenever Connor was away or ill.
Consequently newsmen increasingly used the appellation *Judge* whenever they mentioned him in a complimentary way. It was a special
compliment, indeed, whenever the editor of the *Taylor County News*
called him Judge Legett, since the newsman had editorialized as recently as March 19, 1897, that "the *News* is no toady. No one is going
to be called General, Colonel, Major, Captain, or Professor, who has
not seen service, or who is not legally entitled to the appellation." If
the exception to his rule bothered the editor, he did not admit it. Perhaps he already suspected that the able young lawyer would "see
service" and soon earn his right to the title.

[42] *Abilene Reporter*, September 24, 1897.

*The wild and woolly desperado, loaded down
with knives and shooting irons, is a thing of the
past . . . on the ranges as well as in the towns.*

CHAPTER SEVEN

# Learning to Sit Sidesaddle

MANY West Texans, including those who thought they knew him best, assumed that K. K. Legett would one day embark upon a political career. His public image viewed from any direction was that of an intelligent, astute, and ambitious young man who knew his talents and who planned to exercise them on a larger political stage than Abilene could offer. Earlier generations of gifted young men often followed careers in politics, since that was virtually the only area where power and influence might eventually become national in scope. After the political disruptions of the Civil War, however, many young men with exceptional abilities found greater challenge and opportunity in industrial careers. As a consequence, by the 1890s some of them had accumulated astronomical wealth and influence. West Texas offered no similar economic opportunity, although there were a few wealthy and influential cattlemen such as Legett's father-in-law, W. C. Bryan. In the 1880s and 1890s Texas offered only cattle raising and politics as means of success. Hence it was taken for granted that W. C. Bryan's young son-in-law would eventually announce his candidacy for political office.

To West Texas Democrats the state and congressional elections of 1894 seemed an appropriate time to launch K. K. Legett's political career, in spite of the fact that he was lukewarm to many facets of Populism, flatly opposed public ownership of the railroads, and had opposed Governor James S. Hogg's candidacy in both 1890 and 1892. The executive committee of the Taylor County Democrats met on Saturday, July 14, and voted to recommend to the full convention K. K. Legett's nomination as a candidate for the state senate.[1] The

---

[1] *Taylor County News*, July 20, 1894.

chairman of the county executive committee, Dr. J. T. Harrington, one of the nominee's closest friends, read the endorsement.

When Legett arose at the convention and declined the nomination, every member—including his brother-in-law, John Bryan—was astounded. They had looked upon his numerous public addresses, his readiness to assume civic responsibilities, his gregariousness and congeniality as stepping stones to public office. Until the moment of his startling rejection, they were unaware of one dimension of Legett's complex character and personality: he was, they would realize later, extremely secretive about his personal goals and ambitions. Every friend knew that Legett carefully planned day-by-day detail, but only Lora Bryan Legett knew his hopes and designs for life's major goals. Only she could have predicted his abrupt rejection of the committee's recommendation. Only she knew that he did not adjust easily to unexpected changes in plans or designs; that, in spite of his almost constant public activity, he was at heart a family man; and that he had decided some years earlier that the rewards of public office were too uncertain to subject his family to the whims of election-day decisions. Political offices were for others to hold.

Legett's impoverished childhood and the financial inadequacies he obviously felt when he married into a wealthy family spurred his ambitions to provide his own family with the security he had lacked. He seemed determined to provide for his wife in a manner to which she had been accustomed as W. C. Bryan's daughter.

For those reasons K. K. Legett linked financial success to family goals rather than to personal goals. It followed, therefore, that his family interests superseded whatever personal ambitions he may have had for a political career. He showed no interest in honors that his family could not share, but he rarely missed an opportunity to draw them into the glow of his own public spotlight. Thus when he addressed Simmons College's first graduating class, he drew attention to his young son, Kade, who sat in the audience.[2]

He wanted the world to see his family and he wanted his family, in turn, to see the world. Long before his children were old enough to dress themselves, they accompanied him—usually only one at a time unless Mrs. Legett went along—on business trips throughout

---

[2] Copy of address in Legett Family Records, file 14, paper 1.

Texas. One of Julia's earliest recollections was that of a trip to Austin where she sat for hours at her father's side at a committee meeting in the state capitol, where secretaries periodically marched her off to the ladies' room, where she and her father walked down the long halls in search of someone who could comb a little girl's hair, and where, on at least one occasion, a distressed male colleague asked her father: "Judge, does this child's dress button in front or in back?"[3]

Whenever the children traveled with him, Legett taught them to observe the changing landscape, to sharpen their curiosity, and to ask questions as the scenes changed. On those journeys when other business associates went along, the young father and teacher encouraged his children to write letters home to mother, and to include descriptions of what they saw. Mrs. Legett carefully preserved one letter that Kade wrote between Abilene and Fort Worth in August, 1900, when he was ten years old:

Dear Mama

The train cam in when we were at the office. I beged papa to hurry. We got on all right. The first station was Clyde and stopped There about 5 minites. The next came biard. We passed over a creek ceveral times between there and Putnam.

In the meantime we passed a frait train on a switch. There was a whole lot of hills.

Mr. Sayles and Mr. Kirk went to Fort Worth with us. There were a lot of Elms between Putnam and Sisco and one section house.

We passed another switch but there was no train on it. We passed a camp in a pasture between Putnam and Sisco.

When we came to Sisco I saw two boys holding a goat at the crossing. . . .[4]


By such exercises in recording their observations, the Legett children developed a learning technique that their father practiced throughout his lifetime. Earlier that year, for example, on January 19,

---

[3] Interview with Mrs. Julia Legett Pickard, Abilene, Texas, July 16, 1973. This and the other incidents are based on information gained from Mrs. Pickard during the interview or from her collections of Legett newspaper clippings, or from Mrs. Ruth Legett Jones, whom I have interviewed and from whom I have received letters dealing with the Legett children's childhood. (Kade Legett, the son mentioned in this chapter, is deceased.) All other sources are cited in separate footnotes.

[4] Miscellaneous paper no. 517, Legett Family Records.

1900, the *Abilene Reporter* printed on page three Legett's observations of the changing scene in Fort Worth, where he was attending a convention. He favorably compared the delegates of that convention to those of earlier days. Their appearance and deportment, he reported, reminded him more of a religious delegation. He claimed that he had not met a single intoxicated delegate, nor one who was profane or boisterous. The men of the West, he concluded, were becoming "fine Gentlemen," which "speaks in no uncertain language as to the progress of the great West in everything that tends to build up and dignify a people. The wild and woolly desperado, loaded down with knives and shooting irons, is a thing of the past . . . on the ranges as well as in the towns."

Much earlier in their lives than most children of that era, the Legett children were allowed to travel alone. In September, 1899, when they were eight and six years old respectively, Julia and Ruth rode the Texas and Pacific train some forty miles west to Sweetwater to visit Fay Trammell, their cousin. A local newsman thought their unchaperoned journey was so unusual that he mentioned it in a news item. He watched for their return three days later and succeeded in getting a follow-up story: "Miss Julia and Miss Ruth Legett returned home this morning from visits to Sweetwater. Miss Ruth certainly made an impression on one young man, as she carried home a very appropriate and valuable present, a beautiful canary bird in a pretty cage. We advise the little Miss that cages catch others than canaries, as she will learn later on."[5] K. K. Legett delighted in such evidences of local interest and affection toward his family.

Predictably, the father sometimes placed his son and two daughters on pedestals from which they occasionally fell. As a consequence, their mother frequently found herself caught between the father's ideal and the reality of three active pioneers comfortably at home in an environment where the rough edges were still evident. She was a mother and wife with a great capacity to understand both the weaknesses of children and the consternation of a father who hoped for perfection.

One of their earliest and most enduring temptations loomed every morning as they looked across the street at their grandparents' red-

[5] *Abilene Reporter*, September 22, 1899.

topped second-story roof. The urge to climb the steep roof and slide
down its red surface to the first-floor porch top never faded, but the
opportunity to enjoy that forbidden fruit rarely occurred. Sometimes
their mother and grandmother left the house at the same time, but
never without the mother's admonition that they were not to climb to
the roof. Invariably upon her return she had to punish them for dis-
obedience. In spite of their loud denials, she somehow knew that they
had disobeyed. Years passed before they realized that she needed only
to look at the red seats of their clothing to learn the truth. She usually
"forgot," however, to mention some of those infractions to the children's father. One should avoid apoplexy in the home whenever one
could, she later explained.

Like most responsible pioneer settlers, Legett was sensitive to the
West's wild and woolly reputation, even after a decade and a half of
physical and social improvements. Adults attempted to enforce upon
all youth a rigid discipline, but their Victorian attitudes toward the
different roles in society expected of males and females caused them
to preach much more discipline to the boys than the boys actually
practiced. Local newsmen editorialized almost weekly about the row-
diness of the local male population. The following series of newspaper items are typical of those which appeared in the *Abilene Reporter* throughout the 1890s:

(November 9, 1894) The noise made by some of Abilene's boys at the
opera house would put to shame the gang that holds down the peanut roost
of a third rate theatre in a large city.

(August 23, 1895) Abilene has a few young men and boys whose chief
occupation seems to be holding down street corners. . . . They would be
better off at work. . . . Idleness breeds more cussedness than anything else.

(March 25, 1898) We warned the boys that they would be fined if they
did not quit running their horses through the streets. . . . Many only
thought it funny and . . . this morning were fined to the tune of $25 each,
plus the costs. . . . Now we want to warn the boys that this is not a city
but a state law they violated. . . . It is about as expensive as a six-shooter
case.

Warming to the subject, the editor lectured the twelve-year-old male
population of Abilene as well:

There are a few twelve-year-old boys who have taken up the silly and offensive habit of yelling in the streets at night. . . . Sunday night a lot of them squalled like Comanche Indians as they left church, and unless their mamas turn these kids over their knees . . . until they learn to act like civilized boys . . . there will be big fines to pay.

Legett generally shared these views, and whenever the opportunity arose the editor quoted him. His address to the first meeting of the Taylor County Teachers Institute on Friday evening, January 6, 1899, therefore, received more than the normal amount of newspaper space. During the course of the address, he reported that he recently lost an old client because of a teacher's efforts to discipline a student. The teacher had struck the client's son and the client then reported the incident to Legett. According to a lengthy item in the *Taylor County News,* "Mr. Legett said he had no doubt that he should have been struck many times instead of once, and he advised the client to go down to Welche's harness store, buy a strap and wear it out on the boy for lying about his teacher. 'Though it is true that the hand that rocks the cradle is the hand that rules the world, yet that hand must be sustained by the teacher in order that its beneficent rule may continue!'"[6]

The social environment in which the Legett children grew up and the restrictions of a proud father who expected them to avoid the rougher influences of the frontier subdued Kade, Julia, and Ruth but did not seriously inhibit them. Of the two daughters, Julia was perhaps nearer in conduct to the little-lady image that their father had in mind. Older than Ruth by eighteen months, she was by nature less tomboyish than her fiercely competitive younger sister. It was Julia, for example, who dressed her doll Lucy in pale blue China silk with lace and silver passamenterie and won first prize at the Doll Fair that Mrs. J. M. Wagstaff sponsored at the Cumberland Presbyterian Church.

Ruth, on the other hand, idolized her big brother and tried to please and to emulate him at every turn. This relationship led to a variety of incidents that Mrs. Legett "forgot" to mention to her hus-

[6] *Taylor County News,* January 13, 1899.

band. He did not hear immediately, therefore, about the bronco-busting game that Kade and Ruth invented. There was a shed with a low, sloping roof under which one of the two held a calf while the other climbed to the roof, slid lickedy-split off the edge, and landed on the surprised calf's back. The animal never failed to go into a brief bucking and twisting routine that resulted in the bronco-rider falling to the ground. This kind of rambunctiousness usually sent Julia back to the house in tears. At such times, father's little lady was just a sissy in her brother's and sister's eyes. The sympathetic mother, conscious of the situation but unaware of the irony of her statement, frequently admonished Ruth to "be nice to your little sister."

One incident went unreported even to the mother. A huge willow tree grew at the edge of a small pond on the far side of the Legett's forty acres on Pine Street. In absolute secrecy Kade and Ruth climbed the tree and tied a rope to the topmost branch. Each day before their father returned home, they hid the rope among the branches. Day after day they swung back and forth across the pond, muddying their clothes in the process. Mrs. Legett knew about the rope and did not prohibit the swinging, but she eventually tired of their muddy clothes. At first she cautioned them, but finally had to prohibit them from swinging across the pond. The children held council and agreed to a solution: they would, henceforth, remove their clothes before they played around the pond. For a while the scheme worked, but one day Eugene and Tom Pearce, and several other neighborhood boys, observed the fun from a distance and ran to join in. They appeared at the pond while all three Legett children were stark naked and just as Ruth, who clung to the rope, reached the midway point across the pond. There was nothing for her to do but release the rope and seek cover in the muddy water below. Kade had long since convinced both girls that the pond was a thousand feet deep, and Ruth knew that she would drown, but her Victorian training required her to choose death in muddy water to nudity high above the heads of the neighborhood boys.

Such periodic traumas subdued the children for brief periods during which they struggled to entertain themselves in less boisterous games. One day during their best behavior, one of their many pets, a Belgian hare, died. Kade and Ruth agreed with Julia that the animal deserved an appropriate funeral. Having won their cooperation, Julia deftly retained control of this quieter activity. First, she played upon Ruth's momentary grief and got her to give up her favorite pirate's cache (a tin box) for the rabbit's casket. For a shroud, Julia contributed her own embroidered handkerchief. Kade conducted the service. Unfamiliar with the lyrics of the familiar church hymns, Julia led the singing of every verse of "My Country 'Tis of Thee." A few days later, Ruth's grief subsided. She regretted her rash contribution to the recent funeral and notified her sister that she planned to retrieve her tin box. Over Julia's protests, Ruth dug up the box, but its odorous contents quickly convinced her that for once Julia should have her way.

Mr. and Mrs. Legett believed firmly in the axiom that an idle mind is the devil's workshop, and so each fall they welcomed the first clangs of the schoolhouse bell. The opening of a school session, however, did not always assure calmer and quieter days in the Legett household. The Legetts' second family home, on Pine Street, was not far from ward school, but one opening day the parents allowed Kade to ride his pony, Nell, to school. The girls pleaded for a similar privilege, and their parents finally agreed to allow them to ride the donkey.

That beast, unfortunately, was a typically stubborn donkey; indeed, it was the only animal in the pasture to which the children refused to give a name. Julia and Ruth exchanged pungent comments upon the cards that fate had dealt them, but the compromise was the best they could gain under the circumstances. As the youngest girl, Ruth's "hand" was hardly worth playing: she would have to ride behind her sister. For several days the sisters accepted the unsatisfactory arrangement, although, day by day, the donkey walked more and more slowly toward the school. The girls usually arrived late and frustrated but determined to outlast Kade. On the return trip home, the stubborn animal's slow gait gradually accelerated to a near-gallop. He had learned that someone would feed him shortly after his arrival at the house. A silent, undeclared rivalry developed between the girls as each struggled to be the last to fall to the rocky earth, and every day they arrived home embroiled in the same debate: were Ruth's frequent falls from the donkey's rear end accidental, or the result of

Julia's deliberate crowding? Inevitably, Ruth fell on her right shoulder, broke her collarbone, and put an end to further donkey rides to school.

The Legetts claimed that after-school chores built character. It followed that the children had plenty of character-building opportunities upon their return home. Lora Bryan Legett insisted that cleanliness is next to Godliness, but her children often wondered if the two characteristics might rule the Legett household coequally. A tireless worker herself, Mrs. Legett rarely kept domestic help for more than a few weeks. Since she expected the help to work with her own zest and enthusiasm, she simply wore them down. To compound the problem, there were few domestic workers for hire in Abilene, as the population was overwhelmingly male.

Lora Legett refused to look upon housework as dull and routine, so she made every chore a character-building exercise. Perhaps her most disagreeable outdoor task was that of cleaning the henhouse and dipping the chickens in a carbolic solution to kill bluebugs. Mrs. Legett still looked upon its bright side: first it helped the children to burn up much excess energy chasing down the chickens, and second it provided her an opportunity to compare the docile manner in which the hens submitted to the dipping to the deafening squawks which emitted from the roosters. Just the way most men and most women respond to personal outrage, she concluded.

Mrs. Legett made a songfest of the hours spent in her vegetable garden. Her only assistant, Mr. Lambkin, enjoyed gardening as much as she and, unlike her female employees, remained a faithful worker for many years. While the two worked, they combined their voices in endless duets of such old hymns as "Amazing Grace," "In the Sweet Bye and Bye," and "Just As I Am." In a different mood and alone, she practiced her dance steps while she swept the porches, floors, and sidewalks. With the cane-handled broom as her silent partner, she kept time to her own renditions of the popular polkas and foxtrots.

K. K. Legett's long hours at his office did not exempt him from his share of the homework. He assumed full responsibility for milking the cows, cutting the wood for the stoves and fireplaces, mowing the lawn, feeding the horses, cleaning the lots and barn, and tending the acetylene tank.

Of all the character-building chores assigned to the children, they hated churning most. It was the dullest job and the one they tried hardest to avoid. When they finished the onerous task, they might gather eggs, pick up chips for the fire, "wipe the stairs down," spade the garden, pick and string beans, shell black-eyed peas, shuck corn, dig potatoes, pick berries, "chunk" (with a broom handle) the clothes under water in the boiling washpot, make lye soap, or dig up Johnson grass. The grass-digging work was perhaps the second most boring chore, but Mrs. Legett awarded five-cent prizes each week for the finder of the longest Johnson grass root and for the highest pile of roots. Mrs. Legett looked upon dusting and dishwashing as parts of routine living and did not allow those tasks to become "chores." Every member of the family did his share of dusting and dishwashing every day.

In spite of busy schedules about the house and school, there was still time on any given day for the unexpected crisis or trauma. One Sunday afternoon, just as Legett prepared to leave Abilene to attend a court case in Aspermont the following morning, Kade rode Nell out to the pasture to drive in the other horses. Shortly after he reached his destination, a gray mare, old and always gentle until that moment, kicked Kade to the ground. The blow broke both major bones in one leg, and after Kade fell to the ground, his startled pony stepped on his arm and broke the bone just above his wrist. The injured youth lay in critical condition for sixteen days. The initial injuries and a later complication (a bone had to be reset) kept him bedfast for several weeks.

Periodic outbreaks of rabies kept children and adults constantly on the alert. When farm and ranch animals, which were so vulnerable to rabid coyotes and wolves, became rabid, it involved financial loss, but when a family pet was the victim, the crisis had the potential for human tragedy. The Legett household experienced such a nightmare in the spring of 1900. A stray dog wandered about the neighborhood in northwest Abilene in mid-May and attacked several family pets. Later that day Major John Girand stopped by the Legett house on Pine Street and informed Legett that the stray was frothing at the mouth and that Girand and several other men in the area had decided to destroy their own dogs. Someone had told Girand that the Legett dog was also among those attacked by the stray.

Legett thanked his neighbor for the information and agreed that every dog under suspicion of possible infection must be destroyed. The Legett children, who were ten, eight, and six years old at the time, wept and then pleaded with their father to spare their pet's life. Moved by their distress, Legett agreed to tie the dog to a post and to keep him in total isolation for twelve days. The children in turn promised to stay a safe distance away. After the twelve days passed without sign of rabies, Legett released the forlorn prisoner. All day the joyous pet followed the children about their play. Shortly after Mrs. Legett called them into the house for dinner, however, the dog, left outside, suffered a series of convulsions that left no doubt that it had a genuine case of rabies. Legett immediately shot the animal. That close brush with tragedy reminded him that sentiment must never again prevail over sound judgment.[7]

As in most households, the Legetts learned to expect the unexpected, and both parents struggled to remain calm and composed during most times of stress. One was never to display his emotions in public. Nor should one's daily life grow so hectic that there was no time for activities away from the home. Mrs. Legett was not as socially active as her husband, but she nevertheless pursued several of her own interests. Her major church activity centered around the Ladies Aid Society of the Baptist church. Several times each year she hosted the group at her home, and now and then she represented them at their annual state conventions. She continued her interest in painting, and when she entered her oils in contests at the West Texas Fair, more often than not she won a ribbon.

Parental efforts to develop a more refined social environment on the West Texas frontier sometimes seemed hopeless. Frequent local disputes, such as the one about the town cows' right to roam Abilene's public streets, competed for the younger generation's attention. Periodically the editors of the *Taylor County News* and the *Abilene Reporter* demanded that town officials banish the town's most irritating nuisance. A typical editorial on the subject appeared in the *Abilene Reporter* on October 7, 1898:

We have been following the custom of rural editors in calling our burg a city, but we shall have to go back and use the term village, instead. . . .

[7] *Abilene Reporter*, May 25, 1900.

So long as our streets are used for grazing purposes we are only a village—a kind of string-town, in fact.

Some enterprising man ought to start a hog ranch with headquarters near the city hall. Hogs would really do well in Abilene, and as scavengers they are less objectional than cattle and horses. True, they could not rob the farmer's wagon, but they could root up the lawn after the cows have destroyed the trees.

From time to time the issue appeared on the ballot in local elections, but throughout the nineties the town cow won the right to remain a nuisance. Just before the turn of the century, the argument became a heated letter-to-the-editor war. In one of the published letters, Dr. J. W. Keeble announced that he had built a small pen behind his house and that, henceforth, any cow that broke into his yard would be penned up and deprived of her milk.[8]

Another local dispute arose between tobacco-spitters and non-spitters. Local ladies who dreamed of Abilene as a center of cultural refinement complained that the floors of the best business houses in town ruined their skirts. Unless the disgusting habit ceased at once, one irate lady complained to a newsman, she and her friends would abandon their skirts and their femininity and wear bloomers to do their shopping.[9]

The more sensitive female citizens never abandoned their determination to raise the town's cultural level. They strove to improve the West Texas Fair with educational attractions for the younger generation; thus a float prepared for the 1897 fair parade depicted a scene from Longfellow's "The Village Blacksmith." Their inspiration originated with the discovery that Torrey Hancock, the New England blacksmith who inspired Longfellow's famous poem, was the father of Abilene's own H. A. Hancock. Hancock drew from memory a sketch of his father's shop, Abilene blacksmith John Martin loaned his tools, and Hancock posed on the float in his father's historic role.

Christmas provided annual opportunities to add color and gaiety to the children's lives. During the 1895 Christmas season, Kade and Julia had reached their sixth and fourth birthdays, respectively, and

8 Ibid., December 1, 1899.
9 Ibid., June 12, 1896.

Ruth approached her third. Each was young enough to catch the spirit of Santa Claus, but all were old enough to watch, entranced, as a Christmas parade moved from the corner of Cypress and North Second streets southward to the opera house. The Abilene Brass Band (almost frightening to Julia, it was so noisy!) led the way, followed by toy soldiers come to life (the Abilene Light Infantry Company), and then followed by hundreds of other men and women wearing the funny hats and dressed in the colorful uniforms of the fire company, the Foresters, the Independent Order of Odd Fellows, the Knights of Pythias, the Knights of Templar, and the Daughters of America.

After the parade, the crowd gathered about the speakers' stand in front of the opera house at South First and Chestnut streets. Normally this would have been the part of the festivities the Legett children liked least, but their father was one of the people sitting on the stage. They recognized also the preacher, Mr. G. W. Smith, who walked to the front of the platform and said some funny things about their father and the people laughed; and then Papa stood up and said some funny things and the people laughed harder. Abruptly their father turned serious and talked at length about charity. When he sat down, other men collected money, which, their mother explained, was for the needy people—not their father. After everyone sang Christmas carols, their father jumped from the platform, rejoined his family, and took the children home in their mother's new buggy.[10]

Mrs. Legett explained to them that she needed to talk to Santa Claus at his downtown location. They looked forward to Christmas morning, and to dolls and toy soldiers, but the parents also used the occasion to replenish winter clothing of all sorts for every member of the family. In 1895, Mrs. Legett could purchase play overalls in Kade's size for thirty-five cents, and heavy, lined pants ranged in price from fifteen to thirty-five cents. Buckle shoes in the girls' sizes cost seventy-five cents, stockings ranged from three to five cents, and wool hats averaged twenty-five cents each.[11] Such were the items received on Christmas morning with a few toys and stockings bulging to overflowing with candy, nuts, and fruits.

During the summer months, the annual camp meeting served both

[10] Ibid., December 13, 1895.
[11] Prices listed in advertisements in the *Taylor County News*, November 1, 1895; *Abilene Reporter*, November 15, 1895.

the spiritual and social needs of West Texans. Sometimes it also provided another source for the children's education. The 1895 meeting
gathered about two miles southeast of the town, on the east bank of
Lytle Creek, during the last week of June. To the children, it was one
of those exquisitely exciting times when all parents filled their buggies and wagons with food, clothing, and other necessary items—
always first-aid supplies—and spent the day out-of-doors. It was a
huge and prolonged picnic interlaced, unfortunately, with interminable speeches. Nevertheless, the day differed from the usual routine.
They enjoyed the ride to the creek, but the arrival among so many
people excited them most. A large structure, which their parents called
a tabernacle, stood at the center of the throng. Several smaller buildings surrounded the tabernacle, and their mother called them, in
hushed tones, "bath houses." Long tables, where people ate and
talked and laughed, filled one area of the camp grounds. Tents of all
sizes and colors encircled the entire space. Their father explained that
the people who came from Snyder, Mt. Pleasant, Ennis County, Marshall, Fort Worth, Henrietta, Loraine, and many other distant places
slept in the tents during the meeting.

At the 1895 meeting they saw a man named W. B. Godby who
had just returned from the Holy Land; they saw also a lady preacher
from Albuquerque, New Mexico, named Josie Tennyson. Both went
to the speaker's platform and talked and talked and talked, but, first,
those two had to wait until a little man named Thomas Nishikawa
told the children about life in Japan.[12] The parents listened, too. Kade
thought that Mr. Hancock, who came from New England and who
knew how to build boats, was the most interesting man at the camp
meeting. Hancock built four rowboats, bought the boating concession
on the creek, and then rented his boats to any West Texan who
claimed he could swim. Kade could swim and so he accompanied his
father for a ride on the creek.

In such a fashion the Legett children grew up in West Texas
while it was still a frontier region. They were kindred parts of their
environment and all were profoundly influenced by it. They received
an uncommon quantity of care and guidance from parents who took
advantage of every opportunity to increase their knowledge, to diver-

[12] *Taylor County News*, June 28, 1895.

sify their experiences, and to broaden their horizons. They spent the summer of 1905 in Colorado, California, and Vancouver, and the summer of 1907 in Virginia, where they attended the Jamestown Tercentenary Festival. Narrow provincialism had no opportunity to develop as Kade, Julia, and Ruth Legett grew interested in the world beyond the borders of their own region.

But they did not entirely shake themselves free from the dust of their native West Texas. A favorite family anecdote illustrates the point: Sometime during the 1890s, when the children were still small, Mr. and Mrs. Legett attended a public function and found themselves seated next to Dr. and Mrs. J. H. Bass. Mrs. Bass was the girls' piano teacher. Both Julia and Ruth, unfortunately, were tone-deaf—a fact known to Mrs. Bass for several months. The kindly teacher could not bring herself to admit that disturbing fact to the parents. Mrs. Bass tried to guide the conversation to other subjects, but eventually Mrs. Legett asked the inevitable question: had Mrs. Bass been able to further the girls' instruction at all?" she wanted to know. "Yes, indeed," the teacher answered sweetly, but too quickly, "Ruth no longer straddles the piano stool like a pony. She's learned to sit sidesaddle!"

*The demands on my time are very, very great
and it is with much reluctance that I yield to this
call for an increase in public service. The hope
has been entertained that I had already reached
the limit.*

# CHAPTER EIGHT

## Money, Man, and God

ON Friday, August 26, 1898, the *Abilene Reporter* announced: "Abilene has been honored in the appointment of one of her popular citizens to the important office of Referee in Bankruptcy for the Abilene district, consisting of twenty-five counties. In the selection of that well versed and conscientious lawyer, Judge Legett, the government has, by going outside of parstisanship for the best material, done itself credit and conserved the best interests of justice. We congratulate our neighbor, also, upon this recognition of his ability and integrity."[1] The newspaperman had failed to conceal his surprise that a local Democrat had received a coveted judicial appointment during a Republican presidential administration.

Abilene Democrats had known for some time that K. K. Legett was lukewarm, even hostile, toward his party's stand on the silver issue. They understood his open opposition to Populist and Democratic efforts to regulate railroads, since such regulation could discourage railroad construction in West Texas. Some of them shared Legett's general suspicion and distrust of William Jennings Bryan's Populism. These conflicts did not lead to a break with his party, however, nor did his appointment as referee in bankruptcy represent an attempt by Republicans to lure him into their political camp. The Democratic newsman concluded, therefore, that the Republicans, for once, had appointed a man to office on the basis of his ability and integrity.

Legett accepted the offer without hesitation. He had, in fact, vigorously sought the appointment from Judge Edward R. Meek. The duties of a referee in bankruptcy should not require lengthy trips

[1] The following month, Judge Edward R. Meek designated the *Abilene Reporter* as the official organ for the court of bankruptcy (see *Abilene Reporter-News*, September 16, 1898).

away from home, nor interfere with his private law practice, nor hinder the expansion of his sundry activities in real estate, cattle ranching, and grain and dairy farming.[2] Terms of appointment were for seven years, with no restrictions on reappointments. Though locally prestigious, the position would provide only a nominal fee for each case in bankruptcy; nevertheless, the additional income was not a factor the enterprising businessman-lawyer overlooked. He believed that a family's prosperity, just as a nation's, was more secure if based upon diverse sources of income.

No other local attorney, whether Republican or Democrat, could seriously challenge Legett's candidacy for the position. Legal training and experience qualified a score of Abilenians, but Legett's qualifications were in other ways unique. Both the congressional district and the judicial district that the bankruptcy court would serve resulted, to a large degree, from Legett's earlier work. In 1892, he alone had gone to Austin and convinced state legislators that a new congressional district should be carved from that territory between the Fort Worth and Denver City Railway on the north and the Texas and Pacific tracks on the south (which, at the time, marked the approximate boundaries of the 39th Judicial District). Later that same year, Legett joined the group whom he had represented in Austin (J. V. Cockrell, H. A. Tillett, Asa Holt, G. A. Kirkland, Henry Sayles, and S. P. Hardwicke), to sponsor Judge Cockrell's successful candidacy for the congressional seat of the newly created district.[3] In due time, Congressman Cockrell pushed one bill through Congress that created the United States District Court for the Northern District of Texas and a second that designated Abilene as one of the locations where that court would meet. At every stage, Legett contributed to the Abilene cause and to Cockrell's efforts. It was unlikely, therefore, that District Judge Meek would look elsewhere for a referee in bankruptcy.

Abilene had sought a district court for the past ten years without

---

[2] He would shortly purchase, for example, sixty-one dairy cows from T. M. Willis and begin a dairy farm on land he owned near Trent, Texas (see *Abilene Reporter-News*, September 7, 1900).

[3] From an article written by Congressman J. V. Cockrell, quoted in Ellouise Cockrell Stevenson to W. J. Bryan, Abilene, Texas, February 24, 1938, W. J. Bryan Papers, miscellaneous letters, Hardin-Simmons University. In the same national elections of 1892, a brother of Texas Congressman Cockrell was elected to his fifth term in the United States Senate from the state of Missouri.

success. When word spread that Congress had passed the bill, progressive Abilenians celebrated throughout the night. Cap Taylor's Domino Club postponed its scheduled meeting for the first time since the town was founded. Abilene had been denied, on numerous other occasions, a Texas Civil Court of Appeals, and outraged Abilenians had joined the *Taylor County News* editor, James A. Lowery, in a demand that West Texas secede from the state of Texas. "We have learned by past experience that it is no use whatever to ask for anything from . . . Eastern and Southern Texans," they complained.[4]

Two years had elapsed between the establishment of Abilene's district court in 1896 and the act of Congress to establish a uniform system of bankruptcy courts throughout the United States on July 1, 1898. The long and tedious struggle to push the bankruptcy act through Congress occurred when self-serving members of the House of Representatives debated whether the law should be one favorable to creditors or to debtors. Their compromise bill provided for the first time a national system of bankruptcy laws. The courts would operate under the immediate direction of referees in bankruptcy and within the jurisdictions of the various district courts. Legett, therefore, would work in close collaboration with Judge Meek. Technically his title was Mr. Referee, but from the beginning lawyers throughout the nation recognized the judicial nature of the referees' duties—their judgments in actual court cases—and the referees usually were called judges.[5]

All bankruptcy cases brought before Legett, whether voluntary or involuntary, would originate in Judge Meek's office. A voluntary bankruptcy case would be presented to the court by the debtor himself, but if creditors should instigate a case it would be classified as involuntary bankruptcy.[6] Legett's conjecture that the assignment would demand only a small portion of his time rested upon his familiarity with the area's sparse population, its limited business operations, and its severely limited money-lending agencies. He was probably surprised, therefore, when one of his first cases involved liabilities of more than $150,000 and required a great deal of his

[4] *Abilene Reporter*, June 12, 1896; *Taylor County News*, April 7, 1893.

[5] J. Henry Doscher, Jr. to the author, March 8, 1973.

[6] The word *bankrupt* means, in Italian, *bench-broken* and derives from the old Italian custom of destroying the bankers' benches when their business failed.

personal attention.[7] George Gray of Midland, Texas, was a voluntary
bankrupt, but his many creditors disagreed at length over the selection
of a trustee to handle the various details of their claims. Legett always
attempted to locate a trustee who could gain a unanimous vote from
the creditors, but in this case he was forced to accept a simple majority
ballot. One other aspect of the case turned out to be quite simple:
George Gray's exempt property included nothing more than one
horse and one saddle.

His first case, filed on August 9, two full weeks before Legett's
appointment, more nearly represented the typical case in bankruptcy.
He received the preliminary documents from Judge Meek on September 20 and heard Abilene attorney J. F. Cunningham's petition in
behalf of D. F. White of Midland later that day. White was a farmer
and rancher who had experienced a series of financial difficulties in
Arkansas, Lubbock, and Abilene.[8] As referee, Legett would perform
two major functions: first, he would decide upon a fair distribution
of White's property among his creditors, and second, he would discharge White from the remaining portion of the unpaid debt so that
the bankrupt could begin anew in all business transactions. In performing the first duty, Legett would exempt from confiscation and
distribution certain kinds of personal property. In the White case he
exempted the following: "All household and kitchen furniture, four
cows and two calves branded ⊖F, two horses, one branded W and
the other unbranded; one buggy, and property [claimed as] being the
homestead of the family."[9] In performing the second duty, Legett
would need to satisfy himself that the bankrupt had not committed
any of a lengthy list of offenses as he prepared to petition the court.
The list included any effort by the bankrupt to falsify, conceal, or
destroy his books, to obtain money or credit by false statements of his
financial condition, or to fail to explain satisfactorily any recent losses
or deficient assets.

Judge Legett recommended and the creditors unanimously agreed

[7] *Abilene Reporter,* January 6 and 20, 1899.

[8] Federal Archives and Records Center, General Services Administration, Fort
Worth, Texas, United States District Court Records, Bankruptcy Docket No. 1, FRC
No. 28-4-41 (bankruptcy cases filed in numerical order by bankruptcy case file num-
ber). Hereinafter referred to as FRC.

[9] FRC No. 28-4-41, "Order Setting Aside Exempt Property."

to accept Thomas M. Willis "as Trustee to take, hold, and distribute said estate." The position of trustee was no sinecure. If, for example, White had owned a public business, such as a department store, Willis, as receiver, would have been required to operate that business during the course of the bankruptcy proceedings so that the company's assets could be retained until sold. In due time Willis distributed cash or property valued at $2,530.01 to White's creditors. On January 1, 1899, Judge Legett inserted between the pages of his makeshift bankruptcy record book receipts which show that for their labors in behalf of the D. F. White case in bankruptcy trustee Willis received $5.00, deputy clerk Girand $10.00, and Referee Legett $10.00 plus expenses.[10] The final entry recorded Legett's accumulated expenses during his first bankruptcy case:

Statement of Expenses Incurred by Referee:

Sept. 20th 1898— Record Book ............................ 10 cts
Sept. 20th 1898— Envelope ............................... 3
Sept. 23, 1898— Publication of Notice ................. 2.00
Oct. 24, 1898— Pub. notice final discharge .............. 2.00
Oct. 24, 1898— Cash to Bankrupt ....................... 2.00
    Pd. by the Bankrupt [no date].[11]

During the remaining months of that calendar year, Judge Legett heard four additional cases, and in the following twelve-month period he heard seventeen others. He heard through the years a total of 636 cases. As his other business enterprises grew more complex, Legett systematically reduced the time spent in his private law practice. Income from his bankruptcy cases remained minuscule, but he performed those duties with utmost seriousness and apparently looked upon them as part of his civic duty. Although opponents of the Bankruptcy Act of 1898 charged that its sponsors in Congress wrote the bill favorable to creditors, Judge K. K. Legett built a reputation for fairness among both creditors and debtors who appeared in his West

[10] Legett sometimes varied his rates. In his forty-first case, in 1901, for example, he charged L. S. Cotter only five dollars, but during the same year, on his forty-seventh case, he charged the Star Stove Company fifteen dollars. In 1904, beginning with case seventy-five, he raised his regular fee to fifteen dollars (FRC No. 45396 [Correspondence]).
[11] FRC, "In Re D. F. White, Bankrupt, Statement of expenses."

Texas court. Not a single incident is recorded in court files or local newspapers of an attempt to appeal a Legett judgment in bankruptcy court.

By 1893 Legett had invested all of his accumulated wealth into the development of cattle lands and grain, cotton, and dairy farms, and by the turn of the century he typified the new American whom Frederick Jackson Turner sought to distinguish from his European ancestors. Legett was a fifth-generation American who, in the evolutionary process, also set forth the Horatio Alger dream. His steady climb up the economic and social ladders provided some degree of truth to the mythical tales of Alger's rags-to-riches heroes, Ragged Dick and Tattered Tom. Viewed from any angle as the new century began, Legett was a leader in the true Alger tradition. His colleagues in the legal profession openly admired his self-taught professionalism. Local businessmen respected his entrepreneur instincts, for his investments, sales, and trades rarely failed to turn a profit. Chairmen of various civic organizations recognized his popularity as a platform speaker. Debtors appreciated his expertise in guiding them out of their financial difficulties. Perhaps above all, the academic community at Simmons College, both faculty and students, valued his assistance whenever crises occurred.

He was at once a conscientious family provider and a conscientious civic leader; combined, these two instincts required constant exertion. At many stages of his busy life, Legett was reminded by his wife that his energies and time itself were limited, but there seemed always something else that needed to be done. A typical comment on his problem appears in a letter to Judge Edward S. Clinch of New York City: "The demands on my time are very, very great and it is with much reluctance that I yield to this call for an increase in public service. The hope has been entertained that I had already reached the limit." [12] Legett rarely reached his limit and, when the need involved Simmons College, he always responded.

In 1902 the Simmons community faced one of its many crises: after only one year at the school, President C. R. Hairfield announced that he would resign—a consequence of his inability to solve the financial problems of the college. Shortly thereafter, C. W. Merchant

[12] K. K. Legett to Judge Edward S. Clinch, January 5, 1906, Legett Family Records, file 1, paper 28.

could not continue as chairman of the board of trustees. Through the spring and part of the summer of that year local Baptists expressed alarm at the instability of the college and wondered if it could keep its doors open. Meanwhile the board continued to fill vacant positions. In July they elected Oscar Henry Cooper president of the college, and, at a special meeting on October 3, by unanimous vote they made K. K. Legett president of the board of trustees.[13]

He readily accepted the new responsibility. The office involved God's work, and Simmons College was God's property. With this thinking, Legett had no choice but to accept.[14] Through the years no other public responsibility would demand more of Legett's time, drain more of his energy, consume more of his attention, require more of his talents, or challenge more of his patience. On the other hand, perhaps no other public responsibility contributed more to his sense of accomplishment. Time after time he began letters concerning school matters with the facetious remark: "I have the misfortune to be the chairman of the Board of Trustees at Simmons College." But he never made the remark in a serious vein and gave evidence of pride in the position.

By the time Legett assumed his new duties, the school appeared to be entering a brighter and more hopeful era under its new president. Oscar Henry Cooper's academic background included a Phi Beta Kappa key from Yale University, graduate study at the University of Berlin, the superintendency of public instruction for the state of Texas, and the presidency of Baylor University.[15] His celebrated personality conflict some years earlier with former Governor James S. Hogg, whom Legett never liked, probably paved the way for a lasting friendship between the president of the board and the president of the college.

The 1903 *Annual Catalogue of Simmons College* clearly reflected the beginning of a new era at the school. Cooper tightened the curriculum so radically that students completed in two years the program that previously had required four years. He announced plans to insti-

[13] Simmons College, *Minutes of the Board*, 1:69.
[14] K. K. Legett to Judge Edward S. Clinch, February 26, 1906, Legett Family Records, file 1, paper 35.
[15] Rupert N. Richardson, *Famous Are Thy Halls: Hardin-Simmons University as I Have Known It*, p. 31.

tute at some time in the future a new four-year program that would lead to the Bachelor of Arts degree, and he immediately strengthened the preparatory school by establishing a program similar to that in public high schools.[16]

Other innovations in the 1903–1904 catalogue included commercial advertisements purchased by local businesses and a full-page plea for donations to the college's endowment fund. President Cooper could have suggested the use of the catalogue for advertising purposes, but the possibility is equally strong that the new board president recommended the variation from earlier editions. The request for gifts contains phrases strikingly similar to Legett's writing style, and more significantly the opening sentence was a favorite Legett expression:

ENDOW SIMMONS COLLEGE

A good college is a "possession forever." Tuition and incidental fees never cover adequately its expenses. Annual donations are good, and under present conditions are necessary to Simmons College. The donations of the past year amounted to about ten thousand dollars. . . . The college has about twenty thousand dollars in its endowment funds. This is a beginning. Every lover of Christ, every friend of the college, every believer in the value and need of higher education is invited to add to this fund. . . . Such a gift to a college for Christian education strengthens forever the foundation of righteousness.[17]

This new leadership at the college brought measurable results almost instantly. Enrollment increased at the following rate:

| | |
|---|---|
| 1902–1903 | 189 |
| 1903–1904 | 221 |
| 1904–1905 | 229 |
| 1905–1906 | 249 |
| 1906–1907 | 326 |
| 1907–1908 | 340 |

Dozens of new ministerial students accounted for a significant part of the increase. For the first time, men and women from the community drove out to the campus to enroll in Professor Charles T. Ball's Bible

[16] Twelfth Annual Catalogue of Simmons College (1903–1904), pp. 57–58.
[17] Ibid., back cover.

courses and Professor Lee R. Scarborough's courses in homiletics and missions. A new course in military training for men reflected the nation's growing acceptance of military preparedness following the recent war in Cuba.[18]

Legett soon proved that he enjoyed his duties as a college trustee. The following year he accepted an appointment by Governor S. W. T. Lanham to the board of trustees at the Texas Agricultural and Mechanical College at Bryan. That institution's program to train young men in agricultural and mechanical arts was in Legett's mind second in importance only to the program of religious education at Simmons College. The appointment clearly bolstered Legett's self-assurance among those with more formal education, whom he usually treated with a certain gesture of courtesy similar to that reserved for clergymen and ladies. Perhaps the appointment improved his self-esteem among his own in-laws. The Bryan ancestry included several men of letters, and, in the family tradition, John Bryan held a bachelor's degree from Texas A&M and a law degree from Cumberland College in Tennessee. Possibly Legett relished the thought that he, rather than his brother-in-law, received the governor's appointment. Nevertheless, he continued to devote far more time to Simmons matters than to problems involving Texas A&M.

The Abilene college was small, only eight frame buildings (one main building and seven two-room cottages) on thirty-four acres. In 1903 a new dormitory for girls neared completion, and the college catalogue described the rapid growth of the library collection. Prospective students and their parents could learn also from that catalogue that Abilene was a modern city of five thousand inhabitants and that it was "only" one hundred and sixty-one miles west of Fort Worth. Abilene's modern features, the catalogue explained, included an electric light plant, a waterworks system, a local and long-distance telephone network, an ice factory, a cottonseed oil mill, a cotton compress, a steam laundry, three weekly newspapers, and one daily newspaper. Its message to parents emphasized the fact that Abilene's wild and woolly frontier days had ended: "Abilene has no saloons and is free from many of the temptations to vice found in larger cities, yet it affords nearly all their social and educational advantages. The social

---

[18] Richardson, *Famous Are Thy Halls*, p. 32.

and religious sentiment of the people is, in itself, an influence for good that cannot be overestimated." [19]

Legett's labors for Simmons College covered a broad spectrum: his speeches ranged from formal commencement addresses to extemporaneous lectures to the four literary societies; his travels in behalf of the school ranged from extended business conferences in New York City to train excursions to Brownwood in support of the Simmons debate team in intercollegiate contests with Howard Payne College; his correspondence as president of the board ranged from requests to Andrew Carnegie for financial assistance to letters answering parents' requests for assistance or advice. The following letters written in late 1904, are typical of hundreds of others:

October 14, 1904

Mrs. Aretta Woodman
   Hagerman, New Mexico
My Dear Mrs. Woodman:
   Of course, I will with pleasure do anything I can to assist you and your son. . . . I will see the president of the college and see if there is any [work] to get him in. . . .

Your friend,
K. K. Legett [20]

December 21, 1904

Mr. S. P. Tolleson
   Amarillo, Texas
Dear Sir:
   It is my understanding that all colleges require payment in advance by all students for the term, and that this sum is never refunded except where the student is prevented from attending by actual sickness. I assume . . . Mr. Munsey left without cause. However, I have referred your letter to Doctor Cooper and requested that he do the proper thing by Mr. Munsey.

Yours respectfully,
K. K. Legett [21]

[19] *Eleventh Annual Catalogue of Simmons College*, p. 9.
[20] K. K. Legett to Mrs. Aretta Woodman, October 14, 1904, Legett Letter Book, p. 25.
[21] Legett Letter Book, p. 51.

In other college-related correspondence he pursued every course that might lead to new benefactors. When he learned that Abilene would receive funds from the Andrew Carnegie Foundation to construct a local public library, Legett immediately pressed his friends and acquaintances to write to Carnegie in behalf of Simmons College. He dictated four letters on December 18, 1905, and addressed them to Governor S. W. T. Lanham, Senator C. A. Culberson, David S. Houston (University of Texas), and H. H. Harrington (Texas Agricultural and Mechanical College). All were almost identical to the following letter to Governor Lanham:

Dear Governor:

I have the best reasons for believing that if I can get from you a letter to Mr. Carnegie along the lines indicated in the copy herewith enclosed, we can get a substantial donation from him to the college located at this place. . . .

Governor, I will very keenly appreciate your action . . . if you will send me a letter . . . written on "Executive" letter heads, and enclosed in an envelope addressed to me. . . .

I know you are interested in everything that pertains to the development of the country, and for that reason I . . . make the request.

Your friend,
K. K. Legett [22]

In spite of his efforts on that occasion, the Abilene college did not receive aid from Andrew Carnegie.

At other times, Legett found it necessary to write to personal friends who owed debts to the school. In his drive to secure financial stability for Simmons College, personal matters never hindered his efforts, as the following letter demonstrates:

April 7, 1906

Mr. William Young
Tuscola, Texas.

Friend Will:

On the 12 of January, 1898, you gave a note to Simmons College for

[22] Copy of letter in Legett Family Records, file 1, paper 25.

$50.00 due in five years with 6% interest, on which there appears to have been no payment made.

Please give the matter your prompt attention and relieve the board of the necessity of placing notes in the hands of attorneys, which I would very much dislike to do.

Truly your friend,<br>K. K. Legett [23]

In a positive frame, Legett sometimes used personal friendships to bring outstanding speakers to the campus. Thus, as the 1905–1906 school year began, he wrote to his friend and district court associate, Edward R. Meek:

Sept. 19, 1905

Judge Edward R. Meek,
    Fort Worth, Texas
My Dear Judge:
    . . . I am writing to . . . extend to you . . . an earnest and cordial invitation to stop with us during the next term of court. . . .

    I shall expect you while out here on Monday morning to go with me out to Simmons College and deliver an address to the students. . . . It would not only do you good, but greatly help the students. . . . Let me hear.

Truly your friend,<br>K. K. Legett [24]

As the same school year ended, he pressed another friend to close the session:

April 30, 1906

Hon. W. R. Smith
    House of Representatives
    Washington, D. C.
Dear Judge:
    Some days ago Dr. Cooper, President of Simmons College, requested

[23] Copy of letter in Legett Family Records, file 1, paper 44.
[24] Ibid., paper 20.

me to write you an earnest invitation to deliver the commencement address at the college. . . .

Now, Judge, I want you to do this.

Truly your friend<br>K. K. Legett[25]

Legett's most successful endeavor to bring visiting lecturers to
Simmons College began in 1905 when he collaborated with President
Cooper to organize the Simmons Bible Institute. Its instant popularity
on campus and in the community encouraged the men to conduct the
institute annually, usually in January. Thereafter the annual catalogue
described it as "a great factor for good in the religious life of the
college."[26] An advertisement in a local newspaper explained the program to the public:

SIMMONS BIBLE INSTITUTE<br>Abilene, Jan. 16–27, 1905<br>Program

The following program composed of 15 lecturers and 64 lectures on
many interesting religious subjects will be given at Abilene Jan. 16 to 27.
Preachers, missionaries, Sunday school teachers and other church workers
of all denominations are cordially invited and urged to attend all the
lectures.

Board at private homes, Simmons College, and at some of the hotels
will be $5 for the ten days term. There will be reduced rates at the wagon
yards for teams. There will be no fees nor charges . . . for these lectures.
. . . The lectures in the day time will be at the chapel of Simmons College
and at night at the Baptist church.[27]

The sixty-four lectures included topics which ranged from "The
Pastor's Burdens and Joys," to "How to Take a Collection," and
from "The Culture of Christian Living" to "Money, Man, and God."
Through the years Legett looked upon the institute, its lectures, lecturers, and its many out-of-town visitors as the outstanding event of

[25] Legett Letter Book, p. 430.

[26] See, for example, the *Fourteenth Annual Catalogue of Simmons College*
(1905–1906), p. 13.

[27] *Abilene Reporter*, January 4, 1905.

the school term. Invariably, he filled his home with as many of the
guest lecturers as he could accommodate.

Conversely, his most distasteful task in behalf of Simmons College arose, also in 1905, following the death of Dr. James R. Simmons, the school's most generous benefactor. At the time of his death,
Dr. Simmons's cash gifts amounted to twelve thousand dollars, and
his gifts to the library made up more than half of its total collection.
His son, Dr. Robert S. Simmons, showed an equal interest in the college; he literally created the library during one two-month visit when
he catalogued, arranged, and bound every book. In addition, the
younger Simmons endowed two scholarships, each of which provided
full tuition to a needy ministerial student. Aware of Robert Simmons's independent wealth, Abilenians were not surprised to learn
that the college had inherited the entire James R. Simmons estate.
Genuine distress prevailed, however, when news reached Abilene
that the son might contest his father's will. Equally fond of both men,
the college community had no wish to compound their recent loss by
offending Robert Simmons.

K. K. Legett was especially fond of the elder man. Less than three
years earlier he had written, "your bearing, your manner, and your
purity of thought have been an inspiration to me."[28] A short while
after Simmons's death, Legett received a letter from Judge Edward S.
Clinch, the Simmons family's attorney, who explained the son's position and requested Legett's suggestions. Legett responded at length:

I regret that Robert Simmons feels aggrieved at the testamentary disposition of property made by his father. . . . My want of familiarity with the
laws of your state . . . render it quite impossible for me at this time to
offer a suggestion that would be of practical value.

Without committing myself to any policy at this time, I do not consider it improper for me to say that I am in favor of meeting Robert Simmons in a spirit of fairness and liberality.[29]

The board chairman was perhaps more apprehensive than his letter revealed. In a letter to the Reverend Lee Scarborough, a member
of the Simmons faculty who was at that time on leave to study at Yale

[28] K. K. Legett to James B. Simmons, January 8, 1903, Legett Family Records,
file 15, p. 5.
[29] Legett Letter Book, January 5, 1906, pp. 307–9.

University, he expressed the fear that they were going to have some trouble with the provisions of the will.[30]

Later in January, Legett assured Judge Clinch that "every member of our board has nothing but feelings of kindness for Robert Simmons. . . ." Again he expressed his eagerness to do the proper thing: "I feel that I owe to Robert Simmons as high a duty as I do to the College. . . ." A week later he still seemed inclined to sympathize with Robert Simmons' attitude: "I differ widely with Dr. Jas. R. Simmons as to the provision that a parent should make for a child and . . . I am willing to go further than he did in that direction."[31]

On February 26 Legett reluctantly notified Clinch that he had decided to go to New York, since he could not see how the problems could be satisfactorily disposed of by correspondence. He explained that he would leave Abilene to attend a meeting of the board of trustees at Texas A&M and would travel from there to New York. At that point, his dread of the long winter journey, his anxiety about Robert Simmons, and his failure to devise some solution to the problem strained his patience. Apparently without justification, Legett suddenly grew irritable toward the New York lawyer following an unexplained delay in response to an earlier inquiry: "I do not know why you would not extend to me the common courtesy of a reply to my last letter, and I do not know why you have never directly or indirectly sought the views or cooperation of the college or anybody connected therewith."[32]

The next day's mail brought added pressure. Legett received an anonymous letter in which the sender offered a considerable amount of money, but with strings attached:

February 27, 1906

Mr. K. K. Legett,
   Chairman of the Board of Trustees,
      Simmons College, Abilene, Texas.

Dear Sir:

I own a $3000.00 bond issued by the Continental Oil Company bearing 5% interest, the interest payable semi-annually.

[30] K. K. Legett to Rev. Lee Scarborough, January 6, 1906, Legett Family Records, file 1, p. 29.

[31] K. K. Legett to Judge Edward S. Clinch, January 26 and 30, February 7, 1906, Legett Family Records, file 1, p. 32.

[32] Ibid., February 26, 1906.

I will donate this bond to Simmons College for general endowment, provided the Board will secure $3000.00 of the funds bequeathed to the College by Dr. Simmons. . . .

I am advanced in years and would not leave this proposition open indefinitely. . . .

Yours very truly,

[unsigned] [33]

Legett spent the first two weeks in March conferring with Clinch and Simmons and in traveling to and from New York. Upon his return to Abilene, he wrote to Terry Smith in New York, "I found Judge Clinch a most courteous, elegant gentleman, and had not the slightest difficulty in arranging matters satisfactorily with him." [34]

The New York conferences led to the discovery—somehow overlooked until Legett arrived—that New York state's inheritance laws permitted not more than one-half of the estate of a New York citizen to be willed to any individual or institution outside New York. With this knowledge, Legett and Robert Simmons agreed that the estate should be divided into two equal portions. As a consequence, approximately one year later Legett accepted in behalf of the college a final settlement of $20,000. [35]

Thus the delicate negotiations, fraught with potential hard feelings that could have tarnished the good will and Christian spirit upon which the college was founded, were concluded to everyone's satisfaction. For many years thereafter the Simmons College *Bulletin* emphasized the point that there was no residue of ill will; each edition repeated the identical statement that Robert S. Simmons was second only to his father in his generosity to the college. [36] Without Legett's unselfish involvement in "God's work and God's property," that statement might never have been written.

[33] Letter to K. K. Legett, February 27, 1906, Legett Family Records, file 1, p. 36.

[34] K. K. Legett to Hon. Terry Smith, March 16, 1906, Legett Family Records, file 1, paper 38. Mr. Smith was probably a New York attorney whom Legett consulted in advance of his meeting with Clinch.

[35] *Sixteenth Annual Session of Simmons College* (1907–1908), p. 65.

[36] See, for example, *Bulletin Simmons College* (1920), p. 15.

*I have just built me a real good home. It cost
me more money than I was able to put into a
house, but I did it on account of the girls.*

CHAPTER NINE

## The Mansion

K. K. LEGETT was a proud man, but he was never a boastful man
until he built his mansion. For months thereafter he could hardly resist the temptation to describe it to out-of-town friends, relatives, and
business associates. Early in 1906, for example, he boasted to a client: "I have built me an elegant home, and I think one of the petti-
est homes in Texas. I am sure there is nothing to equal it in architectural appearance in the western part of the state. I wish you could
come and spend a few days with me." [1] It was characteristic also that
he planned the home in such detail that its location marked the exact
point of Abilene's highest elevation. It was perhaps even more characteristic of Legett's pioneering generation that the thought never
seemed to occur to him that Comanches, Apaches, and Kiowas had
occupied the site only a few years earlier.

Since colonial days the elegance of a man's home had measured
his success as family provider, just as land ownership measured his
wealth. Legett's pride and his rapidly expanding landholdings, therefore, dictated the proportions and the quality of his home. For generations to come, the house stood as a symbol of its builder's public
image. Newspapermen rarely described the house in terms other than
"the Legett mansion," or "Judge Legett's palatial home." Legett
stated to many acquaintances that he built the home for his daughters, but one must suspect that his own impoverished childhood in-
stilled in him a need to build a home as elegant as any in West Texas.

He approached his fiftieth year conscious of the fact that he had
passed "from youth into middle age," that his hair was "touched by
the frosts of intervening years," and that God had cared for him

---

[1] K. K. Legett to Dr. R. C. Elliott, Guanacevil, Durango, Mexico, February 5,
1906, Legett Letter Book, p. 352.

"with a lavish hand." [2] As he and his home town grew older, younger Abilenians prepared annual lists of surviving pioneers as part of the town's birthday celebration. Legett enjoyed his status as an original settler. He voiced his full share of bromides and platitudes which, although worn by overuse, reminded new arrivals to take advantage of their town's opportunities: "a town that never has anything to do is on its way to the cemetery"; "any citizen who will do nothing for his town is helping to dig its grave"; "a man who always complains about a town's poverty throws flowers on its grave."

K. K. Legett was an "old-timer" before he was an old man. New settlers usually paid rapt attention when he or some other pioneer offered advice or reminisced about such early history as the January morning in 1886 when temperatures dipped to eight below zero, or the week in November, 1897, when for the first time in West Texas history the Texas and Pacific railroad used snowplows enroute from Fort Worth to El Paso, or the year 1895 when Abilene had twice its average annual rainfall.

Legett's personal success reflected the general prosperity of Abilene during its first two decades. Jealousy between West Texas towns was commonplace, and they belittled more often than they praised one another. It was no idle remark when the editor of the *Coleman* (Texas) *Voice* admitted that "no town in Texas is growing faster than Abilene, and there has never been a time in our knowledge that that town was not ahead of the country." [3] Abilenians never doubted the sincerity of such remarks as they looked about them at the turn of the century and saw a new sewerage system nearing completion, a new water system, a telephone system, free mail delivery service, an electric plant, an ice plant, a college, and a public school system. During its first decade Abilene progressed from a cowboy town to a family village, and during its second decade it grew from a village to "a bustling little metropolis, well and wisely built." [4]

The surrounding farm and ranch lands were correspondingly prosperous. Taylor County settlers assured every new arrival that he was worth his weight in gold. Newspapers included special sections

---

[2] K. K. Legett to Judge John A. Nabers, Vernon, Texas, December 15, 1905, Legett Letter Book, p. 301; K. K. Legett to A. H. Kirby, Fort Deposit, Alabama, July 19, 1905, Legett Letter Book, p. 185.

[3] Quoted in *Abilene Daily Reporter*, August 29, 1904.

[4] *Abilene Daily Reporter*, October 14, 1904.

reserved entirely for real-estate news, and at least one land agent, Eugene Wood and Company, purchased a half-page advertisement in every daily paper throughout the year. The following real estate notices appeared in the *Abilene Daily Reporter* on August 14, 1905, and were typical of that era:

No. 16—160 acres, 155 tillable, one mile north of Nugent, 21 miles from Abilene, 120 in cultivation, no rocks or Johnson grass, fine well water and lasting water in creek, 1000 berry vines, 100 grapes, two-room boxed house and rock chimney. A special bargain at $2,500 cash, $1,000 balance to suit.

No. 42—10,000 acres near Eskota has been plotted out and we will cut you a tract to suit you. Unimproved land from six to fifteen dollars per acre, you can pay one dollar per acre cash, and only interest to be paid the next two years, balance to be paid on six years' time at eight percent.

Every measurable indicator in 1904 proved the area's prosperity. According to government reports, Taylor County farmers produced 22,896 bales of cotton—better than any of its immediate neighbors—during that year. Taylor County banks announced on January 11, 1905, that deposits exceeded $650,000. Abilene's faith that prosperity would continue stimulated plans for a new Texas and Pacific depot, a new library building (with assistance from Andrew Carnegie), an Elks hall, and an electric street railway.

A few extra dollars in the family's entertainment budget provided another barometer of prosperity—a simple lesson in arithmetic not ignored by the owners of Ringling Brothers Circus as they planned their annual pilgrimage about the country in 1904. When the company made its initial appearance in Abilene on Wednesday afternoon, October 12, 1904, a record-breaking crowd of more than 25,000 West Texans came to see its million-dollar street parade, its hair-raising menagerie, its Roman hippodrome races, and its "spectacular reproduction of Jerusalem." More sophisticated West Texans—the "elite theater-goers" as one newsman identified them—filled every seat at the Lyceum Theater on Tuesday evening, February 14, 1905, in spite of deep snow from a recent blizzard. A blue norther was no reason to miss the performance of Millie Des Monda and J. H. Harris in their four-act play, *The Hand of Man.*

With more affluence came more sophistication. A city council proclamation on March 2, 1905, ordained that local cattlemen could no longer build feeding pens and dipping vats within the city limits. Not even Legett could deny, however, that Abilene still had its share of unprincipled knaves whose tobacco spitting soiled the floors of public buildings, whose town cows wandered the streets and chewed green leaves from young maple trees, and whose downtown "privies" brought increasingly frequent letters of protest to local editors. One editor added that the most thoughtless scoundrel of them all was the person who, only one day after the city hauled one hundred and one wagon loads of trash out of town, dumped a huge pile of tin cans near the business district on Chestnut Street.[5]

In spite of such lingering evidences of frontier knavery, civic leaders such as Judge Legett vehemently protested when "jealous Easterners" belittled western progress. Some easterner identified only as Claridge wrote such a derogatory article in a 1905 edition of the *East Texas Farm Journal*:

There's a lot of half-starved pore white trash crawling out of the East Texas "bresh" and hiking out to West Texas. It would be a good thing for East Texans if they would never come back, but they will.

These people can scratch a half-starved living by working a day in a week, but they can't do it on a West Texas "dry section" if they hustle from early morn till dewey eve, six days in the seven.[6]

The Abilene editor resented the "ugly imputation" of "pore white trash" but he was outraged by the suggestion that West Texas was full of dry sections. One would have to travel a great distance west of Abilene to locate such a section, he insisted.

Two weeks later the indignant newsman displayed prominently on the front page an item from the *Palestine* (Texas) *Daily Visitor* that convincingly refuted "Claridge's insult":

On Saturday last, Hon. W. M. Lacy said a final farewell to Palestine and left for his new home at Abilene, Texas.

We spoke in a former issue of Mr. Lacy's bright prospects in Abilene, where he is one of the founders of the Commercial National Bank, and of the universal regret of his departure from our city.

[5] Ibid., July 19, 1905.
[6] Ibid., October 14, 1905.

He has been twice elected mayor of the city, twice treasurer of the county, was assistant superintendent of the Rusk penitentiary and has held other important offices of trust. . . . He has in every sense of the word been a leading citizen, and we know of no man who would be more missed.

He has a lovely family, his wife being ever a social leader, and son Hensely is the pride of our city, being one of the brightest and most popular midshipmen in the U.S. navy; and another son, Dr. Robert Lacy, an eminent physician.

Abilene may well be proud of the citizen she has gained while in Palestine his place and that of his family can never be filled.[7]

Abilenians sometimes admitted a dry spell existed, and now and then they acknowledged the blazing heat of summer, but nature, they insisted, was no harsher in West Texas than in other parts of the country. "Unnamed parties" provided proof for their claims when they went east during the summer of 1905 to escape the West Texas heat but soon returned home with the report that the Virginia mountains were fairly sizzling.[8] Why travel such a great distance when the same summer heat was available at home?

With the possible exception of the weather, Legett and his friends convinced one another that hard work and civic spirit could change anything that needed changing in Abilene. Whatever Abilene needed Abilene could acquire through a well-organized civic association. Such an association could provide plans and leadership for public parks and playgrounds, trees and flowers along streets and railroad tracks, and carts and wagons to haul brush and trash from back yards and alleys. A civic association could do for the entire town what a little cooperation had done already for the folks who lived along Butternut Street. F. W. Chatfield, for example, had filled his yard with young sycamore and maple trees; the Methodists had planted a nice California hedge around the entire church yard; J. D. Stinchcomb, Jr., had planted one hundred and seven shade and fruit trees; editor Shook had forty-seven trees in his yard, which included ten black locusts and an English walnut that he had planted back in 1892; Judge J. V. Cockrell's large trees attracted dozens of mockingbirds to his home;

[7] Ibid., October 26, 1905.
[8] Ibid., August 23, 1905.

ten-foot high sycamore and fruit trees encircled George Widmer's house on the corner of South Fifth; a wide-spreading mulberry tree shaded most of J. P. Daniel's home; and Hon. H. A. Tillett made his home "one of the prettiest places in Abilene by encircling it with trees, shrubs, and flowers."[9]

As the town grew and its citizens prospered, a few of the wealthier pioneers began to build homes commonly called showplaces: the J. M. Radford residence at Hickory and North Second, the Henry James place at Elm and South Sixth, the C. B. Scarborough home on South Sixth, and the J. M. Wagstaff dwelling on Grape Street. Individually and collectively such substantial buildings demonstrated the town's stability and permanence, and in 1904 K. K. Legett decided that he too could afford to build such a home. In 1904 Kade was a high school teenager and the girls were only a few years behind. They soon would want to entertain their young friends at home, and the home on Pine Street was not appropriate. The year 1903–1904 was especially prosperous for Legett on both farm and ranch lands, his law practice kept him busier than he preferred, and his land speculations proved especially profitable. His income, if not his savings account, justified immediate construction of his dream home.

In August, 1904, Legett sold the Pine Street home to J. M. Chandler, an able young man who recently had purchased controlling interest in a local steam laundry. The transaction merited public notice: "Judge K. K. Legett has sold his home on Pine Street and will build a palatial residence on the highest point in Abilene—Alta Vista —on the site of the Taylor home which was destroyed by fire a few years ago."[10] The Legetts agreed to give possession of the house in January, which, they assumed, provided more than enough time to build a residence.

Judge and Mrs. Legett discovered in *Munsey's Magazine* a picture of a house that both liked. The house was basically Georgian Colonial with certain touches of the Victorian Gothic design then popular in England. Barber and Kluttz, a Knoxville, Tennessee, architectural firm advertised the model and the Legetts ordered blueprints. Later they employed an Abilene man, William P. Preston, to redesign certain interior dimensions. He remained on the job as gen-

9 Ibid., April 24, 1905.
10 Ibid., August 17, 1904.

eral superintendent of construction. Late in August, Legett and Preston employed I. M. Lane, a Dallas builder, to construct the Abilene home. Preston and Lane proved to be good at their trade and Legett remained one of their best references for home, school, and office construction.

The Legett lot covered the entire six hundred block on Meander Street. It was six blocks south of the Texas and Pacific tracks and twelve blocks west of Chestnut Street, which at that time was the center of the southside business district. The center of the lot rose six feet above the street elevation. Legett and his contractors decided that the house should have an east front and that the front entrance should measure exactly one hundred and fifty feet from the street curbing. They designed a driveway that would lead from the street to the south portico. A concrete walk six feet wide would lead from the street to the front entrance. Wide two-story verandas would encircle the house on the east, south, and west sides and four massive columns would accentuate the front entrance. Legett decided to locate the foundation toward the north end of the lot so that a small summer house, a fifty-foot grape arbor, an orchard of several dozens of peach, pear, and plum trees, a large vegetable garden, and an adjoining croquet court could occupy the south and west yards. Elm, pecan, cedar, huckleberry, and oak trees would encircle the house on all sides.

First-floor ceilings would rise twelve feet above the floor, and second-floor ceilings would be two feet lower. A captain's walk would top a full, third-floor attic. The Legetts decided that the first floor should include a combination entrance-library-stairway (with extended platform), a "front room," a parlor, a dining room, a butler's pantry, a kitchen, and a master bedroom suite with separate bath and sitting room. The second floor included five bedrooms, a sun room (a seldom-used sitting room), and a game room. Legett and Preston estimated the costs of building materials (including seasoned lumber from East Texas), transportation, and construction at $10,000, and both men agreed that the structure should be completed within three months. The Legetts hoped, therefore, to move into their new home at 602 Meander Street around Christmastime.

Legett could not have imagined the frustrations and traumas that awaited him. Costs and construction time doubled his original estimates. For a man accustomed to balanced accounts (who only recently

had reminded his wife that "the eggs from just one hen would pay
for a subscription to the local paper" and who then suggested that
she should "dedicate a hen to that purpose"), the costs of chandeliers, heavy oak staircases, and polished mantels staggered the imagination. For a man who saved two hundred and fifty Virginia cheroot
wrappers and Durham tobacco coupons and exchanged them for six
table spoons ("of Rogers standard weight, shell design and satin fin-
ish"), the cost of a grand piano for the front room boggled the
mind.[11]

Legett never lost faith in Preston or Lane, but the difficulties he
encountered as he attempted to deal with distant supply houses caused
him to question, and sometimes to condemn, the competency of
American businessmen. Mrs. Legett generally decided upon needed
items for furnishing and decorating the house, but her husband located and purchased those items. Before long he was involved in endless correspondence with furniture companies located in Galveston,
Chicago, Memphis, and numerous places in between, and with lawn
and garden companies from California to Florida. He rarely placed
an order that did not eventually lead to perplexing complications. Efforts to purchase mantels, tiles, and grates for seven fireplaces brought
hints of the frustrations to follow. In late September he began a series of businesslike, no-nonsense negotiations with companies in St.
Louis, Dallas, Waco, and Fort Worth, but by the time he received
the proper quantities, colors, widths, heights, and styles, fall and
winter had passed and spring had arrived.

The following statements, sifted from a portion of the correspondence during those long months of construction, attest to the
frustrations of a man attempting to build a mansion in West Texas in
the first years of the twentieth century:

(September 28, 1904, Central Mantel Co., St. Louis): . . . Tell me how
much it will cost in plain English. I have no time to dicker by exchange
of letters.

(January 18, 1905, Rick Furniture Company, Dallas): Ship my mantels, tiling, and grates at once. What are you waiting for?

(January 28, 1905, Nash-Robinson Co., Waco): I bought elsewhere. I

---

[11] K. K. Legett to Folordora Tag Company, St. Louis, Missouri, September 28,
1904, Legett Family Records. Other spoons of grape design were added to the collection in exchange for orange wrappers.

shall not soon cease to wonder why you [spent] so much energy in trying
to convince me that neither I nor my contractors knew what tile opening
I wanted.

(March 6, 1905, Rick Furniture Company, Dallas): You sent me only
four sets of tiling when you should have sent five. You failed to send the
"Art tiling."

(March 11, 1905, Louis F. Rick, Rick Furniture Co., Dallas): I have
your uncalled for letter of the 8th. . . . Whenever I make a statement I
tell the truth and if the grates had not been of the kind I mentioned the
statement would not have been made.

I contracted for the Monarch grates, I want the Monarch grates, and I
am going to have Monarch grates.

. . . I am not going to dally with you . . . with any further correspondence.

(March 13, 1905, Rick Furniture Co., Dallas): I received today by
express a box of white Art tile, but when opened, it was found to contain only the tiling for the facing and not one piece for the hearth.

(March 22, 1905, Ellison Furniture and Carpet Co., Fort Worth): I
wrote you some days ago that I wanted a hearth with a blue border. The
sample you sent me is cream colored and we don't want it.

(March 22, 1905, Rick Furniture Co., Dallas): I am nearly fifty years
old and you are the *only* man who has refused to accept my word as true
for thirty years. . . . I am going to have the benefit of the trade I made
with you, if it involves me in a half a dozen suits.

By early December Legett knew that his new home would not be
completed before late January. A letter from Legett to Mrs. M. E. M.
Elliott in Waterford, Ireland, on February 18 reveals his weariness:
"I am building me a good home, but it looks like I will never get it
finished." [12] About mid-March, the Legetts dared to order shipment
of their new furniture. They knew there would be more problems:

March 17, 1905

Rick Furniture Company
Dallas, Texas
Sir: On yesterday we unpacked the furniture you shipped. I find that you
sent us one large chair which we did not buy, and failed to send the one
which we did buy. . . .

[12] K. K. Legett to Mrs. M. E. M. Elliott, Waterford, Ireland, February 18, 1905,
Legett Letter Book, p. 87.

The small dresser was badly damaged. . . . You also failed to send rollers for either the davenport or dining room table. The hall seat is badly scarred. In fact quite a sliver is broken from one of the arms. . . . One of the dining room chairs has a small part of the veneering torn off.[13]

In April, 1905, the Legetts moved to 602 Meander Street, more than three months later than their original estimate. The mansion was structurally complete but contained rooms only partially furnished, some entirely empty, and others unused for lack of lighting fixtures. The yard was barren and empty except for a few scattered mesquite trees.

As summer arrived the Legetts continued to debate whether to install electric or gas lighting. They preferred the cleaner and more convenient electric light, but numerous fires around town—caused by faulty electric wiring—and Judge Meek's strong recommendation induced them eventually to turn to acetylene gas. Still uncertain, however, Legett instructed Lane to construct the house in a manner that would allow easy installation of electric wires at some later date. Having made the decison to use gas, Legett ordered from the American Acetylene Gas Light Company in Fort Worth sixteen ceiling chandeliers. He ordered, in addition, forty-eight white globes and four porch lanterns. Seven fireplaces, a huge Majestic range in the kitchen, and a small space heater in the master bedroom suite provided heat on both floors. Hall and room carpets at $1.25 per yard came from Fort Worth. Through the spring and early summer Legett ordered fencing materials from Kansas City, gates from Chicago, flower seeds from Fort Worth, rose bushes from Los Angeles, and porch furniture from Houston.[14]

By fall the proud owner believed he had "by all odds the prettiest house and location in town." He added to his library shelves such future reading materials as Theodore Roosevelt's colorful six-volume set of *The Winning of the West* and such popular periodicals as *The American Magazine, Suburban Life, Review of Reviews,* and *Cosmo-*

[13] K. K. Legett to Rick Furniture Co., Dallas, Texas, March 17, 1905, Legett Letter Book, p. 115.

[14] K. K. Legett to C. V. Sayles, c/o American Acetylene Gas Light Co., Fort Worth, June 19, 1905, Legett Letter Book, p. 486; Legett Letter Book pp. 373, 428, 364, 331.

*politan.* During the winter months, three different music companies delivered grand pianos to 602 Meander before Mrs. Legett finally decided upon a Baldwin. During the Christmas season, unaware that some of the most hectic months of his life loomed ahead, Legett tried to slow his pace so that he might enjoy a relaxed holiday. On December 19 he sat at a desk in the library and wrote a letter to one of his sisters who still resided in Arkansas:

My Dear Sister:

I have always loved all of my people and the fact that I have not written to you and them is not due to my want of affection. . . .

I was very glad too that Pa and Ma went to live with Tom. They were a great source of anxiety and sorrow to me for a number of years. I have been supporting them for fifteen years. I don't mind this at all if only they could be more comfortable, but it seems impossible. I bought a home for them at Buffalo Gap and saw to it that they had all they needed or wanted to eat and wear, but it was awfully lonesome for them. They will now be well cared for. . . .

So far as I am concerned . . . God has been especially good to me. I have a nice healthy family and enough property to get along on. . . . Our boy is now fifteen years old and our girls are thirteen and twelve. . . . They have all been in school all their lives and all taking music, Kade on the cornet, Julia on the piano and violin, and Ruth on the piano. They play some. After a while we hope to have good music in our home.

I have just built me a real good home. It cost me more money than I was able to put into a house, but I did it on account of the girls. I hope they will appreciate it. It leaves me in debt some but I guess I will get out after awhile.

We all make a stammer at doing our Christian duty. We have a nice little city of six or seven thousand people and it is growing nicely and the country is rapidly developing.

Give my love to all your children. . . .

As ever your brother,
(signed) K. K. Legett[15]

It was characteristic of Legett that he did not mention the trials and tribulations that had accompanied the construction of his home.

[15] K. K. Legett to Mrs. V. A. Hale, Furlow, Arkansas, December 19, 1904, Legett Letter Book, p. 55.

Although he never expressed regret that he had built the mansion, he undoubtedly would have delayed construction if he had foreseen the immediate future. The sudden deaths of Mrs. Legett's parents, only a few months apart, brought both sorrow and disruption to house plans. Mrs. Bryan died early in November, 1904, just as the Legetts realized that they would not move into their new home at Christmas time. In April Colonel Bryan died. His death, although it added enormously to the Legetts' total wealth, brought immediate problems to his heirs. Two years would pass before the estate could be cleared for an equal division between the three Bryan children, but meanwhile miscellaneous claims against the estate must be paid and the Bryan cattle interests must be continued.

Legett had planned to sell a section of land in Falls County— purchased earlier from the Bryans—to provide cash as needed for building materials. A boll weevil invasion of that farm reduced its sale price and forced Legett to withdraw his offer. Simultaneously, cattle and cotton prices dropped sharply as the nation's general economic recession spread to the western states. Legett received $400 for a carload of cattle shipped to Fort Worth in December, 1904, whereas a year earlier an identical shipment netted $700.[16] Reduced cotton prices that winter forced Taylor County farmers to withhold part of the season's crop from the glutted market. Tenant farmers, as a consequence, began to abandon their lands. Such developments intermingled with other events in January, 1905, forced Legett to give his attention to many divergent matters: On January 1 the house was only two-thirds completed and required his constant attention; on the ninth he attended a Baptist convention at Waco; on the sixteenth the first annual Simmons Bible Institute began its ten-day session (out-of-town guests who had been invited earlier to stay at the Legett mansion were housed, instead, at the Bryan home); on the eighteenth the Abilene American National Bank failed;[17] on the nineteenth the New York cotton market dropped twelve points when news of Abi-

[16] K. K. Legett to Charles Crowly, Clyde, Texas, December 1, 1904, Legett Letter Book, p. 44.

[17] Legett wrote to a friend, "the bank failure did not catch me for anything, but, with an indebtedness of a million and a half dollars, it hurt the community very much" (K. K. Legett to Dr. R. C. Elliott, February 18, 1905, Legett Letter Book, p. 93).

lene's bank failure reached the East;[18] on the twenty-third Legett accepted Governor S. W. T. Lanham's reappointment to the board of directors at the Texas A&M College; and on the twenty-fourth, as Legett departed on an eastbound train for Dallas where he had an appointment with Judge Meek concerning a bankruptcy case, Mrs. Legett left on a westbound train for Sweetwater, where her little nephew Wash Bryan Trammell lay near death with pneumonia. These events help explain why a man highly respected and noted for his compassion could express considerable impatience when he received grates too wide for the fireplaces, furniture with handles broken or legs splintered, or chandeliers in every style except "Old Brass"— the only style he would accept.

As winter turned to spring, fences of stone, wood, and wrought iron provided both form and outline to the Legett property. Freshly planted fruit and shade trees softened the lines of the huge house and erased some of the barrenness surrounding it. Bermuda grass carpeted the enormous lawn, and soon flowers of every variety and color bordered sidewalks and driveways. When summer heat arrived, the Legetts learned to appreciate their twelve-foot-high ceilings and wide windows.

Each passing day helped erase more of the trauma of the past year. When he learned that the John Bryan family planned a summer vacation in northern Michigan and the A. H. Kirbys made arrangements to tour the southeastern states, Legett decided his family needed and deserved a long family vacation. As soon as the idea occurred to him, one rationalization led to another: in a letter to his parents he explained that he had had "right good luck the last few months and can go without increasing my indebtedness"; to Lora Legett (who needed no encouragement) he announced that ten years in the kitchen deserved a rest; and to his children he announced that they were old enough to make the trip an educational experience.

Consequently on June 9 Legett requested information from the Texas and Pacific Railway concerning costs for a family of five to travel by Pullman car for a month's tour of the northwest. On July 14 he sought the same information from the Gulf, Colorado, and Santa Fe agent in Fort Worth. The following day he wrote to the

[18] *Dallas News*, January 19, 1905, in *Abilene Daily Reporter*, January 20, 1905.

Rock Island agent in Fort Worth. Eventually he decided to take the Fort Worth and Denver City in early August and transfer later to the Union Pacific line. The family would leave immediately after the return from Alabama of his law partner, A. H. Kirby. A letter to Kirby on July 19 reveals the enthusiasm with which he approached the trip:

My Dear Mr. Kirby: I have not worn more than one sweater any day since you left and the thermometer has not registered above 106 in ten whole days.

Ed [Overshiner] is wearing his white shoes and mottled socks and the Lord hasn't killed him for it yet.

In the midst of all these blessings I have been dreaming of "Kool Kolorado" and the land of Brigham Young, Oregon, Puget Sound, Vancouver, and the Golden Gate. This dream has developed a burning desire to make it a reality, so we have decided to load our "bag and baggage" on your return and strike for the mountains and the Pacific coast. . . . Now don't you cut your vacation short one day on this account.

The following day he informed A. J. Brown, chairman of the board of directors at Texas A&M College, that he could not attend any board meetings before September 20.

On August 3 Legett informed his parents that "the children are on the tip-toe of anxiety to get off." On the morning of August 5 the family departed Abilene on the eastbound Texas and Pacific train. They transferred to the Fort Worth and Denver City line late that afternoon. During the remainder of that month and part of September they visited Colorado Springs, Denver, Salt Lake City, Portland, Vancouver, San Francisco, Los Angeles, and El Paso. "It was," Legett later reported to a brother, "a great sight-seeing trip, very educational. . . ."

In spite of his complaint to A. J. Brown on September 19 that "it looks like the world has come to an end since I came home [and] I just can't catch up," he seemed as proud of his family tour as he was of his new home. Indeed, Legett intended that each should complement the other.

But family pride and interest did not end at his own doorstep. He rarely saw his brothers and sisters and their families, but he never lost contact with them. Upon his return from the northwest, among the letters stacked on his desk was one from his brother, J. B., of

Malone, Texas, informing him that a son, Lander, had enrolled at
Baylor University. In the same stack, from another brother, the Reverend Thomas B. Legett, was a request for a $50 loan, payable within
six months. Portions of each letter reveal K. K. Legett's continuing
concern for them:

Dear Tom: I here hand you not only $50 as you requested, but $100,
and instead of your paying it back in six months, you need never pay it
back.

It gives me great pleasure to help you at this time.

My Dear Brother [J. B.]:
. . . I am glad Lander started to Baylor . . . Don't let him fail for the
want of help. If it develops that he cannot make it let me know and I
will see him through. I know what a little help can do for a fellow, so
don't hesitate to call on me if you see he can't make it without help.

Similar letters through the years show Legett's continued interest
in his brothers' and sisters' families, none of whom seemed to have
his business sense nor his qualities of leadership. A letter written the
following year to his elderly and feeble parents reviews his efforts to
help them and shows his frustration as, in their senility, they continued to move from one location to another:

April 27, 1906
My Dear Father:
The condition of you and mother has and does worry me a great deal. . . .
Nothing that I have been able to do seems to meet the requirement.

I took you in my home. Then I furnished you a home, and that failed.
I sent you to Arcadia and built you a home there, and that did no good. I
then brought you here and bought and furnished you a home at Buffalo
Gap, and that did not serve the purpose. I then sent you to Port Lavaca,
and helped to build you a home with porches there. So I have fitted you
up in a home four times, and you have taken this last move without my
advice and against my judgment. I am quite sure you will not live with
Flemister, and what you will then do I cannot imagine.

It might be well for you now to secure a little place in the town of Keller and get some girl to stay with you. This, however, is a mere suggestion.
You should make some business arrangement at once with Flemister. I
will send $12.50 regularly each month on your expense account. . . . If

this is satisfactory write me immediately and I will begin to make remittances.

Now my dear Father, what I have said to you here is said in the greatest spirit of kindness. . . .

Write me at once about this arrangement.

Regards to all the family.[19]

Throughout his lifetime Legett corresponded reasonably often with his father's family, and there is no record that he ever refused assistance to any of them when they sought it.

Following the family tour, Legett settled quickly in his new home and made it a beehive of business, educational, and social activity. Whenever church conventions, college board meetings, or other gatherings brought out-of-town delegates to Abilene, the Legetts filled their extra bedrooms to capacity and crowded guests around their dining table. He reminded his children that they should take advantage of opportunities to meet people from the other corners of the world and to learn something from them. A letter addressed to J. Bascom Price, Weatherford, Texas, on June 23, 1906, is typical of those which brought a constant flow of visitors to the Legett mansion:

Dear Bascom—

. . . Mr. Pierce will consent for you to go into the grove and camp; and I will today see the management of the lake and get from them a fishing permit.

Your train is due to arrive here at 4:20 in the afternoon, and Mrs. Legett and I not only request, but demand that your party stay all night with us after arriving.[20]

Many years of crowded activity were in store for him, but, as Legett approached his fiftieth year, evidence abounds that he enjoyed equally well those quiet hours at home when he could retire to his study and select something to read from his growing library. Apparently during the family visit to Colorado Springs in 1905 he had met Andy Adams, author of the nationally popular *Log of a Cowboy*. An

[19] K. K. Legett to K. K. Legett, Sr., April 27, 1906, Legett Family Records, file 1, paper 47.

[20] K. K. Legett to J. B. Price, Weatherford, Texas, June 23, 1906, Legett Letter Book, p. 492.

exchange of letters and books in the spring of 1905 suggests that Adams sought Legett's evaluation of his new publications. Portions of two of Legett's letters reveal his views of the West's place in American literature as well as his philosophy and literary tastes:

April 7, 1906

My Dear Sir:

With much pleasure do I acknowledge my personal indebtedness to you for a copy of "Cattle Brands." . . .

Our United States Circuit and District Court meets here next week, and when it is over I am going to read your book, and when I have finished it, I will write to you. I had intended to do this even if you had not asked.

Yes, I belong to the vanguard of civilization that has made many upward leaps in the short span of a quarter-century. The observant pioneer in almost any country has thrilling and entertaining experiences and his memory should be aglow with rare and rich incidents. This, however, is not a land of legend and story, nor is it a land of poetry and song, and yet its history is not sterile and barren.[21]

May 5, 1906

My dear Mr. Adams:

I have read "Cattle Brands." Quite an interesting collection of stories. . . .

The public owes a large debt to the author of this book. In this advanced age . . . it is necessary that a halt should occasionally be made and an hour given to the cheerful and humorous.

It sometimes seems to me that Clemens and Bob Burdett should live as long in the life of a nation as Lincoln or Talmage.

From the standpoint of a West Texas lawyer . . . no collection of stories of pioneer life would be complete which omitted the rare and rich incidents connected with the part played by the judges and lawyers in the formative period of the country's history.

I don't know yet if I will visit the Springs this summer, but I hope you will sometime find it convenient to stop in Abilene.[22]

Legett might daydream about a gentlemanly life of leisure in which he could pursue his literary interests, but he was too pragmatic

[21] K. K. Legett to Mr. Andy Adams, Colorado Springs, Colo., April 7, 1906, Legett Family Records, file 1, paper 43.
[22] Ibid., paper 49.

and too realistic—too much a product of the Texas frontier—to follow such fantasy; therefore, when he received, a few days later, an invitation from the secretary of the Austin (Texas) Literary Society to speak before that group he cast aside his daydreams and replied, "my dear sir, I could never write a speech that would be of any interest to your society or a credit to myself."[23]

K. K. Legett recognized his limitations as surely as he recognized his strengths. In the literary field he would move only as close as his library, where he could sit by the fire and read Andy Adams, Owen Wister, and Emerson Hough; Lora could sit opposite, temporarily lost in the worlds of Honoré de Balzac, Sir Walter Scott, and William Cullen Bryant.

[23] K. K. Legett to Paul D. Casey, May 22, 1906, Legett Letter Book, p. 457.

*I am pleading for the learned to become more
practical and for the craftsmen to adopt more intelligent methods in the exercise of their energies.*


CHAPTER TEN

# The World of Theory and the
# World of Practice


K. K. LEGETT'S quarter-century of service to Simmons College as a
founder, trustee, and chairman of the board had inherent rewards.
The college attracted to Abilene a small cluster of genuine intellec-
tuals whose scholarly backgrounds he sometimes envied and whose
company he often sought, and as a Baptist institution, the college attracted to Abilene church leaders from every part of the state. Legett's
gregarious and affable nature led him to seek variety in his daily routine, and Simmons College provided part of that variety.

He accepted Governor S. W. T. Lanham's appointment to the
board of directors at the Agricultural and Mechanical College of
Texas for less personal reasons. The appointment obviously satisfied
a need for recognition, but Legett's eight-year dedication to the demanding tasks of director outlasted any personal satisfaction he may
have had. During these eight years—the last four as president of the
board—he served the state's oldest public institution of higher learning with loyalty, devotion, and responsibility. Texas A&M provided
a meeting ground where the fragments of his personal philosophy
could merge and become reality. "The best two worlds," he often
said, "are the world of theory and the world of practice." A lifetime
of diverse experiences accentuated a natural tendency to seek a practical solution to every problem. Such solutions, he insisted, resulted
from the deliberate consideration of "all theoretical possibilities."
That creed served him equally well before a venire of jurymen or at
the head of a conference table.

The recent emergence of industrial power and its challenge to
America's agrarian mores created problems that intrigued Legett. He

always had lived in sparsely settled agrarian areas. Through the years he had come to accept many of the traditions and customs of an agrarian society, but he had no patience with those who consistently resisted change and sought to return state or nation to agrarian controls. Legett branded them "Populists." In his view they were not reformers but "negative people" and poor candidates for roles of political or economic leadership. He remained a lifelong Democrat, but he gave only lukewarm support to such party leaders as William Jennings Bryan and James S. Hogg. Each man, Legett believed, would destroy the railroad industry by excessive regulation. Without the railroad, he argued, West Texas could not survive. In political theory Legett was a moderate committed to a diversified economy, whether personal or national in scope. He managed in every speech he made to reach into his repertoire of clichés and plead for a diversified economy: "One nation or one farmer should never place all the eggs in a single basket."

In 1905 he received an invitation to address the graduating class at Texas A&M. He was both surprised and flattered, and he accepted at once: "I doubt the wisdom of your committee, but I have decided to yield to its judgment. In accepting this invitation I am reminded [that] 'fools rush in where angels fear to tread.' "[1] The following day he wrote about business matters to his friend (and District Court colleague) Judge Edward R. Meek but characteristically succumbed to the temptation to add a final personal note: "I have accepted an invitation to deliver the commencement address at the A&M College and I am quite busy getting up an 'off hand unprepared speech.' "[2] The local editor also spread the word:

The *Reporter* is glad to announce that one of our citizens has been honored by an invitation to deliver the baccalaureate address at the commencement exercises of the A&M College, Judge Legett.

While honoring our town the institution has done itself honor in selecting a gentleman of such high standing in moral, social, legal, and intellectual matters, and has assured itself of an address which will be long remembered. While Congressman [Thomas H.] Ball and Senator [Joseph W.] Bailey have recently addressed the same institution, The *Reporter* does

[1] K. K. Legett to Professor H. H. Harrington, May 12, 1905, Legett Letter Book, p. 148.
[2] K. K. Legett to Judge Edward R. Meek, May 13, Legett Letter Book, p. 149.

The presidential electors for the state of Texas, 1884. K. K. Legett stands at the center of the second row. He was twenty-seven years old. *Courtesy, Julia Legett Pickard.*

K. K. and Lora Bryan Legett with children Julia, Kade, and Ruth, 1894. *Courtesy, Julia Legett Pickard.*

Kirvin Kade and Minty Berry Legett, parents of K. K. Legett, at their fiftieth wedding anniversary, 1892. *Courtesy, Julia Legett Pickard.*

Lora Bryan Legett, circa 1903. *Courtesy, Ruth Legett Jones.*

K. K. Legett, circa 1903. *Courtesy, Julia Legett Picard.*

K. K. Legett witnessed the construction of the first jailhouse at Buffalo Gap, where he began his law practice in 1879–1880. *Courtesy, Abilene Reporter-News.*

Taylor County's first courthouse, built in Abilene after Buffalo Gap lost the County Seat War in 1883. *Courtesy, Abilene Reporter-News.*

Abilene as it appeared about the time of K. K. Legett's marriage to Lora Bryan in 1886. *Courtesy, Abilene Reporter-News*.

Abilene in 1911, about the time Judge Legett ended his frequent railroad journeys to College Station (via Fort Worth) as chairman of the Board of Directors at Texas A&M. *Courtesy, Abilene Reporter-News*.

Abilene, circa 1900, looking south from the Texas and Pacific tracks. The old county courthouse looms in the background. *Courtesy, Abilene Reporter-News*.

Theodore Heyck's Shipping and Commission, about 1900. Abilene's original town lot auction was held on a platform near Heyck's warehouse in 1881. *Courtesy, Abilene Reporter-News.*

Abilene Volunteer Fire Department, circa 1892. *Courtesy, Abilene Reporter-News.*

West Texas sandstorm, circa 1900. Pioneers insisted that Abilene's weather was ideal, "since sandstorms, blizzards, and drouths don't count." *Courtesy, National Archives.*

Wind, hail, and rain damaged buildings on Pine Street in July, 1911. *Courtesy, Abilene Reporter-News.*

Early Abilenians had access to a complete line of saddlery and harnesses at Peter S. Kauffman's shop on Pine Street from 1892 to 1922. *Courtesy, Abilene Reporter-News.*

Abilene's City Livery Stable on North Cypress, circa 1906. Courtesy, Abilene Reporter-News.

The old Federal Building, erected in 1903 at Pine and North Third streets, Abilene. *Courtesy, Abilene Reporter-News.*

The H. B. Smith cotton gin in Abilene, 1912. Judge Legett's farm diversification plan encouraged West Texas farmers to avoid too much reliance on a single crop. *Courtesy, Abilene Reporter-News.*

Ringling Brothers visited fast-growing Abilene every year. Great crowds turned out to see the "million-dollar street parade, its hair-raising menagerie, its Roman hippodrome races, and its spectacular reproduction of Jerusalem." *Courtesy, Abilene Reporter-News.*

Shoppers from farms, ranches, and villages throughout West Texas joined Abilenians during holiday festivities. *Courtesy, Abilene Reporter-News.*

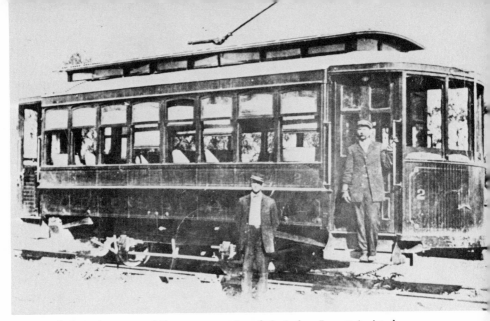

Convinced that the automobile was a passing fad, Judge Legett insisted that the street railway was an "infinitely superior mode of travel." *Courtesy, Abilene Reporter-News.*

In the 1920's automobile travel in Taylor County was not always easy. Despite his mistrust of the "machine," Judge Legett eventually supported a bond drive to pave Abilene's business area. His children later took driving lessons from young Eddie Rickenbacker. *Courtesy, Abilene Reporter-News.*

The original building on the Simmons College campus, constructed in 1891–1892. Judge Legett wrote the original draft of the school's charter. *Courtesy, Abilene Reporter-News.*

In 1923, McMurry College occupied this one building, Old Main. Judge Legett, a Baptist, Henry Sayles, Jr., a Presbyterian, and J. M. Cunningham, a Methodist, donated land for the Methodist school's campus. *Courtesy, Abilene Reporter-News.*

## ANONYMOUS CARTOON CIRCULATED
## IN EFFORT TO INJURE ABILENE'S
## CHANCE FOR NEW STATE COLLEGE

Abilene's success in building three church-related colleges—Simmons, Abilene Christian, and McMurry—proved a liability when other West Texans argued that locating a proposed Texas Technological College in Abilene would destroy the denominational schools. This cartoon appeared on the front page of the *Daily Reporter* in April, 1923. *Courtesy, Abilene Reporter-News.*

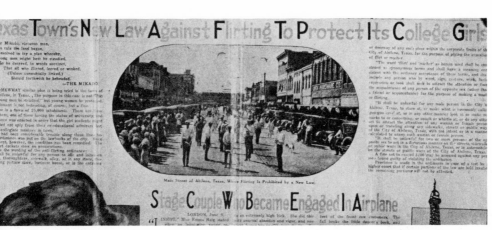

During the 1920's Abilene passed an antiflirting ordinance to protect the female students of the three colleges not only from their "coeducational admirers but from non-collegiate mashers in town." *Courtesy, Abilene Reporter-News.*

"Tent row" at A&M College, 1908. Judge Legett worked hard as a member of the college's board of directors to provide less primitive housing for A&M students. Construction on Legett Hall, a new dormitory, began in 1910. *Courtesy, Texas A&M University Archives.*

Texas A&M cadets on parade. Texas A&M's land-grant college goals combined in the best way Judge Legett's "world of theory and world of practice." *Courtesy, Texas A&M University Archives.*

The Legett Mansion, built in 1904–1905 at 602 Meander Street, Abilene. *Courtesy, Ruth Legett Jones.*

Judge Legett's younger daughter, Ruth (*center foreground*), was first editor of Abilene High School's yearbook. Here she sits with other student officers in 1910. *Courtesy, Abilene Reporter-News.*

Judge Legett mowed his own lawn until his death. This photograph was made in the early 1920's. *Courtesy, Ruth Legett Jones.*

The eight-column banner headline marked the enormity of Abilene's loss with the death of Judge Legett. *Courtesy, Abilene Reporter-News.*

HOME EDITION

# The Abilene Daily Reporter

5 CENTS PRICE

VII.     ( ASSOCIATED PRESS REPORT BY LEASED WIRE )     ABILENE, TEXAS, SUNDAY, JUNE 6, 1926—FORTY-FOUR PAGES     (For Abilene and vicinity Sunday generally fair and warmer)     NUMB

# JUDGE K. K. LEGETT DIES SUDDENLY HER

## est Texas Lumbermen Will Assemble In Convention Friday And Saturd

## ggings On City Farm At Houston Charged In Testimony Satur

**tending for Iowa's Senatorial Nomination**

**Sent Bomb**

### NAME COMMITTEES TO ARRANGE PLANS FOR MEETING HERE

With all committees appointed and other arrangements practically completed, a highly successful showing is being anticipated for the West Texas Retail Lumbermen's association, which convenes here June 18 and 11, according to detailed plans made by public history, by Thomas Bains, manager of the Burton-Lingo Lumber Company, and president of the association.

Judging from previous meetings of the organization, approximately are handled fifty delegates are expected for the convention, which will include two business meetings, a banquet and luncheon, and a number of other entertainments. Chief speakers named for the two days meet are Dr. J. W. Hunt, president of McMurry College; Dr. J. D. Sanders, president of Simmons University; J. A. Kirkpatrick of William Cameron & Company, Inc., Waco; and J. d. Payne, vice-president of the Frazier Brick Company, Dallas.

The first business session will be held in the afternoon of June 18, of which time Mr. Kirkpatrick is address the convention on "The Rights and Remedies of the Employmentman." On their will follow in address at a banquet to be held in the First Methodist Church the evening of June 18 and Dr. Sanders will speak Friday noon at a luncheon to the Abilene Chamber of Commerce. Dr. Payne's speech will be heard at the second business session Friday morning.

Other entertainment will be an occasional morning picture show of the Burtled Theatre Thursday evening and an automobile ride through the city Friday evening at eleven o'clock. In the perhaps it will be shown at the steps of the

### GUARD IS HELD IN $7,000 BAIL IN DEATH OF PRISONER

HOUSTON, Tex., June 6—(AP)—Stories of flogging were recited here Saturday by prisoners of the city Farm, testifying at the examining trial of W. J. Hill, 34, guard, charged with having beaten to death Wiley Ziegler, inmate. Hill was held in the grand jury under $7,000 bail by Justice of the Peace Campbell H. Overstreet.

Prisoners who said they had seen the whip used upon Ziegler as sworn expressed when he thought Ziegler was not working fast enough and knocked him down with the whip. They accused Hill of beating him as he lay on the ground, begging for mercy and asking that he be permitted to get up.

A few moments afterward, the prisoner's statements set forth, Ziegler fell unconscious and was taken to the end of the field where he was left nearly two hours in the boiling sun.

Hill, in his statement to Justice Overstreet, denied violence had been done the prisoner and said he flogged while in the field.

W. F. Buckalow, 24, of Houston, serving a five day sentence, was the principal witness for the prosecution.

"I saw it," he testified. "The officer just got the belt beat out of her by the guard when he told him to go on his row, which was going wrong.

"I was working a little ways ahead of Ziegler. He appeared to be in good health. First I heard was when Hill told him to go on his row and cursed him." Buckalow said. "Still then knocked him down with a buttonhole and kept on

**DIES SATURDAY**

Judge K. K. Legett, resident of this city for many years, who died suddenly here Saturday night.

### FEDERAL INQUIRY IN CHICAGO STATUS

PROBE, REFUSED BY CONGRESS, IS BEGUN DURING SATURDAY AT CHICAGO

CHICAGO, June 5—(AP)—A federal inquiry into Chicago's crime situation refused overtly ago by congress, was begun today. Though no one had so experts sitting from another source at liberty, made up the crime which was investigations.

### CEREBRAL HEMORRH BRINGS END TO PION LAWYER AND CAPITA

**6 CHILDREN DIE IN TUCSON FLAMES**

FAMILY OF FOUR IS ASPHYX-IATED AT EVERETT, WASH., SATURDAY

TUCSON, Ariz., June 5—(AP)—Six children, trapped by flames, perished here late last night when the home of Chefalain Villa burned to the ground while a frenzied crowd stood powerless to aid. The mother, her oldest daughter and a baby escaped.

The fire is believed to have started by a spark from a stove.

The crackling of the flames awakened the mother, who screamed frantically to save her family and who was forced to leave the missing structure only after she had been badly burned.

EVERETT, Wash., June 5—(AP)—A family of four, McCreaon Thayer, 48 years old, his wife, Mrs. Nortine Thayer, 47, a son, James, 21, and a daughter, Corinda, 12, were found dead on the second floor of their home here today. Death was caused by asphyxiation.

Gas was discovered to be flowing from a main supply line in the living floor which was opened

While he laughed with his children, relatives gathered at his home Saturday night for a day dinner for three of his lawyer, former president of national lawyer, a friend of higher education.

Death came suddenly at 7:40 o'clock, before, as he was seated he had made a hard move to the general national telegraph communications of his chin dropped and he down most each dead.

Dr. L. J. Pickard, was hardly three with his children was gathered at the home near a new Judge Legett's chair. He spoke is already had ended without making a Judge Legett, serious health, the family stated, throughout the business of the somewhat better in that usual. Death came last few minutes stilled.

Judge Legett was with his children's at the time of his born November 4 graduated. Drew and Texas coming to Texas, and coming to the 50s where he one of Drew in the county and in 4

Funeral services arranged deelander-

**OFFERS ESTRANGED WIFE $125 MONTH**

NOTED ARCHITECT SEEKS TO SETTLE DIFFICULTY —WIFE REFUSES

SPRING GREEN, Wis., June 4

not fear a comparison between what has gone before and the forthcoming speech.[3]

Legett had served for two years as a director of the college when he received the invitation. He thoroughly approved of the institution's goals. Long before his appointment to the board, he looked upon all agricultural and mechanical colleges as proof that worthwhile, practical innovations could result from the industrial revolution. Similarly, the carloads of West Texas cattle headed for eastern cities via the Texas and Pacific rails were proof that industry and agriculture could complement each other. He praised the Morrill Bill of 1862 and the land grant colleges that resulted, and he agreed with the effort to train industrial and agrarian laborers in the newest production techniques.

Almost a decade had passed before Texas, recovering from the Civil War, was able to take advantage of the Morrill Bill and request endowment land of approximately 180,000 federal acres. Another year passed before a legislative committee in 1872 designated a tract of Brazos County land as the future site for the 2,416-acre campus that now constitutes Texas A&M University. The Constitution of 1876 recognized all previous plans and made the agricultural and mechanical college an official branch of the future University of Texas system. On October 4, 1876, the college formally opened its doors to one hundred and six students. The small cluster of new buildings—a combination dormitory-classroom building, a mess hall, and five faculty residences—constituted the first state-supported school of higher education in Texas.[4]

The first board of directors of Texas A&M invited former Confederate president Jefferson Davis to become president of the college,

[3] *Abilene Daily Reporter*, May 11, 1905.

[4] The University of Texas at Austin did not begin its first term until 1883. For the early history of the Agricultural and Mechanical College of Texas see George Sessions Perry, *The Story of Texas A and M*; Clarence Ousley, "History of the Agricultural and Mechanical College of Texas," *Bulletin of the Agricultural and Mechanical College of Texas*, 4th ser. 6, no. 8, (December 1, 1935); Austin E. Burges, *A Local History of A&M College, 1876–1915*; David Brooks Cofer, *Early History of Texas A and M College through Letters and Papers*; David Brooks Cofer, *First Five Administrators of Texas A and M College, 1876–1890*; Henry C. Dethloff, *A Centennial History of Texas A&M University, 1876–1976*.

but Davis declined. He recommended instead Thomas Sanford Gathright, the state superintendent of schools in Mississippi, who eventually received the appointment. Gathright had neither the physical equipment nor the philosophical inclination to administer the study of agriculture and engineering. With his five colleagues he proceeded to teach the classics and belles-lettres. Students shared several large dormitory rooms on the upper floors of Main Building. They cut their own wood and carried their own buckets of water. Regulations required that they should complete such chores before nightfall. Darkness transformed the campus—variously described as "a wild waste" or "a black piece of prairie land"—into a serenade stand for howling wolves. The primitive conditions created discipline problems, and, although military training was a planned part of the curriculum, the understaffed faculty had no more interest or talent in that discipline than they had in agriculture or engineering. Many wayward sons enrolled at the school precisely because their parents heard about the school's advertised military training. When the unruly youths found no such training, they quickly demonstrated a variety of reasons why their parents had banished them from home.[5] Inevitably Gathright and his colleagues departed, but in 1879 John Garland James, a new president, organized a new faculty, who in turn developed a new program of instruction.

Discipline had improved when Legett attended his first board meeting on February 11, 1903. Enrollment had climbed to three hundred and seventy-eight students, and the college had awarded approximately four hundred baccalaureate degrees. Improvements to the original school plant included several dormitories, workshops, and classroom buildings and such modern conveniences as electric lights, sewers, and telephones. President David F. Houston still complained to the board about discipline problems just months before Legett's first meeting: "The college has been hampered by the presence of a large number of immature untrained boys. In many instances these boys were sent here by parents who did not know what else to do with them."[6]

[5] Cofer, *Early History*, p. 10.

[6] *Biennial Report of the Board of Directors of the Agricultural and Mechanical College of Texas, 1900–1901 and 1901–1902*, p. 6 (hereafter referred to as *Biennial Report*).

Legett was ill-equipped to comprehend serious discipline problems created by college-level students. His veneration for higher education in any form and his deferential regard for those who had been exposed to formal training blinded him to the possibility that such fortunate young men could stoop to acts of vandalism, insubordination, or disorderliness. When Houston continued to mention "immature untrained boys," Legett apparently listened with scant attention. His own spirited son, Kade, was mischievous, teased his sisters unmercifully, and was accident-prone from infancy, but he never required rigid discipline. Legett had come to know the young men at Simmons College as they worked their way through school and trained for the ministry, teaching, or other professions, and he looked upon them as upright, law-abiding citizens.

He found other peripheral features of his board duties more annoying. Travel between Bryan and Abilene was so inconvenient that a two-day meeting required a four-day absence from his Abilene office. The board met in other cities as often as it met on the A&M campus, and, with the single exception of a meeting in Abilene in 1909, all meetings required considerable travel. The first board meeting he attended, for example, convened in Austin at the Driskill Hotel. The Driskill, a delightful place to meet, was in many respects the very heart of Texas political and social affairs, but it, too, was difficult to reach from Abilene.[7]

Legett attended his second board meeting at the Prairie View Normal School, a branch of Texas A&M and the only college for blacks in Texas. Thus Legett did not visit the campus of the Bryan school until the third board meeting on June 8–9, 1903. To travel there, he left Abilene on an early morning eastbound train, changed at Fort Worth that evening to the Houston and Texas Central rails, and arrived in Bryan around three o'clock in the morning. The college provided room and meals for the board members, but Legett frequently slept on a cot in the conference room where the board held its meetings.

He discovered that most A&M board meetings lasted all day and into the night. At a called meeting in July, 1904, for example, the board adjourned at 11:30 P.M., reconvened at 8:00 A.M., recessed at

[7] See Joe B. Frantz, *The Driskill Hotel*, for the best picture of activities there.

5:30 P.M., returned at 8:00 P.M., and adjourned at an unspecified hour that evening. Legett explained on one occasion that the problems before the board ranged from "the overwhelming to the ridiculous." Routine issues such as faculty and staff salaries (each considered on an individual basis) and competitive bidding for wood, fuel, fresh meat, and mules (also considered individually) consumed endless hours and frequently frustrated him. More challenging problems to Legett included the establishment of a textile school, a state farmers' institute, and a system of agricultural experiment stations. On major issues the board sometimes requested personal assistance from members of the faculty, members of both houses of the legislature, and the governor. Whenever Mrs. Legett protested the long train rides to Bryan, her husband replied that those hours usually provided his only opportunities to sit down and catch up on his thinking. At Bryan he could concentrate exclusively upon A&M problems without inconvenient interruptions. At Simmons College, on the other hand, the briefest board meeting might be interrupted by callers who needed to confer on matters at the office, at the ranch, at one of the farms, at the church, at the courthouse, at city hall, or at home.

Mrs. Legett or Kade sometimes accompanied him to Bryan, but he never invited either of his daughters to the all-male campus. He refused to break that rule even as he made plans to deliver the school's commencement address on July 13, 1905. Legett averaged two or three public-speaking engagements each month, but he sometimes spoke more frequently than that in one week. Although he prepared each speech in advance, he liked them to appear extemporaneous. His papers indicate that he prepared more thoroughly for his 1905 address to the Texas A&M graduates than for any other audience during his lifetime. His frequent references to the forthcoming speech, scraps of research materials, and numerous revisions of the final draft testify to the great amount of time and thought he spent on the project. The copy from which he delivered the address contains numerous Legett revisions in blue ink, in black ink, and in pencil. Mrs. Legett's clear, obviously feminine script appears in the margins and between the double-spaced lines. This is the only manuscript of a Legett address that contains evidence that Legett sought his wife's assistance in preparing his speeches. She made eighteen changes of words or phrases and a half-dozen spelling and grammar corrections.

A few scribbles along the margins suggest Legett's deep concentration as he strove to polish and to clarify every statement.

On June 7 he still wrestled with the manuscript and on that date informed Charles S. Potts, a member of the faculty and sponsor of the campus newspaper, that "it will be impossible for me to finally shape up the forthcoming speech in complete manuscript form before Sunday. If nothing interferes . . . I will mail you a copy."[8]

No "off-hand remarks" appeared on the final copy. It was indeed the most formal and perhaps the most self-revealing speech he made during his public career. As he stood before the graduating seniors, their parents and other relatives, their friends, and spectators, his baccalaureate emphasized the following points:

It is my aim today to impress upon you the importance—the necessity—of bringing into closer relations the "Theoretical and the Practical."

If I can but give you the impression that . . . theory and practice must go hand in hand, then I will be satisfied. . . .

The weakness of this age is found in the fact that this combination does not often exist in the same person. . . .

The relations of capital to labor, the question of transportation, . . . and the matter of social and domestic disorder are the principal conditions demanding attention in this society.

Every opportunity is afforded you for making the highest order of men, and my candid conviction is that the world has a right to expect more of the graduates of the Agricultural and Mechanical College of Texas than of any other class on earth. . . .

The government under which you live has done its duty by furnishing adequate facilities for the development of mind and muscle. On this institution alone the state and federal governments have expended millions for the cause of mental culture and manual labor. Your gratitude should find expression in an unfaltering determination to lift humanity to heights hitherto unknown.

At no other school of learning is the system of instruction so well calculated to turn out theoretical, practical men.

*I am pleading for the learned to become more practical and for the craftsmen to adopt more intelligent methods in the exercise of their energies.* If we do not, a later generation will gather a fruit we did not intend to plant. . . .

[8] K. K. Legett to Charles S. Potts, June 7, 1905, Legett Letter Book, p. 163.

Society demands that you put on the whole armor of representative citizenship. . . .

God demands that you build up a civilization that will be crowned with the honors of coming centuries.

Make yourself what God intended you should be.[9]

The *Abilene Reporter* informed its readers two days later that newspapers throughout the state quoted large segments of Legett's address and praised its instructive and learned quality. Such public response undoubtedly pleased the self-educated Abilene lawyer, but by the time he reached Abilene he was back in the "world of the practical" and he carefully enumerated his expenses for the four-day trip to the college:

R.R. fare going and returning .......................... $16.80
Sleeper fare going and returning ........................  4.00
Hack fare .............................................  1.00
Other bills ...........................................  2.00
                                                       $23.80[10]

Later during that summer of 1905, while the Legetts toured the Pacific Northwest, David Houston submitted his resignation as president of A&M and accepted an invitation to serve as president of the University of Texas.[11] Legett could not attend the emergency meeting of the board called for August 24 at Fort Worth, but he returned with his family in time to attend the meeting on September 8 at the Oriental Hotel in Dallas.

The minutes of that session reveal none of the complexities usually associated with sudden administrative resignations and their replacements. Indeed, no board meeting proceeded more routinely. Board president Marion Sansom called the meeting to order at 10:00 A.M., introduced such agenda items as the need to employ a new corps commander, the purchase of six pairs of harnesses, and the purchase of a

[9] A copy of the original speech is in Legett Family Records, file 2, paper 8.
[10] K. K. Legett to Col. J. C. Harrison, June 16, 1905, Legett Letter Book, p. 170.
[11] Houston was later president of Washington University in St. Louis, and from that institution he joined President Woodrow Wilson's cabinet as secretary of agriculture. Still later he was Wilson's secretary of the treasury.

storage battery for the cow barn. At 12:15 P.M. the meeting adjourned until 2:00 P.M.

At 2:30 P.M. Sansom called the meeting to order for the afternoon session. At that point the minutes state: "On motion, the vote for Professor [H. H.] Harrington as President of the College was made unanimous."[12] A later motion created a three-man committee headed by Legett to notify Professor Harrington of his appointment. The minutes contain no other mention of that major action and, for whatever reason, failed to explain it. The motion for a unanimous vote suggests that the original vote on the matter was not unanimous. The failure to explain an apparent split vote or to mention other candidates for the position suggests also a sensitive issue deliberately omitted. On the other hand, the total lack of public criticism when Sansom announced the board's choice suggests no general disapproval.

President Harrington's first biennial report to the board of directors reveals his familiarity with the history of the college, its purpose, and its internal and external development. His long tenure as professor of chemistry at Texas A&M enabled him to move immediately to the school's pressing problems. Significantly, Harrington's report failed to mention the former president's most worrisome issue, discipline. He centered instead upon public criticism of the geographic location of the college, its untypical Texas soil, and A&M's remoteness from any large city.

Although Harrington raised the issue, he abruptly dismissed it with a brief reminder to the board that the public is prone to criticize its public servants and its public institutions and that they should answer criticism—even when it was destructive—with patience and dignity. The written report appears to reflect a condescending attitude toward the public and toward the board; nevertheless, Harrington's manner apparently belied his words, for the board remained steadfastly loyal to him throughout his tumultuous administration.

Strong but inconclusive evidence implies that Harrington owed his appointment to K. K. Legett's forceful influence. The new president's brother, Dr. J. T. Harrington, was a pioneer Abilene physician who had worked with Legett on the Simmons College board and on many civic projects. Through the years, Legett had come to know and

---

[12] *Minutes of the Board of Directors*, vol. 1 (May 31, 1886 to September 8, 1905), p. 302.

to admire the physician's brother, who was already a professor of chemistry at the A&M campus. Presumably, Legett's personal interest in the school was an outgrowth of that friendship. As early as 1898, following the death of President Lawrence Sullivan Ross, the *Abilene Reporter* strongly urged Professor Harrington's appointment to the presidency:

The board should . . . place an educator and not a politician at the head of that educational institution. Lately his friends have proposed the name of Prof. H. H. Harrington, of the faculty, as the candidate for the presidency. This, to us, seems a wise move, as we think Prof. Harrington peculiarly fitted by education and experience for the position.

Professor Harrington is a Democrat, true, but we had rather see a Republican educator than a Democratic politician at the head of our A.&M. College. Let the board remember that we want no mixture of politics with our educational affairs.[13]

The board on July 1, 1898, exercised its discretion and appointed L. L. Foster as president. After Foster's death on December 2, 1901, David F. Houston succeeded him. Houston's sudden resignation in late August, 1905, and Harrington's equally sudden appointment to replace him suggest that the board knew about and resolved both problems before Legett's departure on the family tour. After the public announcement, Legett wrote to his old friend: "I beg you to accept my congratulations on the victory you scored at Dallas; however, your gain in my opinion is nothing as compared to the gain of the whole State of Texas in your selection."[14] All who knew Harrington seemed to agree.[15] Harrington completed the preparation begun by Houston of new four-year programs in agriculture and in civil, electrical, textile, architectural, and chemical engineering, and enrollment figures steadily advanced.

On the surface at least the campus seemed progressive and tranquil. A student enrolled at that time later described the social scene:

The community was small and everybody knew everyone else sufficiently well for all to mingle freely together. There was frequent social intercourse with citizens of Bryan, . . . especially in lodge and church activities. Some

---

[13] *Abilene Reporter*, April 1, 1898.

[14] K. K. Legett to H. H. Harrington, September 16, 1905, Legett Letter Book, p. 205.

[15] See Ousley, "History," p. 65.

good friends of the college community had plantations in the Brazos bottom less than a dozen miles distant and quite frequently the entire campus community would be invited to a barbeque picnic and open house. . . . The cadet corps gave their formal dances and many young lady friends of the cadets coming to the college for the dance were entertained in the homes of the faculty members. Notwithstanding the many inconveniences, life on the campus was quite enjoyable.[16]

On January 29, 1907, Governor Thomas M. Campbell reappointed Legett to the board for a third two-year term. On March 4, at a reorganizational meeting in Austin, the other directors elected him president of the board. Legett as presiding officer conducted no business at that meeting, but he asked his colleagues to convene on June 7 at the Prairie View campus. He encouraged them to attend the school's commencement exercises, and he expressed the hope that the new members of the board would use this opportunity to familiarize themselves with the physical plant and internal operations at Prairie View.[17] Legett seemed particularly interested in the black institution at Prairie View, and, at succeeding meetings during his first year as president of the board, the body appropriated funds for the school's first sewer system and for an additional dormitory.

In rapid succession the board added to the Bryan campus a new English building, created the office of Dean of the College, increased the student labor budget from $5,000 to $6,000 per year, appointed Thomas Jefferson Wertenbaker assistant professor of history and economics, established a new system of bookkeeping, installed a new sewer system, and adopted a new set of quarantine regulations for all campus residents. No action taken by the board at that time seemed controversial or aroused suspicion, and yet the new quarantine regulations ultimately led to an extremely bitter and prolonged confrontation between President Harrington and the entire student body. At the height of the issue Legett played a central role, and at its conclusion he believed he had saved the school from mindless destruction. The traumatic affair attracted the attention and concern of thousands of people throughout the state.

There is no evidence that President Harrington explained to the

[16] Cofer, *Early History*, p. 84.
[17] *Board Minutes of the A&M College*, vol. 2 (June 12, 1906 to December 15, 1911), p. 21.

board his request for a new set of quarantine regulations, and the directors approved the motion without discussion. The circumstances that led to Harrington's action were in the beginning personal, but, at the time Harrington presented the motion, new circumstances had developed that involved administrative authority. Whether Harrington deliberately withheld information concerning an earlier dispute with Dr. Joe Gilbert, the college physician, is not known, but such knowledge might certainly have alerted Legett and his colleagues to the potential danger inherent in the new quarantine regulations.

The series of events began early in 1907 when history professor C. W. Hutson's married son brought his wife and small child to the professor's home, a faculty cottage, for a visit. During their stay the child developed a case of whooping cough. Upon hearing of the child's illness, Mrs. Harrington became hysterical and insisted that her husband must quarantine the entire family. The Harringtons had lost several children during their infancy, and Mrs. Harrington apparently had developed a morbid fear of all childhood diseases. The beleaguered husband and father promptly quarantined the Hutson household. At that point, Gilbert, the college physician, protested that the quarantine was both unnecessary and unauthorized. Harrington's motion before the board, therefore, was meant to clarify such authority. The new regulation, written in haste, also was ambiguous. The dispute, unknown to the board, quickly spread through the campus, and to Harrington's dismay the students strongly supported Gilbert. Harrington learned that the entire Hutson family were among the students' favorites. As student resentment deepened, other submerged antagonisms surfaced and revealed for the first time that Harrington's aloofness had generated little warmth or support for his leadership. Old rumors that Harrington planned numerous faculty dismissals were revived.

Details of the dispute eventually spread to Austin and to the governor's office. Governor Campbell notified Legett, who was several hundred miles away from the problem. By the time the chairman of the board learned of the dispute, the strained relationship between Harrington and his students was virtually beyond repair.

Judge Legett contacted Colonel Robert T. Milner, whose position as commissioner of agriculture made him ex-officio member of the board. The two directors decided to go at once to the campus where they could conduct a first-hand investigation. The bitterness they encountered shocked Legett, and he wired immediately for the other directors to join him on the campus. As he waited their arrival, he received a student petition demanding Harrington's removal from office. The petition contained no formal charges, nor did it offer reasons for the demand. In Legett's opinion the written ultimatum was both disrespectful and arrogant. The young men's assumption that Legett was an adversary dismayed him.

When all directors reached the campus, Legett described the situation and presented the written ultimatum. Together the board conducted an investigation—"carefully, impartially, and fully"—and finally concluded that the rumors and gossip were without foundation. The board thereupon passed a resolution that expressed their "unqualified faith in the integrity, ability, and absolute fairness of President H. H. Harrington" and concluded with a second resolution that established a procedure for any future handling of student complaints. Such complaints must be submitted "in writing with a statement of facts to the President of the Board." Legett, convinced that "the breach of harmony had been bridged and that the work of the Institution would continue,"[18] then dismissed the board.

To Legett's astonishment, rumors spread among the students that the board had ignored their petition and that Legett had "unceremoniously dropped [the petition] in the waste basket."[19] The following day most students refused to attend classes. Some of them, alert to any excuse to return home, packed their belongings and departed. One chastened young man soon returned and reported to his friends that his father had met him at the Brazos River, pointed a shotgun at him, and ordered him to return to school.[20]

The faculty voted to support the board's position and to notify all students that they must return to class at once or risk dismissal. Representatives of the senior class then requested a hearing before the board. Legett responded, "We have always been willing to receive and carefully consider any specific grievance that may be properly presented," and he called upon the young men to "resume their proper relation as students."[21] The next day they returned to their

[18] Ibid., pp. 67, 68.
[19] Ousley, "History," p. 67.
[20] Perry, *Story of Texas A and M*, pp. 78–79.
[21] *Board Minutes of the A&M College*, 2:70.

classes. Later they presented to the board their specific charges of misconduct against President Harrington:

1. Nathan Powell had been dismissed from the faculty in an irregular manner.

2. The C. W. Hutson household had been quarantined by President Harrington without authority from the board of directors.

3. President Harrington had not paid his laundry bill at the college laundry service.

4. President Harrington had tossed in the wastebasket a request by several seniors to attend a circus at Hearne so that they might "study the different types of draft animals."

5. President Harrington had dismissed Curtis Carson without first consulting farm superintendent W. W. Evans.

6. President Harrington dealt with the corps of cadets arbitrarily, which resulted in a lack of harmony between the corps and the president.

Witnesses stepped before the board to verify each charge, and the board later described their conference with the seniors as "a complete, careful, and patient hearing." One student wrote, however, that it was merely a superficial examination of the complaints.[22] Again Legett announced for the board that the students had failed to submit evidence that showed the president's arbitrary action; on the contrary, the board believed that Harrington showed commendable solicitude for the students' interests and welfare and that he acted wisely in matters of discipline. Legett emphasized that every member of the board concurred.

Within a few days every parent or guardian received the following telegram from the president of the board:

College Station, Texas. February 14, 1908.
Work will be resumed at the college Monday morning. Students will be reinstated on application and promise to conform to college regulations. We invite your cooperation and continued patronage.

(signed) K. K. Legett, President of the
Board of Directors of the A.
and M. College[23]

[22] Clifford B. Casey, *A Baker's Dozen*, p. 94.
[23] *Board Minutes of the A&M College*, 2:75.

On February 22 the Houston Alumni and Ex-Students Association of A&M College adopted a resolution in which they petitioned
the board to reopen the investigation. The board's reply, over Legett's
signature followed by the names of all other board members, stated
that the board had investigated the situation to satisfy itself, that it
had repeated the investigation to satisfy the students, that it, collectively, had devoted thirty days to the problem, that it had invited,
"almost to the extent of pleading," everyone with a complaint to come
forward, and that, on each occasion, it had reported its conclusions to
the public. Therefore, if the Houston alumni still considered the investigation incomplete, the board—which included three practicing
lawyers—was incapable of completing it. Legett in typical style concluded:

Surely it cannot be necessary for us to assure the people of Texas that
we would not see an injustice done to any young man, or that we would
be a party to an investigation that we did not believe was fair and honorable. . . . Under all the circumstances we cannot persuade ourselves that
injustice has been done to anyone. . . .

Neither are we able to understand what beneficial results you gentlemen
expect will follow from the kind of investigation indicated. . . .

In this controversy, as we view it, men have largely ceased to be an issue.
The question involves a principle . . . that lies at the base of a well regu-
lated civilization. To yield the principle contended for by the Board—the
supremacy of law and order—would be the equivalent to an endorsement
of a principle which destroys organized society and undermines governments. We will not do it. We cannot do it. If the corps of cadets can force
the retirement of a President over the judgment of the Board of Directors,
they could with equal propriety force the selection of his successor.

You gentlemen have been the beneficiaries of the State's bounty at this
Institution, and above all classes of citizens, as it appears to us, should
stand to a man in upholding the Board in its efforts to grapple with a trying situation.[24]

For a few weeks, Legett's sharp response to the Houston alumni
seemed to settle the issue, and conditions on campus returned to a
normal routine. When the weary president of the board returned to

[24] Ibid., p. 80.

Abilene, his home town seemed to support his position. On March 6 the following editorial appeared in the *Weekly Reporter*:

"NOTHING IS SETTLED TILL SETTLED OUR WAY"

The *Dallas News* is just now engaged in telling the democrats what democracy is. . . . A few days ago it stated that it is a principle of democracy that "no question is settled until it is settled right." That means that no question is settled until it is settled to the satisfaction of the *News*.

This doctrine seems to have been adopted by the rebellious students of the Texas A. & M. College, who are learning from the *News* . . . "Nothing is settled until it is settled our way. . . ."

Under this doctrine, when the state prosecutes a citizen for a crime, it is her duty to keep it up, no matter how many juries acquit him until he is convicted. It is a monstrous doctrine. . . .

A vital principle is at stake in the A. & M. College matter, and the law abiding people must stand by the directors in enforcing it.

In April, campus rumors accelerated. Students passed the word that President Harrington had told an Austin newsman that the recent unpleasantness at the college was forgotten. The next issue of the student newspaper, the *Battalion*, printed a stinging rebuttal:

We are not a set of headstrong fanatics, as some people would insist. . . . If we are wrong let some personage give us some consistent proof of our mistake. . . . Then we will hasten to make amends. . . .

Otherwise the fire that smoulders in every bosom in the course of time will gather fuel and burst forth in such a conflagration that nothing short of a deluge can quench it.

Let no man deceive himself.[25]

President Harrington and every member of the board received a copy of the newspaper, but each chose not to comment. Unfortunately Governor Campbell called public attention to the *Battalion* article with the curious observation that it was "unwise . . . since it will only widen the breach already existing between the students and the president."[26] Inevitably the governor's comment generated the result he claimed to fear. At the May 20 meeting at Waco, the board directed

[25] Casey, *Baker's Dozen*, p. 94.
[26] Ibid.

President Harrington to determine "the responsible parties . . . and adequately punish" them. Harrington promptly returned to the campus and suspended seven members of the *Battalion* staff.

Again the "Trouble of 1908" spread like a prairie fire, and alumni groups around the state bombarded the board to reopen the case. Reluctantly, the directors agreed to hear more testimony beginning on June 10 and continuing "for such lengths of time as may be necessary to develop the facts." The third investigation lasted eleven days, and at its conclusion Legett announced that the board still found Harrington innocent of all charges. The alumni representative, Dallas attorney Hatton W. Summers, had presented no new complaint. The board regretted the widened breach between the president and the corps, assumed its share of responsibility for originally failing to apply a more drastic remedy, admitted that Harrington no longer held the esteem of the students, but insisted that the president had not demeaned himself so as to forfeit their confidence and respect. Even so, the directors explained,

If the fact be conceded that personal unpopularity with the student body is sufficient within and of itself to justify the removal of a College President, then we could not for a minute accede to it. . . .

We would close the school before we would set the precedent of permitting a student body to rise in open rebellion and in open and bold defiance of constituted authority. . . . This board will never establish such a precedent.

Legett's hometown editor continued his support for the board's action and called on all Texans to accept the final decision without comment. At Bryan approximately seventy-five local businessmen met at the opera house and called upon all citizens to accept the decision. They praised the board's diligent efforts and added:

They have given not only two or three weeks to the investigation, but have had it on their minds and consciences for five long months. Not a man on the board had entered into the investigation with any other motive in view but . . . the good of the institution and the good of Texas.

. . . We pledge to the board of directors, to the faculty, and to the president, Dr. H. H. Harrington, our hearty cooperation.[27]

---

[27] In *Abilene Daily Reporter*, June 27, 1908.

In spite of similar resolutions around the state, President Harrington met with the board at its August 7 meeting in Corpus Christi and
tendered his resignation: "I realize," he explained, "that my continuation as President of your college may serve in some degree as an embarrassment to you."[28] The board accepted his resignation but assured
Harrington that "Texas is losing one of its most accomplished and
painstaking educators."

His replacement was neither an educator nor a political figure.
Colonel R. T. Milner was in fact a member of the board (by reason
of his official position as commissioner of agriculture). A long tenure
as a newspaper publisher had schooled him in the state's agricultural
and industrial problems, and his friendly, affable disposition made
him a favorite among faculty and students while he served on the
board. Harrington's immediate appointment as director of the Experiment Stations caused a ripple of adverse comment, but Milner's
popular appointment diverted much of the campus attention from the
beleaguered educator. Legett publicly praised both appointments at a
news conference in Austin on August 16 and declared that "the
troubles that have vexed the college during the past few months are
now happily passed."

Nevertheless, Legett did not soon forget the Trouble of 1908. He
never fully understood the students' bitter attack upon his quiet, dig-
nified, and distinguished friend. It was incomprehensible that a group
of young men with so many opportunities and so much talent could
temporarily degenerate into such disrespectful rowdies. He believed
that he had dealt with them honestly and on an adult level: the board
ordered partial refunds for room and board for those students who
left the campus before the end of the term; it ordered free room and
board for those who returned to testify during the investigations; and
it financed all travel expenses for all who participated in the investigation.

The ordeal disillusioned and sometimes even shocked Legett, but
it had no lasting effect upon his interest in higher education or his
concern for the young men at Texas A&M. His biennial reports to the
governor prove beyond question his loyalty to the students, and his
vigorous pleas for improved living quarters on campus stand as clas-

[28] *Board Minutes of the A&M College,* 2:99.

sics in the art of expressing righteous indignation. Ever since Legett's tenure as board president, students have turned to his biennial reports to read his unique appeals for more state aid. The following plea, for example, reached the governor just a few months after the Trouble of 1908:

> This is the only institution in the civilized world where a number of its students are forced to live in tents during the entire school year. Our remote ancestors lived in caves and subsisted on the spontaneous products of the earth, and were not at all aesthetic in their tastes concerning dress, but all proprieties of modern civilization demand that our educational institutions, at least, shall not encourage such primitive methods of living.[29]

Legett added a novel dimension to the traditional profusion of colorless, uninspired, bureaucratic reports delivered every year to the governor's desk. He made his reports position papers. He emphasized the need for more housing by ridiculing "tent row"; he emphasized the need for a new mechanical engineering laboratory by describing the "crumbling walls and broken bricks which can be removed by hand"; he emphasized the need for a central heating plant by describing the inconvenience and danger inherent in wood stoves; he emphasized the need for more student aid funds by expounding upon the belief that young men willing to do anything for an education make the best students; he emphasized the need for more library funds by attacking the two preceding legislatures for their failure to "make any appropriations whatever" for that purpose; and he emphasized the needs in the entomology department by explaining to a presumably weary governor that "the green bug destroys five times as much grain in one of its invasions as it would take to equip and run this Department for the next twenty-five years."[30] Unsure that Governor Campbell appreciated the real value of Texas A&M, Legett lifted many passages from his 1905 commencement address to inform the governor that the school's greatest mission was to combine the practical and the theoretical.

Through the years, Legett's biennial reports have not lost their sense of urgency, for Legett never exhausted his store of impressive

[29] *Biennial Report, 1907–1908*, pp. 4–5.
[30] Ibid., p. 9.

statistics. In November, 1910, he informed the governor that the number of students still living in tents exceeded the school's total enrollment in March, 1908. Later he sought to impress the governor by informing him that the Texas A&M cadet corps outnumbered the corps at the United States Military Academy at West Point.

If his extra effort gained additional appropriations for the needs of the two colleges, Legett could ill afford the enormous amount of time he devoted to such matters. During his eight years on the board, he averaged six meetings each year, and each meeting required a minimum four-day break in his Abilene activities. At a conservative estimate, he spent one hundred and ninety-two days on meetings. In addition, records indicate that hardly a weekday passed without some minutes or hours given to A&M affairs. Virtually every mail delivery brought letters from job seekers: professors, administrators, college physicians, plumbers, chefs, wholesale suppliers, or building contractors. His frequent complaint that "the demands on my time are simply terrific" rarely referred to educational problems, but he finally had to admit that he was rapidly exhausting his energies. He would have rejected a fourth appointment to the board in late 1908, but he feared it would be misinterpreted as a surrender to the recent critics of the school. He attempted to resign from the Simmons College board in 1910 but allowed local church leaders to dissuade him. He promised Mrs. Legett to reduce his civic responsibilities but agreed within a few weeks to serve on three separate Abilene committees that sought to gain a new high school, a new state normal school, and a new Baptist sanitarium. He insisted that he had no time to campaign for gubernatorial candidates in the 1910 elections, but he then agreed to join the bandwagon when an old Cleburne friend, Judge William A. Poindexter, announced his candidacy. He promised to preside at the opening exercises at Simmons College in September, 1910, but cancelled that commitment following an emergency call from A&M, where heavy enrollment required another enlargement of "tent row."

Enroute to the emergency meeting at Bryan, Legett decided that he would not accept another appointment to the board and, at the close of the meeting, so notified President Milner. He could step down in good conscience, bolstered by the certain knowledge that he had contributed significantly to the growth of the school in size and stature and that, according to James Wilson, secretary of agriculture, "the A. & M. College of Texas was more nearly fulfilling its mission than any similar institution in the nation."[31] Prairie View State Normal in physical equipment alone had added several dormitories, an administration building, a classroom building, and a sewer system.

At College Station similar classroom buildings, workshops, and dormitories enlarged the physical plant, but under Legett the schools' internal growth was even more impressive. He had presided over the board as it developed a systematic program for faculty promotions and salaries, approved the first correspondence courses, added the departments of education and economics, endowed the first chair of highway engineering, revived the summer-school program, negotiated the first contract for rail transportation from Bryan, instituted a more accurate bookkeeping system, expanded the student-aid program, added a chaplain and an athletic director, and banned smoking on campus. In eight years he had watched enrollment increase from 378 to 1,133.

Combined with his quarter-century of service to Simmons College, Legett's work at the Agricultural and Mechanical College of Texas and at the Prairie View Normal School made him one of the most experienced spokesmen for higher education in the state of Texas. He took his responsibilities seriously and never seemed to tire of dealing with educational matters. Above everything else, perhaps, he envied those young students whom God had called to build up a civilization.

[31] Ousley, "History," pp. 64–65.

*There are two things which I always hated to do
worse than anything else. One was to churn. The
other was to make a speech.*


CHAPTER ELEVEN

# A Fraternity of Contrasts
## and Contradictions

AN honor student at Simmons College in 1910 received a certificate
and twenty-five dollars in cash for writing the best answer to the question: "Who is the Successful Man?" The prize was called the K. K.
Legett Award, and presumably Legett provided the cash and selected
the winning essay. The winner, Conrad A. Lamb, wrote of a successful man as one who "cannot be bound by circumstances to any prescribed sphere. He bursts asunder the bonds of environment and cre-
ates for himself a new environment."[1] Perhaps neither the young
student nor his benefactor consciously made the comparison, but the
winning description precisely characterized K. K. Legett.

By his fiftieth birthday, Legett's environment was almost totally
unlike that of his boyhood days in Arkansas and East Texas. A small
saddlebag contained his only personal possessions when he arrived in
Buffalo Gap in 1879; by 1910, however, he was one of the wealthiest
men in West Texas. The Legetts inherited from the Bryan estate a
sizeable fortune in ranch land, but the major portion of the Legett
wealth resulted from Legett's own talents and ambitions.

Legett differed from many self-made men of his era in one particularly significant way: he learned to adjust to his acquired wealth
and to enjoy the comforts and opportunities that accompanied it. He
habitually feigned shock and surprise at the cost of practically everything, but he paid the price asked for items he really wanted. As his
home comforts increased and his son and daughters passed from childhood into adolescence, he grew increasingly reluctant to spend long

[1] *Abilene Daily Reporter*, May 29, 1910. See also *Eighteenth Annual Session of
Simmons College*, 1909–1910, p. 52.

periods of time away from them. His wish to share the experiences of their adolescent years, and Mrs. Legett's conviction that travel was an indispensable part of educational development, culminated in several family trips similar to their tour of the Pacific Northwest in 1905. In 1907 the Legetts visited the Jamestown Tercentennial Exposition in the tidewater Virginia area, and still later they toured the northeastern states, New York City, and the Great Lakes area.

As the younger Legetts looked toward college, their parents encouraged them to attend distant schools where they might study and, simultaneously, observe the mores of different sections of the country. Although each of them eventually matriculated at the University of Texas, Kade first enrolled at Culver Military Academy in Indiana before he moved on to Vanderbilt, Julia attended Belmont College in Tennessee, and Ruth spent her first two years at Randolph-Macon Woman's College in Virginia.

To K. K. Legett's considerable disappointment, none of the Legett children, during their young adulthood, shared their father's fascination for academic life. Church and secular scholars visited in the Legett home, and such familiarity apparently made the children less impressionable than their father. Kade enrolled for his junior year at the University of Texas on three different occasions, but a car wreck, an almost fatal case of typhoid fever, and a bout with pneumonia ended his efforts. Julia attended Simmons College in 1909–1910 and then enrolled at the University of Texas for her junior year but found little there to interest her. An extended tour of several western European countries completed her formal education. Ruth returned to Texas after two years in Virginia and enrolled at Austin. Her horse stumbled and fell and, for the second time in her life, she broke her collar bone. She returned to Abilene and, primarily to please her father, enrolled at Simmons College, where she completed her junior and senior courses in a single year and received a bachelor's degree.

Everyday life in Abilene and activities in the Legett home proved so satisfying that the Legett children felt no strong desire to declare their independence from parents or home town. They returned to Abilene during college holidays, and their parents welcomed them with joyous enthusiasm. Indeed, the entire town centered its holiday festivities around the college young folk. Early in December young men and women at Simmons College presented recitals, pageants, and

parades throughout the community as they left for their own home-
towns, native Abilenians arrived from other campuses. Thus the
Christmas season dominated the Abilene social scene from late November until the first week in January.

The holiday spirit literally permeated the Legett mansion during
those years when Kade, Julia, and Ruth returned from distant schools.
Festivities began on the morning of Thanksgiving Day after the family attended special church services at the First Baptist Church and
gained momentum during the holiday dinner when the John Bryans,
the Sam Youngs, and the Walter Trammells joined the Legetts. Festivities continued through the following weekend as male members—
and some of the females—spent the remainder of the weekend hunting quail and dove in the hill country of south Taylor County or in
the shinnery of Jones County.[2]

The Thanksgiving activities set the pace for the Christmas season,
and almost immediately thereafter Mrs. A. M. Robertson's daily news
column, "In the Social Realm," included the names of collegians as
they arrived at the T&P depot. Her lively reports generated greater
holiday excitement as she welcomed the students home: "The arrival
of the young people from the various universities and schools has
given an added interest to the Christmas celebration, especially among
the younger society set who have practically all dates filled with dinner parties, dances, etc." By December 23 last-minute arrivals made
front-page news. When a reporter checked off the final name on his
roster of collegians, he exclaimed, "Sure, it ought to be a great old
Christmas!" With everyone present or accounted for, Abilene families filled the church pews to hear their pastors' annual reminders
that "the spirit of Christmas is the spirit of Christ."

Usually Judge and Mrs. Legett awaited their children's arrival
before they decorated the house. In December, 1910, however, Kade
recuperated at home from a recent seige of typhoid fever, and Julia
returned from an extended tour of Europe. By the time Ruth arrived

---

[2] At times the numbers of wolves and rabbits increased so greatly that hunting
became a pressing necessity rather than a sporting pasttime. In the winter of 1910–
1911, two wolves and more than one hundred rabbits were killed in a single day on
Legett's Elmdale ranch, southeast of Abilene. During particularly bad years, the
county paid bounties for each pair of rabbit ears. In 1912–1913, in Taylor County
alone, 19,864 sets of ears were collected (see *Abilene Daily Reporter*, February 2,
1913).

from Randolph-Macon Woman's College, therefore, the Legett's elegant home, according to Mrs. Robertson, was already decorated for the season:

The reception hall, corridors, and parlor are exquisitely decorated with all kinds of greenery, red berries, and New Year's bells, while in the dining room garlands of greenery, showered with sweet peas are draped from the ceiling to the four corners of the room. The table is laid with cluny lace on which rests cut glass vases filled with red carnations. Crystal sticks hold crimson tapers with red shades. Cut glass compotes hold red and white mints.[3]

It remained, however, to decorate the tree—a ritual at the Legett home that varied little from year to year. Judge and Mrs. Legett, after considering all options, usually agreed that the family Christmas tree must be a native cedar from the hill country around Buffalo Gap. Judge Legett then invariably asked if a six-foot tree would suffice. Mrs. Legett invariably insisted that the cedar must reach within one foot of the twelve-foot ceiling. Judge Legett and Kade never failed to locate an eleven-foot tree. As father and son constructed a sturdy platform, Mrs. Legett determined which side of the tree should face the center of the room and which should be turned toward the wall. The tree in place, Ruth and Julia strung dozens of yards of cranberries and popcorn from the topmost branches to the cotton apron that concealed the platform. Finally, every member of the family attached dozens of tiny candles, each in its own metal holder. The candles remained unlighted until such special hours of the holiday season as receptions, dinners, and parties.

Mrs. Legett usually asked Frank Weaver, whose girth suited the character, to dress as Santa Claus. It was Weaver's duty at exactly the right moment to roll back the huge sliding doors between the reception hall and parlor and reveal to the delighted guests the brilliantly lighted tree. Later all helped themselves to Mrs. Legett's special Christmas treat at the buffet: coconut and caramel cake.

House decorations usually remained in place until the Legetts held their traditional New Year's open house. On December 26, 1910, the family mailed an announcement similar to those of earlier years:

[3] *Abilene Daily Reporter*, December 28, 1910.

Mr. and Mrs. K. K. Legett
at home
on the Afternoon of Monday
the Second of January
Nineteen hundred and Eleven

Mrs. Robertson's lengthy description of the event soon followed:

A curtain of greenery veiled the orchestra on the stairway and was sprinkled with a shower of incandescent lights. New Years bells in smilax and flowers hung at intervals from the ceiling.

Mr. and Mrs. Legett with true southern hospitality welcomed their guests in the reception hall. They were assisted by Mr. Kade Legett, Mr. and Mrs. Sam Young, Mr. and Mrs. John Bryan, Bernard Bryan and Juel Bryan. . . .

Mesdames Bass and Holt introduced the receiving line in the parlor. . . .

Mesdames Cooper and Robertson led the way to the dining room where they were greeted by Mesdames Bradfield and Coats who served a dainty salad course. . . .

Mrs. Arch Wood presided over the register table. . . .

Mrs. Sayles and Mrs. Hardwicke served coffee in the living room. . . .

Although the weather was very cold, the warmth and glow inside made all forget all unpleasantness outside. Notwithstanding the very cold weather, there were quite a number of callers.[4]

As Mrs. Robertson strove to make her society page a reflection of Abilene's changing social scene—from a frontier town of yesteryear to a culturally enriched community of almost ten thousand citizens in 1910—the editor's front-page stories mirrored a similar transformation. Following a single performance by the Ringling Brothers Circus, the editor called Abilene's attention to "a startling fact": although the circus had drawn thousands of West Texans to Abilene, there was not one arrest for disorderly conduct "during the entire day and night." Similarly, during a full week of the West Texas Fair, he observed that not a single person landed in jail during one twelve-hour period of that week. Editorials frequently criticized capital punishment and frequently demanded statewide prohibition. Civic leaders applauded efforts to erase lingering memories of the early-day six-shooter and saloon.

[4] Ibid., January 8, 1911.

Such civic zealousness to change Abilene's cowboy image explains in part why culture-conscious citizens would, in 1913, fill to overflowing the First Baptist Church to hear Yale University's professor of English, William Lyon Phelps, deliver an address entitled "Culture and Happiness." It might account also for the fact that the audience "broke into a roar of applause" when Phelps expressed his opinion that the three greatest books ever written for children were the Bible, Bunyan's *Pilgrim's Progress*, and the works of William Shakespeare.

The majority of Abilene's pioneer generation, the K. K. Legetts included, were among those who worked tirelessly to establish Abilene's reputation for cultural refinement. Their concern centered principally about their children, the first generation of native Abilenians. It was not enough for them to reproduce a social structure similar to that which the parents had known in an earlier day; they must improve upon it. Legett's counterparts in the East—attorneys, land developers, and farmers—were not likely to make a habit, as Legett did, of clipping newspaper items on various subjects of etiquette and filing them for future reference among his business papers. Paragraphs from two typical clippings demonstrate the way Legett felt toward his daughters in his role as protector and adviser:

Girls, it's allright for you to have a "fellow" and go here and there with him, but don't be everybody's girl just because he asks you to be. . . .
Don't cheapen yourself girls, but pick some really good young man, a fellow with an ambition beyond cigarette smoking, booze, fighting, and gambling and tie to him.

The second item offered advice on "When a Girl Should Marry":

There is nothing in life sadder than the fate of the girl who marries when she is a child and who outgrows her youthful romance and the husband to whom she is bound.
No girl should marry at eighteen.[5]

Such social admonitions led Judge and Mrs. Legett to discourage their daughters' early romantic interests and to encourage their partici-

---

[5] Unidentified newspaper clippings in Legett Family Records, File 3, papers 1, 2.

pation in a variety of social activities at home. Between holiday seasons, Mrs. Robertson's social items included descriptions of typical home entertainments:

(June 20, 1909) The beautiful lawn of the elegant Legett home presented a lovely picture last Friday evening when the XYZ club entertained in honor of the Sans Souci club at an "apron and overall picnic." The lawn was a picture from fairy-land, with its innumerable lights, its shrubbery and trees, and the handsome home in the background.

(September 12, 1909) The young ladies of the XYZ club were informally yet delightfully entertained Monday evening in the handsome Legett home on the crest of Alta Vista addition by Misses Julia and Ruth Legett. Misses Fannie Preston of Austin and Corinne St. Martin of Louisiana were the guests of honor. Mrs. Legett, assisted by her daughters and Miss Ruth Bradfield, served the guests on the lawn with an ice course.

(May 16, 1910) A delightful musical was given by Mr. and Mrs. K. K. Legett and children at their handsome home last Wednesday evening. Several brilliant musicians, with Mrs. Legett's elegant new grand piano, made an evening of rare enjoyment for music lovers.

(May 25, 1910) Wednesday afternoon the Legett home was thrown open to the music lovers of Abilene when the Rosenfeld club entertained their friends with an open meeting.

(July 16, 1911) Complimenting Miss Mattie Belle Davis, a house guest, the Misses Legett entertained with a lawn fete and reception at their lovely home on Sixth and Meander Streets Wednesday evening. The lawn was beautifully illuminated with incandescents, while myriads of swinging lanterns hung at the gate, along the walk, through the grounds, and around the porch.

Mrs. Robertson's descriptive paragraphs typify the average West Texan's appreciation of a green, well-kept lawn. A large shade tree, even the thin, lacy mesquite, was a prized possession and in some respects more valued than the home itself. One afternoon in May, 1909, for example, the large new home of the M. M. Mayfields at Pine and North Twelfth burned to the ground. When a reporter asked Mrs. Mayfield to evaluate her loss she responded, "All I can think of now is all those trees and that beautiful shrubbery burning. The home can be rebuilt, but it will take years to get the trees back again."[6]

[6] *Abilene Daily Reporter*, May 16, 1909.

Sometimes during a lull in social activities, Mrs. Robertson used her column to inform others of Abilene's social mores and to help erase the frontier image:

Withal you shall not find her people lacking in elegance and refinement, nor lacking in the necessary niceties and amenities of social life; but you will find that broad open-handed frankness and hospitality. . . .

Her people are still possessed of that democratic simplicity that knows little of social distinction and graded castes. Her people have that easy-to-get-acquainted-with air.[7]

Informal dances, Forty-two parties, study clubs, chicken fries, and a steady variety of impromptu socials often provided opportunities to welcome house guests or new residents to town. Thus, when a young Welshman named Percy Jones arrived in town as a guest and future employee of his famous uncle, railroader Morgan Jones, Catherine and Virginia Guitar invited the Legett sisters and a score of other friends to a chicken fry. On such occasions the guests sat in circles under the bright stars and discussed any topic of current interest.

Personalities interested them most, and the name Lillian Eubank often emerged as a favorite subject. Miss Eubank was the daughter of Taylor County commissioner J. J. Eubank. In 1908 the young woman left Abilene to study music in New York City. Within a few years she joined the Metropolitan Opera Company and her debut in Mozart's *The Magic Flute* won instant accolades. Her Abilene friends followed her career with interest and never tired of discussing the latest news release about her.

Other personalities who attracted local comment in 1911 included Mrs. Carrie Nation, the renowned temperance leader, whose death on June 11 reminded Texans that she once lived at Richmond, Texas, and Sarah Bernhardt, the French tragedienne, whose special train stopped briefly at the Texas and Pacific depot on April 6. Her visit provided social comment as expected, but her white French poodle up-staged the famous actress. During an interview with a local reporter, the ribboned and jeweled canine abandoned her life of pampered lux-

---

[7] *Abilene Daily Reporter*, no date given. Pictures of several of Abilene's larger homes, including the Legett mansion, suggest that the newspaper was a special edition.

ury and joined a pack of unpowdered hounds for a stroll down Pine Street. According to local observers, sixty-one members of Miss Bernhardt's stage company scampered about town in search of the disgraced poodle. The distraught actress abruptly ended the interview, but the enterprising reporter, meanwhile, had witnessed one of Miss Bernhardt's most emotional performances.

"Guess who went through on the T&P today?" was a favorite party game among young Abilenians. During the first stage of the game, participants took turns guessing until someone correctly identified such celebrated visitors as Jay Gould, C. W. Post, or Buffalo Bill. The game entered its second stage if someone could add other information of interest about the celebrity. Jay Gould, for example, was a personal friend of Percy Jones's uncle, Morgan Jones, and had named a room in his New York mansion "The Morgan Jones Room." C. W. Post stated, according to one observer, that West Texas was the "greatest country in the world—finest climate, finest land, and finest people on earth."

Kade Legett added extra information following Buffalo Bill's visit. Both had traveled on the same train enroute west. Cody admitted that his shooting eye was not as good as it used to be, but he hastened to add that he did not mean to imply that he "couldn't hit a barn door at twenty paces with a load of bird shot." [8] Cody described the Abilene country in earlier years (a subject Kade's father knew a good deal more about) when it was the home of the buffalo. Cody marveled at the recent changes but commented that he hardly knew whether to rejoice or regret the difference.

Theodore Roosevelt's brief stopover excited everyone, but the Legett children later referred to it as the time Uncle John [Bryan] almost got his head shot off. Senator Bryan had met the former president during an earlier visit in Austin, and, as Roosevelt's train pulled into the T&P depot, Bryan jumped, uninvited, onto the rear platform where the Rough Rider stood. His unexpected movement startled several bodyguards, who moved immediately to surround Bryan. The former president restrained his men, however, and Bryan eventually managed to introduce Roosevelt to the crowd.[9]

Former presidential candidate William Jennings Bryan created a

[8] *Abilene Daily Reporter*, November 22, 1910.
[9] Ibid., March 4, 1911.

social stir in 1909 when he was the house guest of Judge and Mrs. J. V. Cockrell on South Fourth Street, but perhaps no national celebrity more completely held Abilene's attention than Tris Speaker, the famous baseball star, whose sister lived at Caps in south Taylor County. After his visit to Abilene with the Boston Red Sox team, Abilenians of all ages talked only about baseball and the "whupping" administered to the local team by Tris Speaker and the professionals. Young ladies soon tired of conversations limited to the Boston Red Sox, the Chicago Cubs, or the latest Tinker-to-Evers-to-Chance double play, until Tim Murnane, a nationally syndicated sports writer, reported to his readers that Abilene's young women were as lovely as June roses in Vermont. Murnane complained, however, that every man in Abilene insisted upon showing him the city and the surrounding prairie at sixty miles an hour.[10]

When Lillian Eubank's operatic career or Tris Speaker's baseball heroics failed to keep conversations alive, a third West Texan with celebrity status, named Larry Chittenden, might become the topic. Known as the ranch poet, Chittenden was a former cowboy whose royalties from book publishers allowed him to spend much of his time in Bermuda. He frequently returned to West Texas and usually visited the George W. D. Coats family at their Alta Vista home. News reporters enjoyed Chittenden's visits because he always praised his native state and commented favorably about the improvements since his last visit.[11]

Once each year, during the pre-Chirstmas season, Abilenians played another guessing game, appropriately called "surprise package." On the first or second Saturday morning in December, hundreds of men, women, and children gathered at the warehouse behind the Morgan Weaver hardware store, where the postmaster had stacked several scores of unclaimed packages. Their various sizes, weights, and shapes created enormous curiosity. Each package bore a number, but the auctioneer called for bids without further identification. An unwritten law required the highest bidder to open his package on the spot. Most packages contained white elephants of worthless value and the auctioneer underscored that point when he declared "unfortunate winners" rather than highest bidders. Now and then real bargains ap-

[10] Ibid., April 7, 1911.
[11] Ibid., June 9, 1911.

peared, but the crowds gathered to laugh at and to applaud the absurd items. Throughout the day, periodic outbursts of laughter drew larger and larger crowds. An Abilene observer once described a bewildered young man who could not identify the prize he unwrapped and held in his hands. An older man, better informed in such matters, sauntered toward him and explained with the utmost seriousness and authority that the unfortunate winner's prize was an item intended by its makers to be worn "under the northern part of a south-bound skirt." A few feet away, an equally bewildered winner who could not read the label, poured the full contents of a bottle of "Mrs. Stickums Bust Developer" on his shiny bald head.[12]

Abilenians of all ages enjoyed such earthy humor. Their culture at the turn of the century was, according to their newspaper editor, "a fraternity of contrasts and contradictions"—a curious mixture of eastern refinement and western cussedness, northern reserve and southern hospitality, European sophistication and cowboy simplicity. The unique combination created a West Texas congeniality that crossed all age groups and all social classes.

Sometimes contrasting customs and manners failed to blend into compatible social patterns. On such occasions ludicrous contradictions created havoc with "good manners," and, as a consequence, the younger generation heard more than their share of lectures upon proper social conduct. Ruth Legett's secret solution to a collision of East-West mores, just as she completed her prepartions for travel to Randolph-Macon Woman's College, would have distressed her parents. Mother and daughter had spent many weeks assembling the proper wardrobe for Ruth's year at the elite Virginia college, and for the journey by train they had agreed upon a tiny but fashionable purse, large enough for face powder but small enough for easy handling. As Ruth dressed for the trip she vaguely recalled a West Texas adage: "Play it safe in a strange country." She hurriedly decided that a hand gun would provide safety, but, having made the decision, she was confronted by another dilemma: the tiny purse was too small for face powder *and* a gun. After another moment of indecision, she emptied her purse and packed the gun. Only then did she feel prepared to hold her own in that strange country.

[12] Ibid., December 2, 1907.

Her cowboy rationale would have distressed both parents, and yet her distrust of strangers probably resulted in part from her father's frequent claim that Abilene was "the best place in the world, next to Paradise." Another Legett truism, "Be careful what stand you take, you may run across the man who wrote the book," contributed little to her self-assurance. Thus she embarked for the East acutely aware that for the first time in her life she must provide her own defense. A gun, she reasoned, was more important than a purse full of face powder.

While the children were away, Judge Legett tended to accept new civic responsibilities in spite of the most sincere promises to Mrs. Legett that he would curtail them. In 1909 he accepted an appointment to the board of directors of the largest and oldest banking firm in Taylor County, the Farmers and Merchants National Bank. Before the year ended, he agreed to serve as the first president of the Taylor County Bar Association. He could afford neither the time nor the energy for either responsibility, but he accepted both with the forthright admission that the honors in each instance were too attractive to reject. His acceptance speech before the members of the Taylor County Bar Association revealed also a deep need to remain active:

There are two things which I always hated to do worse than anything else. One was to churn. The other was to make a speech. (laughter) . . .

I don't know whether I can be classed as an attorney or not. I have been trying to retire from the practice for a great many years. . . . It is justice to say the public has issued no great protest.

As perhaps all of you know, I am not an applicant for public patronage. I, however, feel at home with lawyers. . . .

The strength, gentlemen, of every civilization is dependent upon the strength of its judiciary. . . .

The older I grow the more respect I have for the courts of our country. I have heard criticism in my time of the courts, especially some of the Federal courts . . . even the Supreme Court. But I believe it is the greatest body of men in the world.[13]

A month later, thirty-six members of the Taylor County Bar Association held their first official meeting at the Legett mansion. A newsman explained that Legett threw open the doors of his palatial

13 Ibid., October 11, 1909.

home to lawyers and newspapermen, who enjoyed a supper served in several courses while they determined organizational procedures. At the following monthly meeting in December, attorneys and their wives from Dallas, Houston, El Paso, and other Texas cities attended the inaugural banquet at Abilene's Grace Hotel. Several out-of-town guests were original Taylor County lawyers who first practiced at Buffalo Gap, but only Legett continued to reside in Taylor County.[14]

As Abilene's list of surviving pioneers grew shorter each year, the *Abilene Daily Reporter* expanded its coverage of those who still made their homes in Taylor County. On September 4, 1910, a feature article included brief character sketches of many of them:

K. K. Legett—Here is a man without an enemy. Judge Legett's chiefest characteristic is a rare old essence of camaraderie with a sprinkle of kindly humor and a flavor—a most pronounced flavor—of incorruptible honesty. He came from Arkansas thirty-seven [*sic*] years ago. His purported age is somewhere in the neighborhood of fifty, but in reality he is not a day over twenty-one.[15]

Legett's remarkable ability to participate in virtually every political, social, economic, or religious activity "without an enemy" was not lost upon local and state politicians. From El Paso to Texarkana, candidates for public office sooner or later made their way to the Legett mansion. The Democratic primary in the gubernatorial campaign of 1910 brought the usual pilgrimage to his door. The overriding issue in Texas that year was prohibition, and, in the scramble for a prohibition amendment to the state constitution, prohibition Democrats plotted to gain control of the party. Among the leading contenders for the

---

[14] Charter members of the Taylor County Bar Association were H. L. Bentley, Thomas L. Blanton, T. A. Bledsoe, John Bowyer, Harvey Brigham, W. J. Bryan, J. H. Calhoun, Fred Cockrell, B. A. Cox, B. L. Cox, J. F. Cunningham, W. J. Cunningham, Edwin Dabney, T. W. Daugherty, Will Daugherty, T. P. Davidson, Eugene De Bogory, C. H. Fulwiler, W. L. Grogan, A. S. Hardwicke, S. P. Hardwicke, C. L. Hailey, R. W. Haynie, D. G. Hill, George Bass Hill, H. N. Hickman, Abdon Holt, B. K. Isaacs, T. G. Jackson, H. Rob Keeble, Harry Tom King, A. H. Kirby, E. N. Kirby, W. M. Lacy, W. C. Laskey, K. K. Legett, W. P. Mahaffey, J. W. Moffett, D. M. Oldham, Bruce Oliver, E. M. Overshiner, W. T. Potter, Henry Sayles, Sr., John Sayles, W. D. Scarborough, W. H. Sewell, M. W. Shelley, Jr., A. Stamps, Arthur Swan, I. N. Taylor, H. A. Tillett, J. M. Wagstaff, and T. M. Willis.

[15] *Abilene Daily Reporter*, September 4, 1910.

nomination, Cone Johnson favored prohibition by legislative statute, William Poindexter favored prohibition by constitutional amendment, and O. B. Colquitt favored the continuation of the local option law.

Legett favored Poindexter's solution, but his hopes to avoid active participation in the campaign ended as soon as Poindexter entered the race. Poindexter was an old Cleburne friend who, in 1879, served on the examining committee when Legett passed the bar examination. On March 26, therefore, Legett headed the Abilene reception committee which awaited Poindexter's train.

"How are you, old friend?" Legett inquired as the travel-weary candidate, umbrella clutched in his left hand, stepped from the train into a blinding West Texas sandstorm. An admiring newsman observed and reported Legett's sensitivity to his friend's uncomfortable situation:

> The distinguished visitor, sand covered and travel-stained, found himself the center of a throng eager to shake his hand.
> Buffeted by the wind and sand, Judge Poindexter looked longingly at the red front of the Grace Hotel, and Judge Legett, quick to catch the wistful glance of the visitor, led the way to clean water and something to eat.[16]

An hour later, Legett led his guest from the Grace Hotel to the courthouse, where approximately one thousand Abilenians waited to hear his address. Legett's introduction was characteristically humorous:

> Gentlemen, if you don't come to order I will make a speech. Now I don't want to make a speech and you don't want to hear me make one. (laughter)
> I present to you the next governor of Texas (cheers) and I have known him one hundred years. . . . He is as straight as a string. . . . He stands for everything that Christianity and morality uphold.[17]

A slightly smaller Abilene delegation of Democrats, headed by A. S. Hardwicke, met O. B. Colquitt a month later. Legett agreed to appear with the platform committee. Colquitt, the local-option candi-

---

[16] Ibid., March 27, 1910.
[17] Ibid.

date, was expected to win the nomination and the election because
Cone Johnson and Poindexter would split the prohibition vote. Local
politicians understood and accepted Legett's position: he would support Poindexter's candidacy for the Democratic nomination, but as a
loyal party man he would support the Democratic nominee in the general election.

Colquitt's supporters, scheming to take maximum advantage of
Legett's appearance at their candidate's rally, seated Legett on the platform and immediately to the speaker's left side. After a typically unsubtle announcement of local interest (that Miss Ellen Beach Yaw,
"the world's highest soprano," would appear in recital that night),
Hardwicke introduced his guest. A local newsman, obviously biased,
reported that Colquitt, "in a condescending manner," reminded his
"fair sized audience" of the "few little things" that he had done for
Abilene and "western" Texas during his public career as the state's
railroad commissioner.

When Colquitt shifted his address to an attack upon Poindexter,
Legett shifted his position in his chair, gazed at the ceiling, listened
to the tick of his watch, uncrossed his legs, crossed them again, tilted
his chair back—too far—and sprawled backward with a great clatter
to the floor. The speaker and his audience froze in shocked silence and
then burst into wild applause and friendly laughter as the unruffled
judge scrambled unhurt to his feet, waved his hand toward the speaker and said, "Go right ahead, Governor." The following day a Poindexter supporter suggested that Legett had shrewdly timed his pratfall
to coincide with Colquitt's attack against Poindexter, but Legett never
admitted that he had deliberately staged the interruption.[18]

On election day, July 23, the local editor stretched a huge white
canvas across the wall of the Mingus and Dellis building opposite the
*Abilene Daily Reporter* office, then adjusted his new "stereopticon
machine" and prepared to flash each candidate's vote upon the im-
provised screen. A reporter proudly described Abilene's first election
party:

Probably the largest crowd ever gathered in the city for any occasion
thronged the streets for more than a block in both directions. Just as dusk
came on the moving picture machine was lighted up and the big show be-

18 Ibid., April 30, 1910.

gan. . . . The crowd was an orderly one and not a single disturbance took place to mar the pleasure of the evening.

At times when favorable returns for favorite candidates came in, wild cheers rent the air and throughout the night people appeared to enjoy the occasion to the fullest extent. [Between reports of the returns] six reels of moving pictures were used and this served to keep the interest up until long after midnight.[19]

For many years thereafter, the downtown election party remained a favorite community event.

Colquitt won the gubernatorial election by a statewide landslide, although Poindexter won a plurality vote throughout most of West Texas. The wide margin of Poindexter's plurality in Taylor County suggested a strong local influence generated by Legett and other members of the Taylor County Bar Association who worked collectively in Poindexter's behalf. The official county vote registered 1,094 for Poindexter, 822 for Colquitt, and 488 for Cone Johnson. The following year, when Texas defeated a proposed prohibition amendment, West Texas voted for the amendment by a two-to-one margin.[20]

In 1912 Legett supported Woodrow Wilson's efforts to unseat the national Republican party. He explained to local voters that Wilson, unlike William Howard Taft, had no blind devotion to private-interest groups and that Wilson, unlike Theodore Roosevelt, seemed level-headed enough not to attempt the impossible.[21] Legett's interests in public issues never faltered, but as the years passed he directed more and more attention to local issues, especially to those involving Abilene's physical growth.

No other man in Abilene paid closer attention to Abilene's construction projects. Public buildings excited him most—possibly because they provided a skyline—but he would detour for many city blocks just to inspect the construction of the smallest barn. Often in good weather he drove straight home, picked up Mrs. Legett, and conducted a tour of each new construction site as though she were a stranger in town.[22] When, in 1910, the First Baptist congregation

---

[19] Ibid., July 24, 1910.

[20] Sybal Hazel, "Prohibition Campaign of 1911," *West Texas Historical Association Year Book* 18 (October, 1942): 92–115.

[21] *Abilene Daily Reporter*, August 17, 1912.

[22] Interview with Julia Legett Pickard, Abilene, Texas, July 17, 1973.

built their impressive $42,790 structure, he drove to the site several evenings each week. It was an especially good year for his favorite pastime: from the First Baptist construction he drove a few blocks north and west to the new site of the St. Paul Methodist, then south and east again to the new T&P depot between North and South First streets, and finally west on North First to the location of Childer's Classical Institute (now Abilene Christian College). Elsewhere in town a girls' industrial home, valued at more than $40,000, added to the town's modest skyline.

Every structure represented growth and prosperity, and Legett reveled in it. His family tried to take advantage of his frequent tours by horse and buggy to encourage his purchase of an automobile.[23] Despite his customary acceptance of inventions and innovations, Legett reacted negatively to the "machine." With the single exception of the railroad, he neither understood nor trusted mechanical devices. His family pointed to his contradictory attitude; he was the first in town, they reminded him, to support the installation of telephones, the sewer system, and the lighting system. Nothing could convince him, however, that the automobile was more than a passing fad. When they argued that the machine provided better transportation about town, he countered that the street railway—which he supported—was "an infinitely superior mode of travel." When they argued that the automobile would transport people across country in areas not serviced by the railroads, he pointed to the new Morgan Jones railroad line from Abilene to Ballinger and predicted that Texas would eventually build a network of railroad lines to serve every town in Texas.[24]

Legett was not impressed by Sam Young's new Firestone, John Bryan's Stevens-Duryea, W. B. Guitar's Locomobile, or John C. Wise's Buick. When his family quoted statistics to prove that the automobile was a safer form of transportation than the horse and buggy, Legett pointed to a front-page news item that described in considerable detail the painful injuries of three machine passengers who drove their vehicle over a steep embankment. The children countered that the accident occurred in a small New Hampshire village and claimed that the item made Abilene's front page for the simple reason that the accident was a rare occurrence. When he reminded them of the ma-

[23] Interview with Ruth Legett Jones, Abilene, Texas, July 16, 1973.
[24] Ibid.

chine's fiendish odor of gasoline, they replied that it was a city odor that reminded them of Dallas.

Legett's resistance slowly weakened. He supported a $50,000 bond drive to pave Abilene's major business area (two blocks on Pine, Chestnut, North First, North Second, South First, and South Second), but he insisted that his horse and buggy could benefit from the smoother surface just as surely as a smelly, noisy machine. Later he allowed the children to take driving lessons from an instructor named Eddie Rickenbacker, but he refused their invitation to enroll in the class with them. When they returned from their first instruction and reported that Uncle John (Bryan) was among Rickenbacker's students, Legett was not impressed. His brother-in-law was a good state senator, he admitted, but, since Bryan had never learned properly how to harness a horse, ride a horse, or drive a buggy, he was not likely to learn much about the machine from Rickenbacker.[25]

Inevitably Legett's resistance collapsed, and predictably his first automobile was one of the finest in town. Behind the wheel of his Buick, he soon proved to his children what they had suspected all along: he had no understanding whatsoever of mechanical contraptions. Indeed Legett and his brother-in-law soon established reputations as the worst automobile drivers in town. Unfortunately, Kade and Julia inherited their father's deficiency in things mechanical, and a year later Mrs. Legett proved to be no better.

To her lifelong satisfaction, only Ruth understood Rickenbacker's driving instructions. For several years thereafter she was the only Legett who could locate, unscrew, empty, clean, refill, and replace the grease cups. Her ego at full throttle, Ruth bragged to one and all that she could locate, service, and replace *every* grease cup—*with her eyes closed.* Her father retorted that locating grease cups on a Buick required a contortionist, not a mechanic.

Year after year, as nearly every male and many females learned to drive, demands increased for more improved streets. As a consequence,

---

[25] Legett's low opinion of Senator John Bryan's riding habits was soon proved correct. A year or two later, Bryan rode his horse off a bluff as he and a ranch hand mended fences on his Jones County ranch. He suffered a severe concussion and almost lost his life. See *Abilene Daily Reporter*, August 19, 1912; and Samuel Luther Robertson, Jr., "The Life Story of William John Bryan, 1859–1948" (M.A. thesis, Hardin-Simmons University, 1973), p. 58.

road crews plowed up the dusty, uneven streets, leveled them, covered them with liquid asphalt, and topped the odorous mixture with crushed rock. Abilenians found the process, according to one newsman, as interesting as attending the fair and as exciting as an aviation flight. After North Second Street turned into a smooth, dustless thoroughfare, Abilenians promptly dubbed it "Young Wall Street." [26]

For a few years automobile travel and paved streets were such novelties that newsmen emphasized the mode of transportation as they reported activities and events. Thus, on one occasion Legett, Judge Meek, and city marshal George H. Green "took an automobile ride" to their favorite fishing hole, and on another occasion, Legett, John Bryan, Sam Young, Kade Legett, and E. E. Griffin traveled in Young's "new Firestone automobile" to the Bryan ranch near Hamlin for a weekend of quail hunting.

Newspaper references to Legett's leisure hours marked a milestone. With the exceptions of social events at the mansion and family tours across country, Legett was fifty-three years old before reporters mentioned his leisure time. As usual, they reported his resignations from the boards of directors at Texas A&M and at Simmons College, and perhaps they sensed his desire to allow younger men to assume part of his heavy responsibilties. His letter of resignation to the Simmons College board indicated a desire to slow his pace:

Gentlemen:

I herewith resign as a member of the Board of Trustees of Simmons College. You doubtless all know that such action has been contemplated by me for a great while. The fact that I have been a member of this Board for about twenty years is a sufficient reason for the action taken. The tenure of office prescribed by law for Director of all State Educational Institutions is only two years. The provision may be a wise one.

I retire from this Board with the unqualified approval of my conscience, and with the deep seated conviction that . . . I have done the best I could. . . .

. . . My most earnest prayers for your success, and for the success of the great college you represent. . . .

Faithfully yours,
(signed) K. K. Legett [27]

---

[26] *Abilene Daily Reporter*, February 14, 1912.
[27] K. K. Legett to Board of Trustees, Simmons College, June 15, 1911, Simmons

Reporters learned, however, that Legett's withdrawal from one responsibility merely created a vacuum which left room for two new responsibilities. Legett never seemed to learn this lesson.

---

College, *Minutes of the Board of Trustees*, 1:213. The board members requested Legett to withdraw his resignation or to withhold it for at least one year, but, determined at the moment at least to lighten his burdens, Legett refused to delay his resignation. He accepted reappointment to the board in 1914.

*I have been criticized for making the statement*
*that this is the best country on earth.*

CHAPTER TWELVE

# Three Cows, Two Sows, and
# Two Hundred Chickens

WHEN K. K. Legett reached his fifty-sixth year in 1914, he was, according to his associates, as physically robust and as mentally alert as many men half his age. Perhaps more significantly, he had lost none of his enthusiasm for life. He seemed to sense that 1914 promised unusual challenges and opportunities as he cut from an unidentified newspaper an article entitled "Some 1914 'I Wills' " and filed it under "Important Papers." By the end of the year, Legett had many reasons indeed to seek guidance from that list of New Year's resolutions, the last of which stated: "I will seek to so shape my influence that it shall enter into the very Eternity of Things."[1]

Records show that Legett fulfilled his fourteenth resolution remarkably well, for in December, 1914, the editor of the *Abilene Daily Reporter* commented upon one Abilene project for which Legett was primarily responsible: "No greater piece of constructive work has ever been done for Central West Texas." The editor referred to Legett's singularly successful campaign to encourage Taylor County farmers to decrease their cotton acreage and increase, simultaneously, their production of hogs, cows, and chickens, and the grain to feed them. Such diversification would free them from "two of the most unpredictable forces on earth—the cotton market and rainfall." Legett was convinced that Taylor County could then become "the richest county on the face of the earth, as well as the greatest."[2]

[1] Unidentified newspaper clipping, January 1, 1914, Leggett Family Records, file 3, paper A.

[2] This appears to be the fragments of an unfinished written address, or perhaps an isolated idea jotted down for future use (in Leggett Family Records, file 3, paper K).

A sharp decline in cotton prices accompanied by an equally sharp decline in rainfall provided the impetus for Legett's diversification campaign. During the first decade of the twentieth century, cotton growers prospered so consistently that many West Texas ranchers cut their pastures into smaller sections, sold them to cotton farmers, and made excellent profits. Plentiful rains for several successive years encouraged farmers with short memories to forget that land west of the 98th meridian frequently received less than twenty inches of rain per year. Land prices climbed higher as immigrants pushed the cotton belt farther and farther west and beyond its natural boundary.

West Texas pioneers knew that a prolonged drought or a glutted cotton market could bring disaster to Taylor County farmers. They recalled the grim years when months passed without measurable rainfall and especially that stretch of twenty-three months through 1886 and 1887 when no general rains fell at all. Most Taylor County farmers had never experienced this kind of prolonged drought. During the wet years, however, no land looked more inviting to cotton farmers. Unfortunately the years 1911 to 1913 were not wet years, and cotton production in Taylor County almost disappeared. The spring months of 1911 were the driest on record. Spirits sank so low in the Abilene area that there was no official celebration of Independence Day on July 4. Continued discouragement through the next two years caused the cancellation of the annual county fair.

Nevertheless, Taylor County folk insisted that central West Texas was a cotton-farming country. Eternally optimistic, they believed the Reverend J. M. Slatton of the Buffalo Gap Methodist Church, who told them that their problems were with God, not with mother nature. The drought was God's method of reminding them of the necessity for better living. Editor George Anderson, the rancher's adversary but always the farmer's friend, convinced himself and perhaps others that droughts were blessings in disguise: "The people are learning that proper soil culture, proper selection of seeds, and proper planting and cultivation will bring results that can be depended upon. . . . Drouths suggest to the farmer better tillage . . . and they compel the tiller of the soil to heed the call for conserving moisture."[3]

[3] *Abilene Daily Reporter*, August 18, 1912.

Improved cotton culture, however, could not guarantee a successful season. During the West Texas drought, bumper crops of cotton in East and South Texas contributed to the glutted world market and forced prices down. Texas cotton farmers in 1911–1913 generally failed to meet expenses whether they had a good crop or no crop at all. As a consequence, the Lone Star State suffered a serious economic recession, which corresponded roughly to Governor O. B. Colquitt's term in office.

In 1911 the governor of Texas called for a meeting in New Orleans of all southern governors to discuss the cotton crisis. At the meeting they agreed upon a program of higher credit supports for cotton growers, increased warehouse storage, and a decrease in cotton production. The conference, unfortunately, produced few concrete results, and the cotton market continued to deteriorate through 1912 and most of 1913.

Torrential rains in November and December of 1913 broke the West Texas drought but simultaneously swept away Lytle Lake dam, which had stored Abilene's main water supply since 1897. Within hours eight hundred million gallons of water disappeared from the lake. The loss was a critical one, but the drought-breaking rain kept spirits high. Editor George Anderson expressed the prevailing attitude that "the old dam will simply be replaced by a better dam." Programs of recovery from the drought commenced before the winter ended.

In February Legett, E. E. Griffin, J. M. Wagstaff, and other Abilene citizens petitioned the Texas game commissioner for permission to restock the county with blue-tops, bob-whites, and quail. They informed the commissioner that such birds were valuable aids to farmers as destroyers of insects. Optimistic as usual, they assured the game commissioner that "the magnificent outlook for the grain crop will give them much to feed on and make it the ideal year to restock the country." [4]

Memories of the dry period rapidly receded. Unemployment in Abilene disappeared as approximately fifty men constructed a new $150,000 courthouse, an equal number paved more downtown streets, and sixty restored Lytle Lake dam. At the same time, civic

[4] Ibid., January 22, 1914.

groups renewed their sponsorship of public programs. A poultry show, for example, brought to Abilene many poultry farmers from local and distant parts of Texas and the Southwest. Farmers from distant counties won most of the prizes, and one farmer from Mississippi won every prize offered for the Plymouth Rock strain.

While Abilenians might lament the lack of high quality poultry in Taylor County, they could applaud the construction by H. M. Vickery of a new creamery on North First Street. Vickery issued a public plea for area farmers to bring their milk to his new processing plant, where they could make a ready sale. Such evidence of Abilene's economic recovery in fields not related to cotton production convinced Legett that more area farmers should engage in occupations better suited to West Texas environment and less dependent upon seasonal precipitation.

Legett's own income from attorney's fees, bankruptcy fees, farming, ranching, land speculation, and banking made a sudden decline from any single source less disturbing. It was a rare year when the income from his business ventures declined at the same rate or during the same season. It followed, therefore, that Abilene's prosperity could become more stable if its sources of income were more diversified and less dependent upon rainfall or warm temperatures.

By coincidence, the Taylor County Farmers' Institute held its annual convention in Abilene in early May of 1914. Among those who accepted Judge Fred Cockrell's invitation to speak at the institute were Judge Ed R. Kone, state commissioner of agriculture, Professor A. M. Ridgway of Texas A&M, Thomas A. McGalliard, state director of farmers' institutes, President J. D. Sandefer of Simmons College, and Judge K. K. Legett. In addition to a speaking assignment, Judge Cockrell, president of the local institute, asked Legett to introduce the principal speaker, Judge Kone. Legett misunderstood Cockrell's requests, however, and believed that his only duty involved his introduction of Judge Kone. Legett learned that he was expected to deliver a major address only after he joined other members of the platform party who sat on the stage in front of three hundred farmers. His speech, therefore, was entirely extemporaneous.

President Sandefer's opening address emphasized the points that all men seek wealth, that such pursuits are honorable, and that most men in history gained wealth through the accumulation of land. It followed, Sandefer argued, that most wealth was based upon some form of agricultural activity in spite of the fact that recent fortunes had been accumulated by industrial tycoons.

Thomas A. McGalliard lectured on the various kinds of soils, the dire effects that result when farmers rob the soil of its nitrogen, the importance of terracing one's land, and the reasons why farmers should adopt a crop-rotation system. Professor Ridgway, a dairy expert, informed his audience that climatic conditions in Texas made the state an ideal one for dairying and yet Texans sent out of the state every year approximately eight to ten millions of dollars for dairy products.

Suddenly inspired by the obvious correlation between these ideas and the ease with which each could be applied to Taylor County's agricultural situation, Legett notified Cockrell during a recess that he would "relate the preceding topics to the local situation." In his opening remarks he stated that his experiences as a member of the board of directors at Texas A&M had provided an opportunity to observe firsthand the enormous research required for the study of agricultural experimentation, that his numerous field trips around the nation in behalf of A&M had proved that theoretical reasoning combined with practical application could solve any problem, and that all farmers in the audience should apply the messages they had just heard to their individual situations.

Taylor County farmers, he continued, should begin at once to practice a more diversified agricultural program; they should double the products of the cow and increase by 25 percent the production of grain crops. He called upon them to follow Ridgway's advice and develop a cooperative dairy system and, while they were about it, build cooperative silos where they could store grain for the dry years. Legett believed that every one of Taylor County's 2,404 farmers could pay his bills through all seasons if he would add three cows and two hundred chickens to his current farm commodities.

If there were farmers in Taylor County who could not afford the initial investment, Legett pledged that he personally would bear the cost or locate a friend or organization who would: "There is no use for farmers to say that they can make no living in this section . . . three cows and two hundred chickens can make any farmer and his family a good living."[5] He informed his audience that bank deposits at the Winters bank had increased during the recent drought, whereas deposits in most other West Texas banks decreased. Upon investigation he discovered that most cotton farmers in the Winters area also raised chickens and dairy products.

On this point Legett ended his address and introduced Judge Kone, the principal speaker. Before Kone delivered his speech ("Cooperation—The Greatest Word in the English Language") he told the farmers who sat in the audience that no people ever had a more noble and good man than K. K. Legett to advise them. When the session ended, an unnamed representative of the Chamber of Commerce stepped to the platform and offered to cooperate with the Taylor County Farmers' Institute and Taylor County bankers to arrange loans for those who wished to follow Legett's recommendations. Thus began the first organized countywide diversification program in the state of Texas.[6]

Although the farmers responded enthusiastically to Legett's address, there is no evidence that any of them requested Legett's assistance in securing a bank loan. In late June, however, Editor Anderson claimed that "the Creator favored the Abilene country . . . as an ideal region for the propagation of poultry, cows, horses, and swine." Referring directly to Legett's May 2 address, the editor continued: "One of the most prominent businessmen in Abilene has agreed to help the farmer if he cannot help himself. If a farmer in this section with two cows cannot make a living from them, this man is willing to make up the deficit."[7] An item on page four of the same newspaper suggests that Legett's advice to build silos had begun to bring results: "Silo talk is rife with the farmer in the Abilene trade territory. . . ."

I. B. Duck's arrival in Abilene on September 5, 1914, provided more convincing proof of Legett's influence. Duck was a dairy expert, a federal government employee, and, for a temporary period of experimentation, a farm demonstration agent for Taylor County. During his assignment, the Abilene Chamber of Commerce provided for Duck an office, an automobile, and traveling expenses. Hence at no expense,

[5] Ibid., May 3, 1914.
[6] Ibid., March 5, 1914.
[7] Ibid., June 28, 1914.

local farmers received advice and assistance from a dairy expert. Duck explained that he would not offer advice where none was requested. He further explained that he could be most useful if local farmers would allow him to coordinate the activities of producers and distributors of dairy products. He offered to check without charge all animals suspected of carrying ticks, and finally he invited all area farmers to meet with him at the county fair and to participate in its agricultural programs.

The 1914 fair was the first in Taylor County since 1910. Its resumption after a three-year interval marked Legett's major accomplishment as president of the Chamber of Commerce in 1913–1914 and signaled the county's improved economic condition. The fair's new title, "The First Annual Central West Texas Fair," reflected Legett's desire to encourage a more widespread participation. Legett served as general director of the fair. Organizational problems after three years af inactivity could have overwhelmed a less determined man, but Legett managed to make the week-long event self-supporting. He announced during the final evening of the fair that every expense had been met. Meanwhile, he had helped to organize a series of lectures, a series of parades, and a daily program of auto races, horse races, baseball games, and aeroplane stunts. He rented scores of exhibition stands for every variety of agricultural product.

Local folk, delighted that the fair had been revived, complimented general manager Fred Wood for its success, but Wood responded that credit should go equally to those Abilene ladies who did most of the work, and to Judge Legett, "one of the greatest and best men in Abilene's history." Perhaps the most significant feature of the 1914 fair grew out of another Legett inspiration—he personally invited Governor Edmond F. Noel of Mississippi, a noted speaker throughout the South and a consistent foe of King Cotton, to come to Abilene and describe to West Texas farmers the evils of a one-crop agricultural system. Governor Noel warned that farmers must cut their cotton production in 1915 or face another depressed market: Why plant and pick cotton at a cost of seven cents a pound, if they were paid only four cents a pound for their efforts? [8]

Within a month, area farmers invited Legett, Duck, and other

[8] Ibid., October 11, 1914.

local spokesmen for diversification to assist them as they organized their diversification clubs. Farmers in the Elmdale area east of Abilene, where Legett owned and operated farm and ranch lands, sought his help. A newspaper item on November 10 announced the approaching Elmdale meeting and that "K. K. Legett, initiator of the diversification plan of Taylor County," would be the main speaker.

More than eighty local farmers attended the meeting, and fourteen of them organized the first diversification club. Three carloads of Abilene businessmen, including young Kade Legett, who worked at a local bank and at the Elmdale ranch, accompanied Judge Legett to Elmdale. A newspaperman also accompanied the group and reported the essence of Legett's remarks:

> His main point was to get each farmer to keep three cows and two hundred chickens. . . . He pointed out to the farmers the success in this line in the North, of which he had made a close and exhaustive study. He stressed that climatic conditions in this part of the country were better.
>
> His talk was interesting throughout and made a deep . . . impression.[9]

The following evening, Friday, November 12, 1914, Legett, as the retiring president of the organization, made the main address at the annual Chamber of Commerce banquet. Considered by Abilenians the major social event of the year, the banquet was highlighted by the keynote speech of the outgoing president. "A great and overflowing crowd" gathered in the enormous basement room of the Radford Building, dined on barbecued goat, held a short business meeting, and then heard Legett speak on the subject "What Diversification Means to the Businessmen of Abilene." A news story in the Saturday morning paper included the following summary:

> This wonderful man told of how Abilene could go on to prosperity through the active efforts of its business men in making Taylor County the greatest dairy section in the state.
>
> He put every person in the audience on record that whenever in the future he was called upon to make a speech, he would talk about dairying and diversification.
>
> He spoke commendably of the men who are now giving their time and endeavors to the organization of the farmers of the several communities

[9] Ibid., November 12, 1914.

into diversification clubs and told of the ultimate benefit that would result if the merchants and business men would cooperate with the farmers to the desired end.

He again suggested the plan of every Taylor County farmer having three good cows and two hundred chickens, wherein is sustenance for each family.[10]

An editorial in the same edition praised Legett's "common old-bay-horse sense."

A week later the Abilene Chamber of Commerce purchased sixteen high-grade Jersey cows and instructed secretary Fred Wood to sell them to any interested farmers at actual cost. Wood devised an installment payment plan and announced that the Chamber of Commerce would purchase additional cows and sell them under the same arrangements if local demand warranted it.

Diversification clubs spread rapidly throughout Taylor County and eventually W. H. Wright, in a feature article for the *Abilene Daily Reporter*, provided another reason for diversification: the recent outbreak of war in Europe would create a drain on American food supplies and ultimately force Americans into more truck farming. He praised the recent organization of diversification clubs at Buffalo Gap, Sambo, and Hamby, and he praised the Abilene Chamber of Commerce for adopting "the great plan of K. K. Legett and his motto 'Three Cows, Two Sows, and Two Hundred Chickens.' "[11]

Legett's delayed inclusion of two sows to his plan for diversification apparently resulted from a conversation with Abilene attorney J. F. Cunningham, who told Legett that Texas Panhandle farmers had gone hog wild over hogs. He told about a tenant farmer in Hemphill County who took one hundred hogs to market and sold them for $2,200. Another farmer in the same county sold forty hogs at $24 each. In Lipscomb County, according to Cunningham, bankers loaned money to tenant farmers to buy hogs and took liens on the hogs for security.

In his next diversification speech, consequently, Legett inserted a new statement: "The worst crime a farmer in Taylor County can commit is to develop a hogless farm. What is the use to raise a big grain

10 Ibid., November 13, 1914.
11 Ibid., November 29, 1914.

crop, sell it at ordinary prices, and then take the money and buy meat at three or four times what the same grain would cost?"

Throughout Legett's campaign for diversification, the Abilene Chamber of Commerce, ably represented by its secretary, Fred T. Wood, provided consistent and vigorous support: It purchased and sold high-grade Jersey cows at cost, it encouraged countywide efforts to organize diversification clubs, it sponsored conventions and brought in farm experts to meet with local farmers, and it underwrote an intensive publicity campaign. In late November, 1914, secretary Wood ordered seventy-five highway signs erected at prominent crossroads throughout the county, each with the inscription:

> MR. FARMER, EQUIP YOUR FARM WITH
> THREE DAIRY COWS, 200 CHICKENS, AND
> TWO BROOD SOWS AND BE INDEPENDENT.
>
> ———— MILES TO ABILENE, WHERE YOU
> WILL FIND A MARKET.[12]

In addition, Wood posted letters to every farmer in Taylor County to explain the benefits of purchasing cows, sows, and chickens. His letter quoted farm agent Duck in detail and included statistics to show how the three cows could profit the farmer $225.00 per year in butter fat and $112.50 per year in skimmed milk, and, at the rate of $20.00 per cow, increase the cows' value for a total of $397.50. Wood explained that the farmer could realize a net profit from his cows of $307.50 each year after deductions of $90.00 for feed grain. The two brood sows should produce an average of twenty-four pigs per year, which, at two hundred pounds each, should bring $384.00 annually. After deducting $150.00 for feed grain, a farmer's net gain should amount to $204.00. Finally, a net profit of $1.00 per hen should provide a total of $200.00 annually. The Legett Diversification Plan, according to Wood's letter, should increase every farmer's annual income by a minimum of $711.50.[13] The farmers' response soon prompted newsman Wright to report that the Legett diversification movement would decrease the 1915 cotton crop in Taylor County by 50 percent.

12 Ibid., November 24, 1914.
13 Ibid., November 29, 1914.

Reports of other responses to the Legett Plan poured into Wood's office. Clarence Ousley, director of the Department of Extension at Texas A&M, congratulated Taylor County farmers for their leadership in the diversification movement; J. M. Cunningham, owner of a farm west of Abilene and another south of Abilene, informed Wood that he had adopted the Legett Plan but on larger scale—he had purchased two hundred registered hogs, one hundred white Leghorn chickens, and hoped to purchase several dairy cows; W. M. Steward wrote that he had not grown up on a farm, but, based upon his success at the Buttonwillow Stock and Dairy Farm, he believed that any farmer who adopted the Legett Plan would succeed; an anonymous Texas firm offered to exchange registered Jersey cows for milo maize, Kaffir corn, and feterita; William P. Sewell brought to Wood's office a four and one-half pound turnip as proof that Taylor County farmers could successfully raise truck crops; O. S. McElroy stated that he had become a diversified farmer "a-la-mode Legett," and claimed considerable success in his experiments with soy beans and peanuts; and E. M. O'Kelly boasted that he had "smashed all records in the poultry raising line." O'Kelly based his claim upon the fact that he had begun with forty hens and within ten months he had netted a profit of $110.70 on chickens, $81.60 on eggs, and he still owned one hundred chickens to begin his second year.

Toward the end of December, 1914, the Abilene Chamber of Commerce announced that it would sponsor a giant diversification meeting sometime in January, 1915. "We plan to have one of the biggest and most interesting programs on the subject ever given in the West," Wood said. He anticipated an all-day program with speakers coming in from all over the state.

The Legett Plan spread to other counties. J. H. Daniels of Clarksville, in the blacklands country of East Texas, called upon Governor O. B. Colquitt to proclaim a "Diversified Week." At Temple, Texas, a mass meeting of farmers called upon the Lone Star State to feed itself "and thus prevent an annual expenditure of $200,000,000. for foods from other states." A few weeks later, a group of Dallas and Fort Worth businessmen responded to the call from Temple, organized a diversification plan, and adopted the motto: "Let Texas Feed Itself." The Texas Bankers' Association pledged its immediate support and challenged every Texas county to feed itself and its livestock in 1915.[14]

As the diversification movement gained momentum, editor Hanks quoted liberally from the pages of the *Texas Stockman*:

Taylor County is leading every county in the state in the matter of diversification. Every community is being organized into a unit of the county system, and when all of the communities shall have been organized, a county diversification organization will be perfected.

United States dairy experts are visiting every community and doing the organizing. As a result the cotton acreage will be reduced fifty percent during the next year and more attention will be given to the dairying and chicken business.[15]

During January, plans for the diversification meeting progressed under secretary Wood's direction, and eventually he announced that the following persons would address the Taylor County farmers at the Jewel Theater on Saturday afternoon, January 30: Judge K. K. Legett, whom Wood billed as "the originator of the Legett movement and its slogan 'Three Cows, Two Sows, and Two Hundred Chickens' "; Professor R. N. Harkey, Department of Extension, A&M College; J. W. Neill, Department of Agriculture, State of Texas; R. R. Claridge, agricultural agent for the Texas and Pacific Railway; Judge E. W. Prescott, Department of Agriculture, State of Texas; and William Ganzer, district farm demonstration agent. Two hundred Taylor County farmers and several representatives of the state organization of "Let Texas Feed Itself" attended.

At the close of the meeting, Taylor County farmers and the Abilene Chamber of Commerce organized a Diversification and Marketing Association similar to several already organized in other Texas counties. Members of the association pledged to encourage farm diversification and seek ready markets for the products from diversified farms. They elected J. M. Miller president of the association, K. K. Legett vice-president, and I. B. Duck secretary.[16]

[14] Ibid., January 25, 1915.
[15] Ibid., January 6, 1915.
[16] Directors were Miller, Dr. J. G. Dodge, U. Collins, G. E. Morris, J. F.

In February, Duck announced that the United States farm demon-
strators for the Central Western District of Texas had judged Taylor
County number one in the district in dairying and poultry and second
only to Comanche County in hog raising. Before the month ended,
Fred Wood called attention to another milestone in the diversification
program: the Gus Roberts Grain Company shipped Abilene's first carload of Red Top sorghum seed to an eastern market.

Other milestones closely related to the diversification program
soon followed. Duck announced the formation of two youth organizations, the Boys' Agricultural Club and the Boys' Animal Husbandry
Club. From time to time Duck awarded prizes underwritten by various civic organizations for the best pigs, chickens, maize, feterita, or
Kaffir corn raised by members of the clubs.

On March 3 the Chamber of Commerce announced that K. K.
Legett had agreed to serve as toastmaster for its annual banquet. Secretary Wood promised that "Judge Legett will see to it that there is
not a dull moment from the time the meeting opens until the last
speaker has had his say." Editor Anderson agreed that "Judge Legett's
qualifications to serve as toastmaster are well known to all Texans,
and his welcoming address alone will be worth going to the banquet.
The man who misses it will regret it ever after." [17]

The event was indeed spirited, and according to one observer "enthusiasm was rampant." More than two hundred members attended,
and long linen-covered tables filled the basement room of the Radford
Building. Newsman Frank Grimes reported:

Judge Legett, whose oratory and good humor has cheered the hearts of
many audiences in the Central West, was never in better form than Thursday night.

As master of ceremonies he introduced the speakers of the evening but
he did some speaking himself that brought the audience to its feet more
than once.

Judge Legett, as is well known, is the original apostle of diversification.
He has worked for it, prayed for it, fought for it, and expects to spend the
rest of his days persuading the farmers of Taylor County to adopt it.[18]

---

Hamby, P. L. Hays, J. E. Hensley, R. G. B. Fain, W. A. Minter, W. B. Hale, K. K.
Legett, H. O. Wooten, Henry James, George L. Paxton, and E. B. Bynum.

[17] *Abilene Daily Reporter*, March 4, 1915.

[18] Ibid., March 5, 1915.

Again editor Anderson praised Judge Legett's energy, enthusiasm, and ability: Legett was the first to introduce the diversification idea, the first to inspire Taylor County farmers, the first to seek the program's sponsorship by the Chamber of Commerce, and the first to request from Agricultural Secretary David F. Houston the appointment of a diversification specialist who could direct the farmers' conversion to diversification.[19]

Area farmers who adopted the Legett Plan eagerly offered their successful operations as proof that the plan worked. Their letters to the editor appeared in nearly every edition as they described their day-to-day operations. O. S. McElroy, who notified the editor at the beginning that he had decided to farm "a-la-mode Legett," proudly announced at a later date that his efforts were entirely successful.[20]

Taylor County statistics on farm export products soon proved that other farmers shared farmer McElroy's success. From February 9 to March 8, 1915, the county's farmers shipped 1,440,000 eggs—ten railroad carloads—to both eastern and western markets. Farm agent Duck claimed that Abilene's egg exports made it the largest egg-shipping center in West Texas if not in the entire state. Based upon Duck's statement, Legett inserted in subsequent speeches the suggestion that the cackle of the hen was Taylor County's clarion of prosperity.[21]

The *Dallas News* informed its readers that Taylor County farmer L. B. Ivy regularly delivered his eggs to the Abilene market in a $2,000 automobile that chickens, hogs, and cows paid for. Ivy claimed that he had arrived in Taylor County from Hill County, Texas, in 1902, $250 in debt, but that he had become a wealthy man by practicing diversified farming on three hundred and sixty acres. At approximately the same time, the first railroad car filled exclusively with Abilene-grown hens left for New York City. The shipment included 54,986 pounds of live poultry valued at $7,385.86.

Abilene banks reflected the new prosperity. Their combined deposits on March 4, 1915, totaled $1,528,296.35—an amount so vast, reported editor Anderson, that the average person would not enjoy the task of counting the money. The report delighted Legett, who

19 Ibid.
20 Ibid., March 7, 1915.
21 Ibid., March 9, 1915.

continued to serve as a director of the largest of Abilene's three banks, and he composed a new letter of congratulations and encouragement to farmers in the Abilene area:

To the Farmers of Taylor County:

I have been criticized for making the statement that this is the "best country on earth. . . ." Considered with reference to healthfulness, the elevation, climatic conditions, fertility of soil, the moral worth and character of the people who dwell here, all in all, the statement is justified.

The last census showed that we have 2,400 farms in Taylor County. . . . The cotton crop of 1914 . . . yielded $1,500,000.00 or $625.00 to the farm. It will thus be seen that the average farm made on cotton last year an average of $1.71 per day.

I believe that there is not a farmer in the county who could not have made at least $2.00 a day out of a respectable size flock of chickens and turkeys. I am equally as certain that there are but few farmers in the county who could not have made $2.00 a day out of a dozen brood sows, and I am fully persuaded that one-half or three-fourths of our farmers could have made $2.00 a day out of eight or ten good cows.

Think of the result if every farmer in the county would arrange to make $6.00 a day out of chickens, hogs, and dairy products. This income would bring to our farmers $5,256,000.00 per year and then add $1,500,000.00 for cotton and we have the enormous income of $6,756,000.00 annually to our farmers.

I do not wish to condemn cotton raising. Far from it. On the contrary, this is a fairly good cotton country, but secondary and subordinate to the main things poultry, hogs, and dairy products. . . .

Very respectfully,
K. K. Legett [22]

The spring months provided new evidence that the Legett Plan worked. The Taylor County Diversification and Marketing Association collected for shipment eighty-eight surplus hogs from seven county farmers. Each hog weighed between 150 and 175 pounds; collectively the shipment required a special railroad car. The association hoped that by shipping in carloads it could secure better market prices. To their great satisfaction the experiment succeeded. Farm agent I. B. Duck announced that Fort Worth purchasers paid good prices—from

[22] Ibid., March 14, 1915.

6.5 cents to 7.5 cents per pound. Two months later another carload of hogs brought 7.9 cents per pound.

By mid-June, farmers in the Tuscola valley of south Taylor County harvested approximately thirty-eight bushels of wheat per acre and thirty-four bushels of oats. On July 7, Richard W. Burrage, a buyer from the Sherman (Texas) Milling Company, claimed that Taylor County wheat was the best he had ever seen. To prove his point he purchased twenty-six carloads for immediate shipment to Sherman. Meanwhile, several carloads of purebred Holstein cattle arrived from Wisconsin. W. M. Steward was so proud of his carload of "animal aristocrats" that he met them at the station, lined them in single file along the railroad track, and hired a professional photographer to capture the scene for posterity.

Before the year ended, dairy-farm production in Taylor County increased to such an extent that the Nissley Creamery Company of Fort Worth inaugurated daily pickup and delivery service for farmers in the area around Nugent, Buffalo Gap, Hamby, Elmdale, Potosi, Dudley, Caps, View, Tye, Iberis, Hawley, Hodges, Cedar Gap, Sambo, Tuscola, and Ovalo. With the new service, Chamber of Commerce secretary Wood urged every cow owner in the Abilene country to produce dairy products.

Other Texans noticed Taylor County's success. In April a special nine-coach trainload of Dallas trade excursionists (businessmen) visited Abilene. Members of the Abilene Chamber of Commerce escorted them to Elks' Hall on North First Street, where more than three hundred Abilene businessmen joined them for refreshments and speech-making. Mayor E. N. Kirby called upon K. K. Legett to explain how the Abilene country had climbed from last place to the head of the list in the matter of diversification. A newsman later claimed that Legett's statistical speech created a small sensation.

Legett claimed that Taylor County farmers increased their monthly income in 1915 above that of 1914 by 30 percent in eggs, 30 percent in chickens and turkeys, and 50 percent in butter and butter fat. He told the Dallas men that no agricultural combination could equal the chicken, dairy cow, and hog combination, and if the trend continued he believed Taylor County could stop worrying about the seasons.

Impressed by Legett's figures, the Dallas visitors reported his claims to R. V. Holland, publisher of *Holland's Magazine* and *Farm and Ranch*, and to E. H. Gray-Crane, the publisher's Chicago-based business manager. The two men traveled to Abilene, toured the area, made detailed notes of its agricultural production, and later wrote that West Texas would eventually become a vast agricultural empire.

Legett's hectic pace worried his family, and they implored him to slow his stride. He insisted that he had never felt better. Indeed his pace quickened as he helped Simmons College—he had rejoined the board of trustees in 1914—take advantage of the new prosperity and begin a campaign to raise money for a new dormitory for women. Throughout 1915 Legett seemed incapable of turning down any invitation to speak in behalf of agricultural diversification or Simmons College.

Finally, on a Tuesday evening in early June, shortly following his address at the formal opening of the Fair Park natatorium, Legett collapsed. His friends rushed him to his home and Mrs. Legett summoned a doctor. A thorough examination revealed that Legett suffered only from heat exhaustion, but the physician prescribed more rest. Mrs. Legett and Ruth eventually convinced Legett that he could rest only by leaving Abilene. He agreed to go to a health resort at Mineral Wells only upon the condition that his wife and younger daughter would accompany him. Within a week he complained that the enforced inactivity bored him. When he heard a report from home that I. B. Duck might be transferred from his Abilene assignment, he announced to his family that he must return to Abilene "to rescue Mr. Duck."

Legett visited town after town to deliver the same proclamation: Duck was Taylor County's most valuable natural asset and should be kept. Such support from Legett and other area leaders produced an arrangement that enabled Duck to remain in Taylor County. The United States government agreed to provide $500, the Abilene Chamber of Commerce pledged $250, and the Taylor County Commissioner's Court pledged $500 toward the farm agent's annual salary.

Prosperity prevailed as agricultural diversification spread and crucial rains continued. With spirits high, Abilene businessmen decided to follow the Dallas example and inaugurated a trade excursion through central West Texas. Representatives of Abilene businesses reserved space on a train—"The Prosperity Special." Their immediate purpose was to advertise the approaching Central West Texas Fair and Fat Stock Show, but in a larger sense they hoped to convince neighboring towns and counties that Abilene was the commercial, industrial, educational, financial, and agricultural center of the area. To assist them in spreading good will at every whistle stop, they would be accompanied by the Abilene concert band and "the very pick of Abilene's colony of orators, noted for their ability to spellbind the crowds."

At eight o'clock in the morning on Wednesday, September 8, the train pulled away from the Texas and Pacific depot with lighthearted representatives of eighty-five Abilene business firms. For three busy days they visited thirty-three West Texas towns along a five-hundred-mile route. Enroute they used the rails of the Wichita Valley Railroad, the Houston and Texas Central, the Kansas City, Mexico, and Orient, the Texas and Pacific, and the Abilene and Southern. Advertised as a comfortable train of Pullmans, the special train assigned each passenger two spaces, a sleeping space and a sitting space. Throughout the journey, however, the aisles were jammed with excursionists visiting back and forth between cars and preparing themselves for the program at the next stop.

Frank Grimes, new staff correspondent for the *Abilene Daily Reporter*, accompanied the delegation and reported their activities. Among scores of items, the following are typical of those prepared for the folks back home:

Hamlin, Tex., Sept. 8—The Abilene Boosters, after their departure from the banner city of the West this morning, everybody in the best of humor and eager for the chance to show the great advantage offered by their home town, arrived at Hamlin at noon today, after visiting Stamford, Anson, and Tuxedo, all of which cities did themselves proud in welcoming the Abilenians. . . . At Stamford the bunch paraded to the square in good form, and the band blazing away for all it was worth.

Loraine, Tex., Sept. 9—Loraine did herself handsome in the reception which she tendered. Iced watermelons were put on the train. W. L. Edmondson made the welcome address and Secretary Wood responded. There was a good crowd present.

San Angelo, Texas, Sept. 10—A magnificent reception and banquet was tendered the Boosters at Hotel Landon. . . . Later, there was an immense crowd at the Orient depot who followed the parade. This marked the red letter day in the history of the two cities.

At six o'clock on Friday evening, more than a thousand Abilenians welcomed the "trippers" home as fire whistles blew, friends shouted greetings, and the throng sang "The Greenest Spot We've Even Seen, Abilene Oh! Abilene." The Boosters paraded to North Third and back to TeePee Park and sang to the tune of "What S'matter with Father?":

> What s'matter with Abilene?
> She's all right.
> What s'matter with Abilene?
> She's in sight.
> San Angelo's wet. Sweetwater's dry.
> We're boosting Abilene high as the sky.
> What s'matter with Abilene?
> She's all right.[23]

To no one's surprise, the directors of the Central West Texas Fair voted to make diversification its theme for 1916. According to reporter Grimes, Abilene had created and thought out more diversification movements than any city of its size in the Southwest, and as a consequence newspaper editors in every section of Texas sent reporters to cover the events of the fair. The *Fort Worth Star-Telegram* dispatched Joe Warren, whose articles and photographs appeared on the front page of the October 10 issue and continued on several succeeding pages. Warren praised Taylor County's "exceptionally fine agricultural products," which, he believed, "prove what can be done by farmers who try."[24]

The publicity centered upon the diversification program attracted to Taylor County many new settlers who bought farm land for the specific purpose of diversified farming. Its influence was soon verified by the United States Census Bureau's report in early 1916 that Abilene's population had increased from 9,204 in 1910 to 13,522 in

23 *Abilene Daily Reporter*, September 12, 1915.
24 In the *Abilene Reporter*, October 12, 1916.

1915. Not all of Taylor County's new farmers came from other sections or states; some native Abilenians merely changed occupations. On March 31, 1915, for example, Joe Hill, longtime head of the produce department at the Hale, Sons, and Keen grocery store resigned his job and announced that he would move his family to a farm at Iberis, where he planned to raise chickens, hogs, cows, and other country produce. More significantly, farm agent I. B. Duck announced a few months later that he would resign his position on January 1, 1916, and move his family to a farm south of Abilene. Having helped so many others change to diversified farming, Duck explained, he wanted to go back to farming to see what he could do.

The Legett Plan thus altered to a significant degree the general direction of Taylor County's agricultural development. Production statistics proved the program's impact: wheat acreage increased 20 percent from 1914 to 1915 and cotton acreage decreased 24 percent. A similar statewide change occurred that year, while nationally cotton acreage decreased by 5,871 acres.[25]

Few farmers in Taylor County questioned the wisdom of shifting from a single-crop system. As early as 1915 merchants reported that their farm customers no longer bought food on credit; instead, the storekeepers were in debt to the farmers for back supplies of eggs and chickens. In 1916 the *Fort Worth Record* claimed that West Texas farmers no longer depended upon cotton as a money crop:

Notwithstanding the light cotton crop, conditions are far better than for several years past. The farmers have been greatly benefitted by the campaign for diversification, and with less cotton are in better shape to pay their bills than in former years.

Cotton has always been the money crop of Texas but this has been changed. Small products of the farm have put the farmers of West Texas on a pay-as-you-go basis.

West Texas is right now in better shape than it has ever been. Money is more plentiful. . . .

Abilene is sending thousands of dollars' worth of cream to Fort Worth every month. . . .

Farmers in Taylor County are shipping carloads of hogs to this market where before there was not a carload of hogs in the entire country.

. . . New buildings are going up, farm improvements under way, and

[25] *Abilene Daily Reporter*, August 2, 1915.

merchants are looking forward to the largest and best fall business in their history.[26]

Legett apparently grew concerned, however, that West Texans might place too much confidence in diversification. He began to re-mind them that the current prosperity was in large part a result of increased precipitation. They must, therefore, guard against those periods when the rains diminished and grain crops—as well as cotton crops—withered in the fields. With such thoughts occupying his mind, Legett entitled his 1916 Fourth of July speech "Frugality" even though the area had never been more prosperous. He suggested to his holiday audience that they should pay more attention to the accumula-tion of property and money and buy fewer of the things they did not need. "A good rule for the farmer to adopt would be that every time a trip is made to town it shall mean an increase in the bank account, or the cash of the family. If there is a need for a sack of flour that costs $1.00, let there be $1.50 of produce sold. If there is a plow to be purchased, let the plow wait until the wheat, maize, or cotton crop is ready for market."[27]

As the war in Europe spread and reports of food shortages reached the United States, Legett increased his pleas for frugality. The nation directed larger and larger proportions of its food production to the warring nations, and Texans stepped up their cultivation of grains and vegetables. In the Abilene area, therefore, Legett's diversification pro-gram quickly merged with the local war effort. He prepared and filed a manuscript (which is undated and appears to be the first draft of a formal address) at the approximate time of the November, 1917, Bolshevik Revolution in Russia, in which he included the following statement: "The most important and patriotic service we can render at this time is to aid the movement for increased provisions and for conserving the supply now on hand. But few people realize the real condition of the world in the matter of foods for human consump-tion. Unless this condition is relieved and relieved by our people, and this done at once, the consequences will simply be fearful."[28]

As Legett reflected upon the diversification program and its place

[26] Ibid., September 18, 1916.
[27] Ibid., July 4, 1916.
[28] See copy in Legett Family Records, file 3, paper 12.

in the area's future economy, he concluded that Abilene must increase its economic diversification. The war would someday end and the rains would eventually diminish; hence, precautions should be initiated to guard against economic recessions similar to that in 1911–1913. He composed an open letter "To the Citizens of Abilene," and, for reasons unknown, he preferred anonymity. The letter was signed "A Citizen." He asked Abilenians to look into the possibilities of expanding business diversification. He reminded them that towns as large as Abilene could not support themselves indefinitely by producing only agricultural products; therefore, if Abilene continued to grow, they must create and develop industrial production. Just as they had made Abilene an educational center, they must make it, also, a center of small factory enterprises. He believed many small businesses would prosper immediately, but he recommended specifically a wholesale drygoods store, a wholesale auto-accessories and electrical-supply house, a cotton mill, a cotton-glove factory, an overall factory, an iron foundry, and a candy factory. Legett added: "Abilene has got to do bigger business from now on. . . . To retain her prestige we have got to become city headquarters and a market for Central West Texas. . . . The people are going to supply their wants from somewhere. WHY NOT ABILENE?" [29]

Thus K. K. Legett demonstrated his inability to narrow his interests, slow his pace, or control his enthusiasm for anything that touched Abilene's present or future needs. The completion of one project merely led to another, but there developed at times situations quite beyond his control. While such situations could never monopolize his concentration, they could sometimes divide his attention. In the midst of his diversification campaign, two events at home engrossed him as perhaps nothing else could—both of his daughters, Julia and Ruth, chose those busy days to inform him of their approaching marriages.

On Christmas Day, 1914, Judge and Mrs. Legett opened their home for their traditional holiday reception. At the beginning, the event differed from those of earlier years only in the sense that it was held on Christmas Day instead of New Year's Day. When all guests had arrived, Judge Legett announced "the coming marriage of Miss

[29] *Abilene Reporter*, March 5, 1916.

Julia to Dr. Luther James Pickard," a local physician, on February 25. Following a series of parties and receptions through January and February, the groom's family and friends (from Weatherford, Texas) met with the bride's family and friends (most of whom were from Abilene and Sweetwater) for the ceremony at Abilene's First Baptist Church. At the reception which followed, the bride's only sister, Ruth, caught the bridal bouquet as she stood at the foot of the stairway. This symbolic gesture indeed proved prophetic. In December of that year, another announcement read:

Judge and Mrs. K. K. Legett
will give in marriage their daughter
Ruth
to
Mr. Percy Jones
on the evening of Saturday the twenty-fifth
of
December
Nineteen hundred and fifteen
Abilene, Texas
602 Meander Street

The groom, Mrs. Robertson reported, was a civil engineer of the Abilene and Southern railway and was held in highest esteem by his many friends. Within one calendar year, therefore, both of the Legett daughters moved from the mansion and into their own homes. Much to the Legetts' delight, they continued to reside in Abilene. Pickard practiced medicine in Abilene and Jones, whose uncle Morgan Jones, was a prominent railroad builder and operator, continued to work with the Abilene and Southern Railroad.

His daughters' sudden departure from the home seemed to spur Legett on to greater efforts in his crusade for diversification. Mrs. Legett, freed from her parental responsibilities for the first time in years, devoted more of her time to hostess duties at the mansion. The Legett home served as a meeting place for endless gatherings of the board of trustees from Simmons College, the board of deacons from the First Baptist Church, the Abilene Bar Association, the church choir, the committees of various diversification programs, the directors of the Central West Texas Fair, the candidates, campaign managers, and directors of local and state Democratic party organizations, the directors of the Farmers and Merchants Bank, and for a constant stream of educators, clergymen, cattlemen, and farmers from all parts of the state and nation.

Mrs. Legett learned to accept the fact that she could not protect her husband from himself. There was never a day when he did not overwork, but no man worked with greater enthusiasm and satisfaction.

*I am going to be very careful, for I must confess that in my youth the greatest temptation for me to resist was a nice, friendly, sociable game of "a nickle ante and a dollar limit." This oil business is playing it with no limit and the joker wild.*

CHAPTER THIRTEEN

# No Booth at the Fair

WHEN warfare erupted in Europe in 1914, K. K. Legett was as surprised as the great majority of United States citizens who paid little or no attention to international affairs. Germany seemed as remote as any other distant land. If West Texans felt any concern about American involvement, President Woodrow Wilson reassured them with his statement that the conflict could not touch this nation. Most Abilenians supported Wilson's diplomatic maneuvers to keep the peace and generally distrusted the war-preparedness program proposed by Theodore Roosevelt and General Leonard Wood. When Germany sought an alliance with Mexico, however, West Texans' attitudes changed. The editor of the *Roby Banner* spoke for most of them: "A sick mule on the border is of more importance to us than the outcome of any of the innumerable clashes across the water." [1]

As Legett approached his sixtieth birthday, domestic issues at home—looking for oil, trying to get West Texas A&M college for Abilene, reintroducing the Legett Plan, and worrying about Governor James E. Ferguson's impeachment—permitted Legett and his Abilene friends little time for warfare in Europe or military intrigue in Mexico City. The statewide search for oil in 1916 attracted most attention on the domestic front. The possibility that great oil deposits lay below the dusty surface of the cattle and cotton lands of West Texas created an excitement unmatched by any news from across the ocean. Abilenians such as Legett wore two hats during the excitement of the search. As loyal boosters of civic enterprises they purchased stock in various oil drilling companies, but as landholders they worked alone to arrange for oil tests on their private property.

[1] In the *Abilene Reporter*, July 21, 1916.

The *Abilene Reporter* oil news items grew into an oil-news section as the industry expanded. Most reports centered upon company activities rather than upon individual searches for oil, and from time to time editor Frank Grimes provided the historical background to the Texas oil discoveries. Texans had believed that huge oil deposits lay beneath them from the time of an accidental discovery in Nacogdoches County in 1867. No major production followed at that time nor after a second discovery in 1889 at Corsicana. A major strike at Beaumont in 1901, however, produced a two-hundred-foot gusher and attracted national attention. During the following twelve months, the Spindletop oil field produced more than twelve million barrels of oil and launched the Texas oil boom. New discoveries in 1904 and 1911 kept interest high as the search spread throughout Texas. Legett purchased a few shares of capital stock in the Hope Oil Company of Abilene on October 30, 1911, but the company never located a producing well.[2] Rumors of new fields multiplied throughout 1912 in spite of meager evidence to substantiate them. As late as December 11, 1912, editor Grimes reported that "the Abilene atmosphere is so filled with rumors of the discovery of oil and gas that they could be stirred with a stick."

Representatives of various oil drilling companies from California caused spirits to rise and fall as they moved in and out of town but, as the months and years passed without a single location in the Abilene area, interest waned. Suddenly in 1916 Frank P. Fox, who represented an oil firm in Indianapolis, rekindled local interest when he drilled a well approximately six miles south of Abilene. Men, women, and children rushed to the drilling site in such numbers that Fox threatened to build a barricade around the area. The spectators, he complained, turned the area into a picnic ground and their children climbed upon the equipment and constantly flirted with death.

Eventually Fox called a meeting at the Citizens National Bank and notified a group of local businessmen that he would abandon the well at 2,700 feet unless he had struck oil at that level. The businessmen offered to donate $2,000 to the project if Fox would continue to drill to a level of 3,300 feet. Fox agreed, and at 3,230 feet a small but fine grade of oil—which contained "37 percent gasoline," a promising

[2] Certificate of title is in Legett Family Records, paper 498.

sign—seeped through the sand and rose to the top of the well. On February 14, 1916, Fred T. Wood siphoned off two quarts of oil and rushed it to town, where he placed one bottle of the greenish-black liquid on a cigar case at the Hotel Grace and passed the other bottle from hand to hand throughout Abilene.

Even as the awed citizens smelled and looked at the first proof of "Abilene ile," Fox dampened their spirits with his announcement that he would abandon the well. He explained that there was not enough oil in the immediate vicinity of the well to produce a profitable flow. As he pulled his casing from the well on March 2, he expressed a conviction that he had drilled at the very edge of a major oil structure. His Indianapolis associates had lost $45,000 on the test, however, and were unwilling to invest more. He planned, instead to commence wildcat operations in the Oklahoma fields.

The strategy succeeded. Local businessmen hurriedly organized an independent oil company, sold shares at $50 each, and raised $11,000 for Fox's second well. Community pride and perpetual optimism kept the shrewd but honest oil man in Taylor County. On March 13 Fox located the second well only one and three-fourths miles northwest of the original test. His procedures clearly underscored the fact that the industry had developed few scientific processes to locate underground oil fields. A local newsman described the scene at the second location:

On a bald hill from which can be seen the entire Abilene country and which is the apex of a vast inverted bowl, a stake was driven at 5:25 Monday afternoon to mark the spot where the second test for oil will be sunk. . . .

The party on location went out in Dr. J. M. Alexander's car. Dr. Alexander, Fred Wood, Cross Payton, W. A. Riney, and a Fourth Estate were members of the party. Dr. Alexander and Mr. Payton, because of their well-known luck in financial ventures of this particular kind, were chosen as stake driver and holder, respectively. Fred Wood went along as High Priest, Mr. Riney as engineer and geologist, and the newspaperman as a sort of "filler." "Luck" was the shibboleth they chose. Each of the five prayed to his own special gods of luck and worked every rabbit foot in sight.

Fred Wood, who was present when the stake was driven at the "dry hole," announced that any man who used any of the hocus-pocus used at the other well would be murdered on the spot.[3]

Earlier, stockholders had named their organization the Hunch Oil and Gas Company of Abilene. When they nominated George L. Paxton president, he declined to serve unless secretary Fred T. Wood could define the word *hunch*. "The nearest I can get to it is that 'hunch' means an inward feeling that we'll all get rich on that oil out there," Wood responded.

Legett purchased two shares of capital stock—the average investment of all stockholders. Their investments were less an expression of confidence in the Fox enterprise than in Abilene's future oil industry. The company was just another civic activity that needed publicity during its early stages of development.

At 1,890 feet Fox's second well struck oil sand, and within minutes a small oil flow erupted. Fox instructed his crew to drill forty feet deeper into the second layer of oil sand. The oil flow increased, but the anticipated gusher failed to develop. Fox estimated a flow of fifteen barrels of oil per day. Abilenians promptly responded to the news: "It was not long until automobiles loaded with men in various states of excitement were burning up the pike to the well site. . . . The gas could be smelled at a distance of 150 yards. Not until they saw the oil in the drain would some of them believe. . . ."[4]

Fox's cautious reminder that the flow was still too slight for profitable production—that he would have to drill deeper to a third sand level—failed to dampen Abilene spirits. Disaster struck before he could drill to the deeper level: a windstorm toppled and destroyed the eighty-two-foot derrick. It was August 19 before Fox could rebuild the derrick, drill to the third level of sand, and install oil pumps. Meanwhile, the price of Abilene real estate, with mineral rights included, spurted upward and created a mild real-estate boom. The June 4 issue of the *Abilene Reporter* advertised both farm land and oil land. The most expensive farm land was offered at $30 per acre, whereas the least expensive oil land was offered at $40 per acre.

[3] *Abilene Reporter*, March 14, 1916.
[4] Ibid., May 23, 1916.

On Saturday afternoon, August 19, 1916, K. K. Legett stood with other company stockholders and watched the pumping of Abilene's first commercial oil. When Fox informed them that the well would produce approximately twenty-five barrels of oil per day, they were clearly disappointed, but they insisted that it was a good little well. They later voted to operate the well for publicity purposes, to increase the stock of the Hunch Oil Company to $35,000, and to drill at least two more wells. A third well, completed in February, 1917, produced about the same flow as the second. Finally, while war raged in Europe and state senators in Austin prepared to impeach Governor James E. Ferguson, stockholders of the Hunch Oil Company met in the offices of the Chamber of Commerce and reluctantly voted to dispose of their holdings. On September 9 they announced the sale of company equipment to Reese Allen, a well-known oil operator in Electra, Texas.

Reports of a major oil strike at Ranger, approximately seventy miles east of Abilene, kept hopes alive, but during the next year no drilling company moved nearer than Shackelford County. More than a score of Abilene businessmen, including Legett, attended the Southwestern Oil Men's banquet at the Metropolitan Hotel in Fort Worth on December 7 and 8, 1918. Editor Grimes solicited a statement from J. M. Radford and Legett as they stood in the hotel lobby:

J. M. Radford: "I do not understand this oil game business, but it's interesting."

Judge Legett: "I am going to be very careful, for I must confess that in my youth the greatest temptation for me to resist was a nice, friendly, sociable game of 'a nickel ante and dollar limit.' This oil business is playing it with no limit and the joker is wild.[5]

Later oil discoveries in Burkburnett, Breckenridge, and Desdemona dramatically raised Texas production and rekindled Abilene interest to such an extent that the eighteenth amendment to the United States Constitution—the national prohibition amendment—attracted less attention than the latest oil news. Editor Grimes praised "the greatest moral accomplishment that the world has ever seen," but his

[5] Ibid., December 8, 1918.

front page carried a single story on prohibition and five articles on the oil industry.

Time proved distressingly clearly, however, that no major oil field existed in Abilene's immediate vicinity. Large landowners such as Legett continued their private search for oil, but collectively they sought other ways to help Abilene benefit from the oil industry. Eventually they secured the construction of a Gulf-Texas refinery plant in southeast Abilene, a Gulf Well Drilling Machinery Manufacturing Company next door to the refinery, and the headquarters of the Burkburnett-Ranger Oil Company.

Legett's personal activities in the oil industry in 1919 included his purchase of stock in the Rosson Oil Company of Fort Worth.[6] He also employed J. E. Carpenter, a geologist, to estimate the possibilities of oil deposits in Legett's Taylor County and Callahan County lands. Carpenter examined the property and submitted the following reports in September and October 1919:

September 18th, 1919: . . . The whole of this tract [Callahan County] lies completely inside a clearly defined giant oil Structure. . . . There appears not to be a single square foot of your holdings that does not show oil paying quantities. . . . The fact that wells near your Callahan lands have all struck more or less oil, shows you are in or near an oil-bearing area.[7]

October 2, 1919: . . . It is conclusively proven that there are pay oil sands in this [Taylor County] section of the country. . . . The reasonable conclusion is that oil will be developed on your property in commercial quantities at depths ranging from 1800 to 2000 feet.[8]

On the basis of Carpenter's report, Legett made two lengthy trips to southern California in search of an experienced and reputable oil drilling company. It was typical of the former Arkansas farm boy that Legett would spend thousands of dollars to bring a California oil firm to West Texas but fret about the price of his rented hotel room while he was in Californiia. In a letter to his son and daughter-in-law on February 21, 1920, he explained that he was giving up his $17 per

[6] Certificate of title is in Legett Family Records, paper 496.
[7] J. E. Carpenter to K. K. Legett, Legett Family Records, paper 500.
[8] Ibid., paper 501.

week room at the Stowell Hotel in Los Angeles and would move to an unnamed hotel in nearby Glenwood where rooms rented for $5 per week.[9]

The family papers fail to reveal Legett's oil activities from this point forward, and he remained uncharacteristically secretive upon his return to Texas. Obviously he had changed to the hat of the private oil speculator. When a local reporter attempted to interview him about his California activities, he commented only upon the California citrus-fruit industry. The purpose of his western trip did not become public until April 18, 1920, when a local newspaper item stated:

Drilling of an oil well on the Legett tract six miles east of the city is to be begun in the very near future according to an announcement made Saturday by E. B. Moore, Secretary and Treasurer of the Texas Treasure Oil Company, which opened offices in the Radford Building this past week. The company also maintains offices in Los Angeles, but now that they are to begin drilling soon near Abilene, the main offices are to be moved to this city.[10]

The initial arrangement apparently collapsed, however, since Legett returned to California in July and, according to a letter addressed to his children, still sought a drilling company willing to negotiate a contract and move to Texas. In the letter he made numerous but inexplicable references to his oil interests, but the following excerpts reveal his determination to explore all possible avenues to an oil contract:

There is not much interest here now in Texas oil. . . . If we didn't have about $16,000.00 in our pockets we would meet with a powerful cold reception. I have not yet sounded out the situation sufficiently to even guess at what I am up against. . . . I may have to spend all the balance of my life over here in order to do business, but I am sure going to make a determined effort.

It is now nearly church time and I am going to try to find a Baptist church. I may run into a dozen different creeds, but I think they all use that wizard board.[11]

9 Legett to Kade and Annie Maude, Legett Family Records, file 4, paper 12.
10 *Abilene Reporter*, April 18, 1920.
11 K. K. Legett to his children, July 25, 1920, Legett Family Records, file 4, paper 13.

In spite of his determination, K. K. Legett did not locate any profitable quantities of oil on his property. A promising strike by Andy Urban in September, 1922, near Legett's Elmdale property later proved to be a dry hole. As time eventually proved, the Abilene Chamber of Commerce had to lower its lofty expectations and work toward making Taylor County "the axis around which the West Texas oil wheel will rotate." As they had done so often in the past, they stitched a silver lining to the cloud:

> Abilene has made this city the administrative oil center by recent completion of the Alexander and Clinton office buildings. . . .
> If Abilene becomes the oil center it seems destined to be it will be the location of the general offices and not the heart of the actual production. There will not be the mad scramble that prevailed at Ranger, but instead an orderly direction of business from this central point.[12]

Still another issue helped to divert Abilene attention from the European conflict. In 1917 and 1918 Abilene competed vigorously, and sometimes desperately, to become the home of a proposed West Texas Agricultural and Mechanical College. Occasionally no other project seemed quite as important, and at times the war news and the oil news disappeared from the front page of the *Abilene Reporter*. At the end, however, Legett and all other Abilenians incredulously watched their apparent victory turn into defeat as the issue became entangled in the impeachment and removal from office of Governor James E. Ferguson.

Legett's exact role in the affair is difficult to assess. Under normal circumstances he would stand at the center of any effort to bring another institution of higher learning to Abilene. In this case, however, his name frequently appears in the records but his activities seem comparatively minor. At the age of sixty, he was perhaps forced by events of 1917–1918 to establish certain priorities. As soon as the West Texas A&M campaign got underway, Legett participated in every petition to state officials and every plea for public support, but with few exceptions he remained in the background.

A longtime friend of Legett's, President W. B. Bizzell of Texas A&M, made in 1916 the first serious suggestion for a similar school

[12] *Abilene Reporter*, January 31, 1926.

in West Texas. The idea won immediate support around the state, including that from representative F. O. Fuller, who subsequently became Speaker of the House. The measure moved quickly through both houses of the legislature, and on February 21 Governor Ferguson signed the bill into law.

In March delegates from a score of West Texas towns met at Sweetwater to agree upon procedural matters. Abilene's four delegates included Legett, Simmons professor O. H. Cooper, state representative Eugene De Bogory, and attorney R. W. Haynie. In May the Chamber of Commerce appointed W. A. Minter chairman of the A&M committee and recommended a tax base of 4 percent on real estate and 2 percent on personal property to underwrite the costs of land for the new campus. A few days later Judge J. F. Cunningham presented Abilene's formal bid to the governor. In June Governor Ferguson announced that he would head the campus-location committee; other members included Speaker Fuller, Lieutenant Governor W. P. Hobby, Commissioner of Agriculture Fred W. Davis, and Superintendent of Public Instruction W. F. Doughty.

Abilene editor Grimes informed his readers that Judge K. K. Legett was intimately acquainted with Davis and Doughty and that Legett's old friend, President Bizzell, would accompany the committee on its tour of proposed locations. The committee visited San Angelo on Monday, June 11, and notified Abilenians that their city was next on the list.

Five carloads of businessmen immediately drove to Ballinger, where they met their guests. At eight o'clock the following morning a caravan of automobiles left Ballinger with the governor in the lead car driven by W. G. Swenson, Speaker Fuller in the second car driven by C. J. Pearce, Commissioner Davis in the third car driven by George L. Paxton, President Bizzell in the fourth car driven by H. O. Wooten and accompanied by K. K. Legett, and Superintendent Doughty in the fifth car driven by city school superintendent R. D. Green.[13]

Enroute to Abilene the caravan stopped at the Elm Creek dam, approximately twenty-five miles southwest of Abilene, where scores of other Abilene businessmen prepared a barbecued lunch. Later, a mile-long parade of automobiles accompanied the visitors to Abilene.

[13] Lieutenant Governor Hobby did not accompany the committee on its inspection trip.

When the travelers reached the city limits at 5:00 P.M., five thousand men, women, and children lined the streets as Abilene's official welcoming party. Pictures and flattering biographies filled the front page of the local newspaper, and articles on the inside pages called attention to the town's "single distinguishing characteristic—its educational atmosphere."[14]

In late afternoon, as the hot June temperature receded and the dust settled, the hosts drove their guests to the proposed campus site approximately one mile southwest of town. The visitors viewed the two-thousand-acre tract from atop a specially constructed two-story observation tower. They returned to the Hotel Grace at eight o'clock for a formal reception and dinner and departed the following morning to visit other West Texas towns.

Two weeks later, on June 28, the locating committee met in Austin to make their final decision. Rumors persisted that only Abilene, San Angelo, Amarillo, Lubbock, and Snyder remained in contention and that Abilene had at least two of the five votes. Back in the *Abilene Reporter* office, editor Grimes awaited word from his staff correspondent in Austin, J. A. Fernandez. At 1:45 P.M. on Friday, June 29, Grimes received the expected bulletin from Austin; he swept aside all other headline news to make space for the major announcement:

ABILENE GETS A. & M. COLLEGE
BIG CELEBRATION SATURDAY

Hundreds of celebrants gathered at TeePee Lawn on Saturday night to hear an impromptu band concert and to celebrate Abilene's momentous victory.

Challenges from the defeated contenders arose almost immediately. They demanded to know the names of those members of the five-man committee who voted for Abilene. The original announcement from the governor's office stated only that Abilene had received the required three votes on the second ballot. However, Commissioner Davis stated that he voted for Snyder on both ballots; Lieutenant Governor Hobby explained that he voted for San Angelo on the first ballot and for Amarillo on the second; Speaker Fuller claimed that he voted for Haskell on the first ballot but refused to reveal how he

[14] *Abilene Reporter*, June 13, 1917.

voted on the second ballot, although he insisted that he had not voted for Abilene. Doughty and Ferguson stated that they had voted for Abilene in each instance. In spite of the obvious discrepancy, Governor Ferguson emphatically declared that his initial announcement was accurate and that there would be no rehearing. The *Dallas News*, nevertheless, demanded a recount.

Editor Grimes reminded his readers that the *Dallas News* was embroiled in a dispute with the governor concerning certain matters at the University of Texas and that the East Texas newspaper would use any pretense to discredit Ferguson. The governor recently had informed the regents at the university that they must dismiss President Robert E. Vinson and certain members of the faculty or risk his veto of all university appropriations for the coming year. The controversy flared into a statewide feud when the regents ignored the governor's demand.

Before most Abilenians realized what had happened, the West Texas A&M location issue had become part of a move to impeach Governor Ferguson. Most West Texans did not question the governor's integrity, but they insisted that he had made a mistake too costly to ignore. Some East Texans made more serious charges that Ferguson had committed fraud in the A&M matter and had acted irresponsibly in the University of Texas matter. Demands for impeachment and demands for a recount of committee votes mushroomed simultaneously. During the hot, bone-dry summer of 1917, tempers grew as heated as the weather.

On July 25 eleven West Texas towns—from Amarillo on the north to San Angelo on the south—sent representatives to a protest meeting at Sweetwater. Judge J. V. Cockrell tried unsuccessfully to convince them that the A&M issue was contrived by Speaker Fuller to justify his demands for Ferguson's impeachment. A majority of the representatives demanded a restraining order that would prevent temporarily the construction of the first college building.

Abilenians continued to express confidence that their original victory would prevail, although Governor Ferguson appeared to weaken under demands for a special session of the legislature. When the call was made, editor Grimes warned his readers to expect a bill of impeachment and a temporary injunction against construction of the new A&M. As the battle raged in Austin, the distressed editor tried to prepare Abilenians for the inevitable defeat: "Abilene expects to go on growing and making friends whatever happens. It is Abilene's way. The West must have a great city and it is Abilene's ambition to be that city."[15]

Two days later the state senate, acting as a high court of impeachment, sustained ten of the twenty-one charges against their governor, James E. Ferguson. On the following day, the new governor, W. P. Hobby, asked the legislature to repeal the earlier move to create the West Texas A&M College. On September 27 the requested legislation reached the governor's desk and Hobby added his signature.

Editor Grimes wrestled mightily to retain his professional composure, but in the end he succumbed to the temptation to express in print his readers' collective feelings:

Born in a storm [West Texas A&M] lived its entire life amid the most tempestuous scenes and died an unnatural death at the hands of envy and malice. That Abilene has lost the institution, for the present, is certain. That it has been treated unfair and unjust is equally certain. But Abilene is a good loser and will not be found crying wolf. . . .

Some day West Texas will have a voice in the legislative halls of Texas. Some day there will be another school to be located in this part of Texas. When that time comes Abilene will be in the fight.[16]

The following day the disappointed editor admitted that "it does hurt and it hurts bad." Although he stated that there was nothing to be gained by harsh criticism, an editorial on October 1 called for a division of Texas into three parts. "The state is too big for any one set of men to handle," he claimed. A day later, Richard H. McCarty expressed similar resentment in the *Albany News*: "Poor old West Texas has got another setback. The West Texas A&M bill was killed by the law makers of Texas. If it had been located somewhere down in the sticks, in a more favored spot politically, it would have stuck, but it fell through. We live by might, either by the sword or by ballots."[17]

Grimes made a final statement in the same issue of the *Abilene Reporter* that revealed another reason for his bitterness: "Governor

15Ibid., August 21, 1917.
16 Ibid., September 28, 1917.
17 *Albany News*, quoted in *Abilene Reporter*, October 2, 1917.

Hobby knew that the West is in the very midst of the most severe drought that was ever known out here since the country was placed upon an agricultural basis and must have realized the need for an institution of that character located in this country to teach improved methods of farming and of adaptation." All of West Texas suffered severely from the drought, and thus no Abilenian publicly voiced resentment toward the other towns in the area when they challenged Abilene's short-lived victory. Instead, Abilene centered its attack upon state officials in Austin. Although most of the protests to Abilene's original selection originated in Sweetwater, the Abilene Chamber of Commerce passed an enthusiastic resolution of support when Sweetwater later entered its bid to become the home of a state asylum for the insane.[18]

From time to time during the next few years, the West Texas Chamber of Commerce called upon the legislature to revive the West Texas A&M College bill, but no legislator outside of West Texas expressed interest. Consequently, when the Reverend J. W. Hunt called a mass meeting of Abilene businessmen and Methodist church leaders to discuss the possibilities of establishing a third church-related college in Abilene, the response was overwhelming. Abilene leaders pledged to donate $100,000 to a new Methodist college, and K. K. Legett, a Baptist, Henry Sayles, Jr., a Presbyterian, and J. M. Cunningham, a Methodist, pooled several of their adjoining lots in south Abilene to form a new campus.

Hunt continued his drive for a church school in spite of the legislature's unexpected vote in 1923 to create a West Texas technological college. In typical fashion Abilenians agreed to meet their prior commitments to the Methodist college and also to make a strong bid for the state technological college. They also reassured officials at the two existing colleges of their continued support by pledging $200,000 to Simmons College and $100,000 to Abilene Christian College. Since no other town in West Texas could equal Abilene's support of higher education, other contenders for the state college attempted to turn her strongest arguing point into a liability. Persons unknown printed and circulated around the state a political cartoon that portrayed a distressed mother (Abilene) pushing a baby carriage filled with four

[18] *Abilene Reporter*, November 19, 1917.

infants. While three infants (the church colleges) screamed with hunger, the fourth child (the state college), obviously sturdy and well-nourished, drank milk (state support) from the only available bottle (the state treasury). Abilenians saw no humor in the cartoon, and W. G. Kinsolving, who spoke for the Chamber of Commerce, called it "a punch below the belt." Bob Miller expressed the typical Abilenian's optimism, however, when he opened a new automobile service station and named it the Tech Service Company.[19]

On July 25, 1923, city officials welcomed the college-locating committee with the same enthusiasm they had shown for the A&M committee in 1917, but no welcoming committee met them beyond the city limits and no crowds lined the streets to observe their arrival. Quietly the committee inspected the proposed campus and departed. While they were in town, the *Abilene Reporter*, as before, placed on its front page pictures and biographies of the visiting group. In an obvious effort to impress the committee with the caliber of men who had built Abilene, editor Grimes also prepared a special four-page section under the banner headline. "The Professional Men Believe in the Future of Abilene as a Real City." K. K. Legett's picture and brief biography headed the list.[20] To counteract the publicity of the baby-carriage cartoon, pictures of the three college presidents—J. D. Sandefer of Simmons, J. P. Sewell of Abilene Christian, and J. W. Hunt of McMurry (the proposed Methodist college)—appeared on page ten with statements of their full support for the new state school.

Abilenians braced themselves for defeat, nevertheless, and insisted that the rivalry between the forty contending towns was friendly and light-hearted. George W. McDaniel, Jr. submitted to the local newspaper a "Dictionary of Words and Phrases Heard Every Day By the Locating Committee of the Texas Technological College":

ACCESSIBILITY—A common characteristic of thirty-seven towns in West Texas, each of which is "easily reached" from any direction whether located on a railroad and highway or not.

AGRICULTURE—A parlor term for farming. Thirty-seven towns in West Texas claim first place in this business.

CLIMATE—An ideal condition of weather that prevails in thirty-seven towns 365 days in every year. Sand storms and drouths don't count.

[19] Ibid., May 8, 1923.
[20] Ibid., July 25, 1923.

COLLEGE ATMOSPHERE—Something that it required thirty-two years to build in Abilene, but which thirty-six other towns claim an abundance of.

MARKETING PLACES—Place where people trade marbles, knives, horses, pigs, chickens, etc. Thirty-seven such places in West Texas.

RAINFALL—A species of water that prevails in thirty-seven towns to such an extent that drouths are unknown.

WATER—Heretofore very scarce in West Texas. Thirty-seven towns now have an inexhaustible supply.

WIND VELOCITY—So slow in West Texas that it doesn't turn the wind-mills enough to water a chicken.[21]


After the state location committee departed, McDaniel reminded his readers that Abilene already had won a prize in the contest; the town, he explained, had never looked prettier: weeds were cut, trees were pruned, lawns were mowed, fences were whitewashed, and tons of trash were hauled away.

Unfortunately, Abilene's clean face was its only reward. On August 8, 1923, the location committee announced in Fort Worth that Lubbock had won the new state college. Lubbock officials later noted that their first congratulatory telegram came from Abilene mayor Charles E. Coombes. Another Abilenian, unidentified, wired his congratulatory message to the governor of New Mexico. The anonymous message stated that Texas Tech should ultimately save New Mexico a considerable sum of money for educational purposes. Editor Grimes agreed. "Mind you, I'm not kicking Lubbock," he wrote, "but Texas seems to have a mania for placing its schools around the rim of this great state." [22]

Abilene's loss of the West Texas A&M College, its failure to locate a major oil field in the area, and the devastating drought of 1917 diverted attention from the European war in spite of the nation's gradual drift toward hostilities. Such preoccupation with local issues during the war was not unique in the western states. A. V. Wainwright, president of the American Public Service Company, toured the nation from Boston to Los Angeles and reported in obvious disgust that the Southwest was shamefully apathetic. Abilenians seemed less apathetic than nonbelligerent, and when Wilson ultimately signed, in April, 1917, the war measure against Germany, they concluded that this ac-

[21] Ibid., August 5, 1923.
[22] Ibid., August 10, 1923.

tion was somehow unavoidable. Nevertheless, when William Jennings
Bryan accepted an invitation to speak at Simmons College in May,
1917, more than three thousand West Texans flocked to the campus
to hear the former secretary of state describe his fruitless efforts to
keep the nation out of war. Bryan's pacifism had not diminished his
popularity among West Texans.

When the United States entered the war, however, most Abilenians gave their loyal support. They applauded young Lieutenant Robert M. Wagstaff's early departure with the Third Texas Infantry, they
met troop trains at the depot and gave food and gifts to the soldiers,
they oversubscribed every liberty-bond drive, they cheerfully observed
meatless Wednesdays, they converted Fair Park into a training camp
for Company I of the Texas Seventh Infantry, they instituted a com-
pulsory course in military drill at Simmons College, and they sent
many of their 1,056 eligible draftees into all branches of military
service.

No man in West Texas claimed to hate war more than K. K. Legett, but while the United States fought in the conflict he was among
Abilene's largest purchasers of war bonds, he served as chairman of
the Taylor County Military Entertainment Committee, and with his
son, Kade, he responded to Wilson's call for greater food production
by raising the largest herd of calves in Taylor County.[23] Although
Kade was eligible for the draft, he devoted his full time to stock and
grain production for military consumption and served during the war
as secretary for the West Texas District of the Texas Farmers' Institute. Legett's son-in-law, Percy Jones, continued to serve as an official
of the Abilene Southern Railroad Company, which was also designated a war-related occupation. Legett's second son-in-law, Dr. L. J. Pickard, enlisted on October 6, 1917, as a first lieutenant in the medical
corps and served throughout the war at Fort Riley, Kansas.

When the war ended Legett sat at his desk and penned a letter to
his daughter and son-in-law at Fort Riley:

Abilene, 11-14-18

My Dear Children—

I have been thinking to drop you a line ever since the 11th but it seems I

[23] Legett Family Records, paper 518, dated January 14, 1918. Notarized statement by Henry James.

never could get to it. . . . My mind ceased to work after 5 o'clock am. on
that date. I heard the news at 4 o'clock, and got up and dressed and sang
hallelujah until daylight. That was the greatest day in the world's history
since the Resurrection of Christ. I have felt like a new man ever since.
Mrs. L. says I look better than I have for years and I certainly feel better.
Yes, we are now in a new, and I hope, better world. We will have new
hopes, new aspirations, and new ambitions. It is *great, great, great.* . . .
    With much love to both, I remain

As Ever, Judge [24]

Legett looked upon the end of the war as a fresh starting point—
the beginning of a new chapter—in his life. He would develop new
hopes, new aspirations, and new ambitions, in spite of the fact that he
had begun his seventh decade of life. He had resigned once again as a
trustee at Simmons College.[25] He wanted to retire as referee in bankruptcy as soon as younger men returned home. Neither action, however, indicated a desire to slow his pace. Instead, he wanted more time
to search for oil, more time to speak out on issues while a new generation chaired the committees and boards, and more time, perhaps,
to convince West Texas farmers that they must return to diversification.

    As the nation returned to "normalcy," Legett's alert mind darted
in many directions: he addressed the Texas Bankers Association at its
annual convention and warned that domestic problems which resulted
from the European war were minor when compared to those that
would emerge with the return of peace. He hosted a lawn party at his
home and then informed his guests that there were people in Abilene
who could not afford medical assistance and thus the guests should
pay for their refreshments with a generous donation to Abilene's free
dispensary. As the postwar recession deepened, he developed a series
of public addresses entitled "Work More but Spend Less." He abandoned that thesis when the city commission, to his dismay, fired a
large percentage of the police, sanitation, and fire departments at a
time when Legett believed those departments should be enlarged. He
developed a second series of lectures entitled "Fiscal Responsibility."

[24] K. K. Legett to Lt. and Mrs. L. J. Pickard, Legett Family Records, file 4,
paper 3.
[25] *Minutes of the Board of Trustees*, vol. 2 (May 11, 1916), p. 15.

Later, when sponsors sought his support for a community celebration of Music Week, he stated that he was for anything that would advance Abilene in the right direction.[26]

Meanwhile, there seemed nothing Legett would not do for the Baptist church in West Texas: he spoke to church groups throughout the area when Simmons College sought funds for a new science hall; he repeated his schedule a short time later when Abilene Baptists decided to erect a West Texas Baptist Sanitarium; and in 1918, at age sixty-one, he volunteered to play baseball for the faculty team at their annual student-faculty fund-raising baseball game. No one could doubt Legett's sincerity when he stated in an address to the members of the Chamber of Commerce at their annual banquet in 1921 that "the world is getting better every day and in time it will become what God intended it to be."

It seemed never to occur to Legett that God's plan might not be equally clear to everyone. He left no trace of a suggestion that his aspirations were unique or in any sense unusual; indeed, he had a score of friends in Abilene who worked as hard as he worked for personal achievement and community betterment. Any man who lived along the 98th meridian learned early that he must face the realities of life with energy and optimism or perish. Those who survived the initial hardships seemed to thrive on challenge. As time passed, many community achievements were direct results of their response to earlier catastrophes. The survivers proved the truth of the cliché which they often preached: every cloud should have a silver lining.

Thus the driest year in Abilene's history, 1917, motivated a vote of 645 to 4 to sell $220,000 in water bonds for a dam at Elm Creek; the loss of West Texas A&M motivated a drive to establish McMurry College; and crop failure motivated the construction of windmills to irrigate gardens and water tanks to water stock. Some of Abilene's "clouds" returned time and time again. Drought was a constant threat, and when it did rain hailstorms sometimes wiped out in ten minutes the most promising crop; tornadoes destroyed towns in less than ten minutes; grasshoppers created their own peculiar cloud and ate crops as farmers watched; and the dread hoof-and-mouth disease wiped out herds of cattle in a single season.

[26] *Abilene Reporter,* May 7, 1922.

In the good years, such as the early 1920s, cotton farmers and cattlemen discovered that their bumper crops only glutted the markets and caused prices to fall. Legett had developed his series of lectures on "Work More but Spend Less" and "Fiscal Responsibilty" in response to that ominous postwar recession and, eventually, returned to his old prewar program of diversification. He correctly anticipated the revival of the business community following its adjustment to a peacetime economy, but he seemed more concerned than ever about the worsening condition among farmers and cattlemen. In his efforts to weave a silver lining, he reintroduced the Legett Plan and offered more tangible assistance to assure the program's success. He addressed a lengthy letter to the Chamber of Commerce in which he explained his plan in detail, and he mailed a copy to the local paper. The letter appeared in full in the June 20, 1922, edition of the *Abilene Reporter*:

Gentlemen:

Our citizenship during the year 1921 voluntarily pledged more than a half million dollars for Abilene enterprises, but not thirty cents for the development and growth of the surrounding country. The policy is a mistake in fact and wrong in principle.

If we had expended $100,000.00 of the $500,000.00 pledged in the effort to [assist] the 4000 farms in Taylor County, the results might have been more satisfactory.

There are two lines of endeavor which have great potentialities for West Texas. I have in mind the dairy industry and poultry raising. . . .

It is my purpose however to direct your attention to the poultry business. . . . There is but one stubborn hindrance to efforts in that direction. That difficulty has been overcome elsewhere and I believe it would be here by three simple methods. First, by raising the greater part of the maize. Second, contracting for the grain in the spring. Third, buying all mixed feeds in carload lots.

I am a great believer in the union of theory and practice and to that end I am going to outline a plan which in my judgment promises success.

I have on my place at Elmdale, by the side of the large lake, one of the best locations for a plant. . . . I will furnish a house for residence, all land needed, wood, water, and the use of approximately fifty acres of farm, without charge, and will give to the enterprise a personal supervision, without charge, if you will furnish the small amount of cash needed to launch the enterprise. . . . A total of about $3,000.00. . . .

I think an opportunity is here furnished for a practical test of what could be done with a poultry farm in West Texas.

Of course you understand this is merely suggestive.

Very respectfully,

K. K. Legett

Editor Frank Grimes commented upon Legett's offer on July 7: "It is a proposition worth considering. . . . In years when the main revenue crop, cotton, fails, the country would have an industry to fall back on." [27] As diversification again gained support, Grimes proposed the immediate organization of a Livestock Breeders Association. Legett suggested that the association could become the nucleus of a general countywide plan to improve the quality of poultry, cattle, and hogs. Grimes later quoted from a *Dallas News* editorial that "a diversity of crops, rather than complete abandonment of cotton, is what the South needs." [28]

Before the end of the year, Grimes reported "a great revival of interest in poultry raising, and this new interest is centered about the better breeds of chickens." He praised the West Texas Poultry Breeders' Association, located in Abilene, for its plans to sponsor a midwinter poultry show for January 24 to 27. With obvious pride Grimes quoted a statement from the *Fort Worth Record* that West Texans were producing some of the finest barnyard birds in the country and an editorial from the *Eastland Daily Oil Belt News* that there was a "well-defined movement in West Texas toward raising pure bred fowls." [29] At the poultry show in late January, Walter Burton, a member of the executive board of the American Poultry Association, declared that the Abilene country was "the best I have seen for raising chickens."

A three-car train exhibit, nicknamed "The Cow, Sow and Hen Special," provided more proof that the Legett Plan was popular once again in West Texas. The Santa Fe Railway donated the train and George P. Grout of Texas A&M stocked the cars with the finest breeds of cows, hogs, and chickens. Grout encouraged West Texans

[27] Ibid., July 7, 1922.
[28] Ibid., December 20, 1922.
[29] Ibid., January 17, 1923.

to replace their scrub animals with the better grades. Later that summer, the Western Produce Company with headquarters in Abilene and branch offices in Sweetwater, Stamford, Lubbock, Haskell, Munday, Snyder, Goree, and Spur boasted that it had shipped carloads of eggs and poultry to such distant points as New York City, Havana, Mexico City, and San Francisco.[30]

In March, 1924, an article in the local paper described how Elmdale farmer Frank Antilley had succeeded as a diversified farmer:

About six miles east and a half mile south of Abilene is located one of West Texas' successful farmers. Here on this 430 acre place diversification is practiced. Good brood mares, Jersey cattle, grain and cotton crops, Bronze turkeys, and last but not least, standard bred poultry. The owner, Frank Antilley, although still a young man, has made a marked success of his undertaking.

Water is piped to all parts of the place, and in the house; a lighting plant furnishes light for the residence, the barns, and also furnishes power for the mammoth incubator. In one of the big stalls at the barn we find a registered Percheron stallion that has carried off highest honors at the Southern Exposition at Ft. Worth and a mammoth Kentucky Jack that has carried off the blue ribbon at several exhibitions. In the pasture we find a small herd of Jerseys, . . . a flock of about 75 Bronze turkeys, 500 white Wyandottes, and 250 white Leghorns.[31]

Judge Legett had at last found one West Texas farmer, his own neighbor in Elmdale, who proved that the Legett Plan could succeed in the Abilene country.

As late as the mid-twenties, nevertheless, West Texans still experimented with ways one might earn a livelihood in a semiarid region. As immigrants moved into the area in increasing numbers, they demonstrated their confidence that a proper balance of farming, ranching, and industry would bring prosperity. Simple survival was no longer the issue. West Texas was not a frontier land and West Texans appreciated any recognition of that fact by others. The *Chicago Herald Examiner* noticed the change in a unique way on November 15, 1925, when it proclaimed in a front-page headline:

[30] Ibid., July 22, 1923.
[31] Ibid., March 9, 1924.

WILD WEST GONE: CAN'T EVEN FLIRT

A half-column article explained that it was against the law to flirt in a public place in the town of Abilene, Texas. Abilenians' reaction to the news item varied sharply. Some were happy that their hometown had outgrown its image as a wild and woolly frontier cowtown, while others stated somewhat piously that no town deserved special recognition for protecting its womenfolk from foul-minded males. Many who responded with letters to the editor ignored the main issue and protested instead that the *Chicago Herald Examiner* called Abilene a town rather than a city.

Judge Legett did not publicly express his sentiments, but he probably shared all three points of view. The "flirtation ordinance," as it came to be known, resulted from the city commission's determination to stamp out "petting parties." National attention focused on that section of the ordinance which stated: "It shall be unlawful for any male person in the city of Abilene to stare at or make "goo-goo" eyes at any female person traveling along any of the sidewalks, streets, or public ways of the city." [32] It was, in a sense, the city commission's unsubtle testimonial to the lingering myth that their city might still be a saloon town—an alcoholic oasis for thirsty cowboys. The myth was an affront to their tireless efforts to bring "culture and refinement to an area far removed from its frontier era" and to cast the workings of the devil from their midst.

A sermon in early October, 1921, entitled "Too Much Jazz but Not Enough Jesus" undoubtedly expressed the attitude of most Abilenians toward the roaring twenties. Those few who missed the Sunday or Wednesday night sermons looked to their daily paper for lengthy summaries. The summaries were no less graphic than the sermons from the pulpit. The headline for the review on April 6, 1919, for example, left little room for ambiguity: "Dr. Scarborough Preached about Hell on Sunday Night." [33]

There were other proofs that the frontier days had passed. When Legett first rode into Buffalo Gap in 1879, the danger of death at the hands of a band of roving Indians was remote but nevertheless possible. In 1922, on the other hand, Legett purchased a ticket at Simmons

[32] Ibid., October 25, 1925.
[33] Ibid., April 6, 1919.

College to hear a series of lectures by Chief Red Feather, a Cherokee Indian. Similarly, when Legett first traveled to Buffalo Gap, he mentioned that sun-bleached carcasses of tens of thousands of buffalo dotted the short-grass prairie like whitecaps on a stormy sea, and yet only four decades later, when O. A. Hale sought to purchase two buffalo for the Abilene zoo, he needed assistance from Congressman Thomas L. Blanton to locate two such animals for sale at Yellowstone National Park.

Another measurement of the changing scene attracted editor Grimes's attention in the early twenties when he discovered that Abilene's young folk showed no interest in the film version of Emerson Hough's "North of 36" until they were told that the cattle trail that inspired the story passed only a few hundred yards west of Abilene's city limits. While Legett's generation viewed with alarm such ignorance of local history, the younger generation abandoned classrooms or churches whenever they heard airplanes (called "thunderbirds" by the youths) pass overhead. When word spread through the schools that the giant United States Navy dirigible *Shenandoah* approached from the east, Abilene schoolteachers recognized the inevitable and dismissed classes. As the huge airship came into view, every whistle and bell in town sounded the alarm. A local reporter caught the mood of the crowd as he described the "awe-inspiring and mighty cruiser's" flight through the air "like a thing possessed." [34]

Abilenians of all ages displayed a more sophisticated demeanor, however, when Simmons College brought to Abilene in recital the famed Polish pianist, Jan Paderewski. The local rush to purchase tickets amazed the college sponsors and forced them to move the concert from the college auditorium to the sanctuary of the First Baptist Church. In spite of the church's larger seating capacity, the sponsors had to return several hundred orders for tickets. On the night of the recital every pew was filled an hour before the musician arrived. Sponsors added chairs in the choir loft, and, when they too were filled, people stood wherever space allowed. When standing space was taken, the sponsors placed 250 chairs in the Sunday-school rooms where one could hear but not see the performer.

For two hours, reported Mrs. Leltie Faucett, Paderewski held his

[34] Ibid., October 10, 1924. Abilenians felt a special loss, therefore, when the *Shenandoah* went down in a storm over Ohio a few months later and disintegrated.

audience in the rarest moments of silence as the throng heard selections from Chopin, Mozart, Haydn, Brahms, and Bach. Mrs. Faucett conceded that "perhaps there has never been anything musical just so perfect and universally satisfying in the history of our community." [35] It was entirely typical of Legett and other civic leaders that they used the crowded occasion to direct attention to the city's "shameful need for a larger auditorium."

A second event only a few weeks later underscored Abilene's "shameful need." When Simmons history professor Rupert N. Richardson introduced a celebrated journalist and early-day muckraker, Ida M. Tarbell, to another huge audience he apologized for the lack of seating space for those who crowded the aisles and doorways. Tarbell delighted her audience, however, with her prepared lecture upon "Women's Contribution to a Finer Public Life" and her extemporaneous comment that the nation's female members could not betray public trust any more spectacularly than the male members currently involved in the Teapot Dome oil scandal.

No Abilenian, and least of all K. K. Legett, doubted that Abilene sailed in the mainstream of national development. As in his younger days, Legett allowed no improvement to go unnoticed. Similarly, every step forward received enthusiastic public support. An announcement by the West Texas Utilities Company on May 18, 1924, is typical of the enthusiasm that never seemed to diminish.

At 8:30 o'clock on the evening of Tuesday, May 20, Mayor C. E. Coombes, standing in the bandstand at Federal Lawn, will raise his hand in a signal. City Commissioner W. D. Mayfield will throw a giant electric switch. Throughout the city long avenues of light will burst into life, flooding with a brilliant radiance more than seven miles of paved streets and boulevards. And Abilene will have reached another never-to-be-forgotten milestone in her triumphal journey to civic progress.

Five thousand West Texans responded to the announcement, gathered downtown for the ceremony, and later joined the auto caravan through the brightly lighted streets of the little West Texas city.

With its own symphony orchestra (conducted by "that temperamental genius, Mr. John Victor"), a nine-hole golf course, a country

---

[35] *Abilene Reporter*, February 24, 1924.

club valued at $50,000, and internationally acclaimed artists perform-
ing on local stages, Abilenians such as K. K. Legett had no tolerance
whatever for those ignoramuses who still believed that their city was
a godless little frontier saloon town. They admitted their hometown's
deficiencies only by their demands for instant corrections. Local enthusiasm and vigorous boosterism were not unique qualities in any
frontier town, but Abilenians always knew they had something special
even before the sponsors of the South Texas State Fair at Houston admitted it in a public statement. In the fall of 1922, the members of
the Abilene Chamber of Commerce forwarded their reservation fee
for a booth at the fair. A few days later, their application was denied
on the grounds that Abilene's booth had won first prize so consistently through the years that other towns refused to participate in the contest. With a great display of condescending sportsmanship, the Abilene Chamber of Commerce agreed to stay out of the race.[36]

[36] Ibid., October 31, 1922.

*A beautiful, beautiful, morning.*

# CHAPTER FOURTEEN

# Old Settlers' Barbecue and General Get-Together

WHEN Howard Barrett, an Abilene newspaperman, wondered why so many West Texas men failed to establish successful businesses, he solicited an explanation from Judge K. K. Legett, who, according to Barrett, in all West Texas was the most likely to know. Legett had served from 1898 to 1920 as referee in bankruptcy for the Abilene division of the federal district court; the division included twenty-six Central and West Texas counties. Upon his retirement, federal officials in Dallas noted that Legett's tenure exceeded that of any other referee in bankruptcy in the nation.[1]

Barrett conducted his interview in Legett's fourth-floor office in the Citizens National Bank Building. The reporter's question was simple: "What makes men go broke?" Legett's answer was far more complex. For more than two hours Legett enumerated and explained eighteen reasons for West Texas business failures. His list included such basic causes as a lack of sufficient capital, which Legett believed constituted the most common cause for business failure. Others included poor location of a business, inaccurate bookkeeping, inability to determine the proper quantity or quality of merchandise, and excessive buying and selling on credit.

Legett was unable to conceal his contempt for businessmen who failed because they could not stay "in communion with the public," or because they were lazy, or because their personal appearance was offensive. Worst of all were those who were pessimistic or fainthearted, i.e., those who were too easily discouraged. "In many stores," said Legett, "you see the proprietor leaning back in a chair smoking his

---

[1] *Dallas Morning News*, June 6, 1926.

cigar. There is no evidence that the floor has been swept in a month."
He had observed other proprietors, he claimed, who "didn't appear to
have shaved or changed their linen in a month." Legett described another failure who "hadn't the energy to rise but sat glued to his chair
until the would-be customer almost begged to know if he had a certain article on hand." Legett seemed most disturbed by the gambling
tendency of businessmen to "buck the market" or play the future markets on margin. Legett claimed that the practice was more common—
even on Pine Street—than the general public would believe and he
worried that "the thing could become disastrous." [2]

He did not spend his later years, however, concentrating upon the
negative aspects of life. General economic growth and prosperity in
West Texas pleased Legett, and hardly a day passed that he was not
reminded of the area's constant and steady progress. In 1920, for example, he assisted three old friends, Henry James, Henry Sayles, Jr.,
and Ed S. Hughes with their sale for $60,000 of three empty lots on
Cypress Street. Only five decades earlier buffalo had grazed the same
land. Legett and other local leaders assumed that Abilene's population
had grown equally fast. They were dumbfounded when the national
Bureau of the Census announced that Abilene's official population in
1920 totaled only 10,274. Surprise turned to outrage and city officials
accused the Bureau of "a glaring inaccuracy." When tempers cooled,
Legett observed that Abilenians must be "the *liveliest* 10,000 citizens
in Texas." He later admitted that the Bureau's report supported his
frequent observation that Abilene had never been a boom town; its
growth had always been steady and expansive. Nevertheless, by the
middle of the decade Abilenians had forgotten their earlier disappointment and predicted that Abilene's 1930 population would number 50,000. Always optimistic, Abilenians sometimes failed to distinguish between their goals and their achievements.

Soon after the disappointment of the 1920 census, the Abilene
Chamber of Commerce decided that the city should adopt a slogan or
motto that would describe its spirit and offered prizes for the best suggestions. The Chamber of Commerce office received hundreds of responses, and on March 24, 1921, a list of all entries appeared in the
*Abilene Reporter*. The contest had provided an ideal opportunity for

[2] *Western Weekly*, January 18, 1925.

local citizens to express the image their town should strive to portray. Legett pencil-marked several entries that, presumably, represented his first choices: "Count on me," "work and win," "boost and build," and "let's go!"

In 1923 Frank Grimes conducted a poll to determine which books had given Abilene readers the most pleasure and reported that Kipling's *Kim*, Stevenson's *Treasure Island*, and the Book of Job headed the list.[3] Legett clipped and filed the list and apparently intended to order the books that were not in his private collection. He clipped items from other newspapers when those articles placed Abilene in a favorable light; hence, he cut an article by Dabney White from the July 19, 1921, issue of the *Dallas News* and marked with a pencil the following statements: "I like this Abilene country. These men have no 'whipped dog' expressions"; "The country is inspiring for it shows how much can be done with so few natural advantages."

In 1923 however Legett's forward-looking attitude changed, and for the remainder of his life he seemed to think only of the past. In February of 1923, Mrs. Legett fell ill. In spite of constant treatment by a team of Abilene physicians, her condition rapidly deteriorated. When the doctors informed Legett that they suspected cancer, Mrs. Legett agreed to enter the Mayo Clinic for further tests. Consequently, on March 6 she checked into Kahler Hospital in Rochester, Minnesota, where for ten days she underwent a series of diagnostic tests directed by Dr. George B. Warne and Dr. William James Mayo. Their examinations confirmed the diagnoses of the Abilene doctors: Lora Bryant Legett was suffering from a terminal cancer.[4] The Legetts returned immediately to Abilene. A few weeks later, at seven o'clock on Wednesday evening, April 11, Mrs. Legett died. Funeral services were conducted the following day at the First Baptist Church.[5]

For the first time in his life K. K. Legett seemed unable to look to the future. For more than thirty-seven years he had depended heavily upon his wife for approval and encouragement in virtually every undertaking. Whether he delivered a lecture before a scholarly assembly or mowed his lawn, Mrs. Legett praised him. He sensed at once

[3] *Abilene Reporter*, June 5, 1923.
[4] Miscellaneous papers, Legett Family Records, nos. 514, 515, 516.
[5] *Abilene Reporter*, April 12, 1923.

the jarring trauma that her absence brought and recorded his silent grief in a small, black leatherbound notebook:

June 10th 1923—The first [wedding] anniversary after Lora's death. I was home, up on the front porch, when the sun rose. It . . . had rained a few hours before. The trees were dripping water. I never witnessed a more beautiful sight. The front yard looked as if set in a million diamonds. A *beautiful, beautiful,* morning.

Abilene, 4-12-24—Yesterday 1 year ago she left us and was buried 1 year ago at this hour, 4:30 p.m. . . . The year does not seem to have lessened my loneliness or my sorrow. . . . How long oh my God will it last. . . .

Abilene, June 11th 1924—Yesterday, 38 years ago, we were married. Today fourteen months ago she left. . . . The fourteen months have not relieved the sting of my bereavement. . . .

Abilene, June 10th 1925—Thirty-nine years ago today I led her to the altar. What memories spring into action of this day! The beautiful, attractive, lovely bride. We walked together 36 years, 10 months and one day.

Their life together since the earliest days of the West Texas frontier were, generally, not unlike those of other young couples who sought their fortunes in the West; nevertheless, their relationship developed unique qualities. From the earliest days of their marriage, Lora shared Legett's interest in land speculation. Buying and selling land fascinated her. During the years when the children were young, it was Lora who suggested that they postpone home improvements or enlargements so that they might purchase more land. In real estate and in other business matters Lora proved to be an unusually competent partner.

Mrs. Legett's death further reduced the number of Abilene's pioneer citizens. Since Judge Henry Sayles' death in 1916, every month seemed to bring its mournful toll for those who first settled in the rugged country.[6] In May, 1917, Legett's old law partner, Samuel P. Hardwicke, died. Hardwicke had come to West Texas from Chatham, Virginia, via West Virginia, Kansas, and East Texas, and had finally settled in Taylor County, Texas, in 1882. Two months later James H. Parramore, known to West Texans as the "grand old cattleman," died at his home at Seventh and Orange streets. A native of Georgia, Par-

---

[6] At Judge Sayles's funeral Legett eulogized his "diligent application, indefatigable labor and fearlessness" (*Abilene Reporter,* June 22, 1916).

ramore moved westward via Mississippi and East Texas and arrived in Runnels County in 1879 just a few weeks ahead of the Texas and Pacific railway construction crew.

John Wesley Wooten, a native of Tennessee and at ninety-three the oldest of Abilene's pioneers, died in March, 1919. He was among the first to settle in Buffalo Gap during the middle 1870s. In May, 1921, Taylor County's long-time sheriff—and Legett's favorite fishing partner—J. V. Cunningham died. Legett's eulogy at Cunningham's funeral revealed some of the criteria by which Legett judged a man's worth in a pioneer era:

I have seen him strive to lift up the downcast and the outcast. And I have known him to restrain the rich and powerful.

I have seen him head the posse that ridded the country of bandits and outlaws. . . .

I have seen him in a distant city in a distant state, surrounded by all the forces of evil, put them to flight and rise like a conquering hero.[7]

The death of J. H. Kershaw in 1923 also extended the melancholy toll. A native of England, Kershaw had established the town's first meat market in a tent along the south side of the Texas and Pacific Railway tracks.

Each death drew the surviving pioneer generation into a stronger bond of kinship. Inevitably, someone suggested that Taylor County should stage an "Old Settlers' Barbeque and General Get-Together" at Buffalo Gap. The idea won the support of all Abilenians. They agreed to hold the reunion on Saturday, July 2, 1921. A few hundred Gappers rushed into action to clean up the "Old capital of Taylor County." Editor Grimes rewarded their labor with an observation that Buffalo Gap was the most beautiful town in all West Texas. He admired especially the hundreds of live oaks, "their mighty limbs casting a dense shade over the streets."[8]

Every Saturday morning through May and June, Buffalo Gap citizens removed unsightly weeds and bushes (but with great care cultivated the wild flowers that grew profusely under the oaks), whitewashed tree trunks, cleared campsites, marked off a baseball diamond,

[7] *Abilene Reporter*, June 10, 1921.
[8] Ibid., May 8, 1922.

and erected a speakers' platform. On July 1—the eve of the reunion —they completed their tasks. The following day, thousands of West Texans of all ages journeyed to the shady village in the hills where Legett had made his first West Texas home. The day-long program commenced at 9:30 A.M. when those who arrived early sang a half-dozen hymns in honor of "those who lie buried in this great section of West Texas." As the day progressed, Legett, J. M. Wagstaff, Fred Cockrell, and John Bryan made major speeches under the general title "Buffalo Gap Forty Years Ago." The celebration continued throughout the day and into the night.

At a business meeting that followed the barbecue dinner, the crowd voted to establish a permanent Old Settlers' Association that would sponsor an annual Old Settlers' Reunion at Buffalo Gap.[9] For the remainder of his life Legett attended the reunions, sat under the great oaks, and reminisced with other old-timers about the days when the summers were hotter, the winters colder, the springs wetter, and the falls drier.

Opportunities to reminisce about the past also arose in conjunction with the annual regional fairs. Abilenians had sponsored a regional fair almost every year since 1884. They housed the first event in the small two-story building west of Abilene State Bank. In 1885 the county courthouse and courtyard served as a temporary fair ground. During the early nineties, the west banks of Lytle Lake provided a picturesque but inconvenient site for the occasion. Eventually, city officials selected a permanent site on South Seventh Street and named the area Fair Park. Each year the fair directors selected a theme around which they produced the six-day event. When, in 1925, directors of the West Texas Chamber of Commerce learned that an average of 40,000 immigrants moved into West Texas each year, they announced that "America's last frontier—West Texas" would soon disappear. With that announcement Olivia Hobgood, dean of fine arts at Simsons University, decided to write "The Vanishing Frontier." Directors

---

[9] The following year a group of local citizens met at the Taylor County Courthouse and organized the West Texas Historical Association. At its organizational meeting on April 19, 1924, the association announced: "Never before has such interest and so much thought been given to the history of West Texas, and never before has there been such a crying need and demand for facts about the history of this section of Texas" (*Abilene Reporter*, April 16–20, 1924, passim).

of the annual West Texas Fair asked Hobgood to present the historical pageant at the 1925 Fair in September. "The Vanishing Frontier"
required the cooperation of more than two thousand amateur actors
and musicians. The pageant divided the history of West Texas into
eight episodes, each of which required elaborate costumes and stage
settings:

*Episode One*: The arrival of Spanish conquistadores to the land of
the Comanches.

*Episode Two*: The appearance of Philip Nolan and other Anglo-
Americans as they blazed new trails into West Texas.

*Episode Three*: A day in the life of the soldiers at Camp Cooper,
Throckmorton County, in 1864.

*Episode Four*: The Indian massacre at Jacksboro as the Red Man
made his final effort to resist Anglo settlers in West Texas.

*Episode Five*: Chief Lone Wolf's visit to Washington, D.C.,
where he pled for the release of his people, the Kiowas, from their
Huntsville prison.

*Episode Six*: Scenes of the cattle era in West Texas in the 1860s
and 1870s.

*Episode Seven*: The arrival of the homeseekers, with their covered wagons and white canvas tents.

*Episode Eight*: "Progress in West Texas." Hobgood used a simple
but impressive format to account for the successful occupation and development of West Texas. Young men and women, dressed as representative members of the pioneer generation, stepped upon the enormous stage as a narrator briefly related his frontier experience.[10]

Legett and other surviving members of the pioneer generation sat
in a section of the grandstand especially reserved for them and, with
five thousand fellow West Texans, watched the reenactment of their
own colorful history. In the concluding episode several hundred school
girls in red, white, and blue costumes formed a "living American
flag" at the rear of the stage. Costumed representatives of "West Texas institutions" stepped upon the huge platform and moved toward
its center: Gilbert Sandefer represented "The Spirit of West Texas,"

10 *Abilene Reporter*, September 8, 20, 22, 1925, passim.

Gypsy Ted Sullivan Wylie represented "Columbia," Roxie Grove represented "Peace," and one by one they were followed by '"Christianity," "Home," "Education," and "Commerce." Then, in appropriate 1880s costumes, representatives of the "Makers of West Texas" moved across the stage: C. W. Merchant, K. K. Legett, D. D. Parramore, J. M. Radford, Will Minter, and a score of other local pioneers. As they stood at the center of the stage, the school girls at the rear sang the finale, "America." The deeply moved audience roared its appreciation for the pageant and for those who sat in the reserved section.

The 1925 West Texas Fair provided other opportunities for Legett and his contemporaries to look into their past. Legett had revived the West Texas Fair in 1914 "to promote regional pride and intercommunity interests." In 1925 the fair still served its primary function. There was a new merchants' exhibition building, a new automobile building, and a new first-aid station. Many exhibits were designed to rekindle memories of earlier years. A printed placard explained, for example, that a wooden churn had been purchased at the Ed S. Hughes hardware store on South First Street in 1882. Legett and every other pioneer knew that the "store" was a white canvas tent, and "South First Street" was in 1882 only a cow trail.

Displays of agricultural products—from wheat, oats, and rye to cucumbers, tomatoes, and watermelons—revealed the continued confidence in diversified farming. An Elmdale neighbor, Eleanor Rouff, won a first-place ribbon in 1925 for the best entry of tomatoes. Another Legett acquaintance, J. M. Wilson of Clyde, won blue ribbons for his peaches and watermelons. J. T. Blanton, another Elmdale neighbor, won first and second prizes with his baled cotton. In the horse and mule show, Elmdale farmer Frank Antilley won blue ribbons for the best draft stallion, the best draft mare, the best yearling mule, and the best yearling horse. Area farmers had entered more than 750 domestic fowl in the poultry show. Barred Rocks, white Leghorns, and Rhode Island Reds outnumbered all other breeds, but W. L. Frank's thirty-five Kiwis, a rare snow-white chicken, won top prize in the 1925 contest.[11]

[11] Ibid., Sepetmber 27, 1925. Historian Rupert N. Richardson stated in a letter to the author on September 28, 1973: "The 'Two Cows, Three Sows, and 200 Chickens' slogan continued to be very popular in the 1920's and was supposed to

Usually Legett walked alone down the aisles of the exhibition buildings so that he might set his own leisurely pace, but in 1925 he had as his guest B. N. Aycock, a Midland, Texas, cattleman. At Legett's urging, Aycock had agreed to come to the fair and serve as judge of the Herefords and shorthorns. The two pioneer West Texans had come to know one another in 1920 when, on July 6, Kade Legett had married Aycock's daughter, Annie Maude. Each day Legett and Aycock rode to the fairgrounds, and at the end of the week Legett noted with considerable satisfaction that Aycock's selections of the best beef cattle were well received, both by the exhibitors and the spectators.[12]

Editor Richard H. McCarty of the *Albany News* described the fair as "a West Texas institution—it fits into the West and it breathes the spirit of the West"; he described Hobgood's historical pageant as "an exhibition of early day history in West Texas [where] men with big ideas had day dreams and with industry and guts and brains made things happen."[13] Legett clipped the editorial and added it to his file.

Legett continued to be concerned about all phases of West Texas development despite his frequent episodes of depression following Mrs. Legett's death. His family and friends worked diligently to lift his spirits and occasionally they succeeded. He insisted upon living alone at his home but refused to allow anyone to assist him in mowing the huge lawn—a chore he had performed from the day he moved into the mansion. A succession of housekeepers tried but failed to perform their duties to his satisfaction. He dined frequently with his children at their homes, and often they prepared the meals and joined him at the mansion. Every national holiday and every family birthday provided other opportunities to visit "Judge." On his own birthdays his daughters arranged surprise stag parties and invited many of his close friends. A local news item described his sixty-seventh birthday celebration: "Judge Legett went for a short ride with his daughter, Mrs. Percy Jones, and upon his return home he entered to find eighteen of his friends assembled. Soon the guests were gath-

---

save agriculture and give it new life. The credo continued on through the Depression, but during the last thirty years specialization has been the policy of farmers. I should say that on the majority of farms in the Big Country there is nary a sow, a milk cow, or a hen."

12 *Abilene Reporter*, September 27, 1925.

13 Ibid.

ered around the dinner table, where a very bounteous turkey dinner was served in four courses." [14]

Early in 1926 Legett's old friends died at an alarming rate. On March 9 Colonel C. W. Merchant, who was the major force behind the decision by Texas and Pacific Railway officials to establish the town of Abilene and who, as a consequence, was looked upon as "the father of Abilene," died at the age of eighty-nine. A month later, on April 11, another old friend, Colonel Morgan Jones, who had come to West Texas from Wales and had built more railroad lines than any other individual in the state, died at the home of Legett's daughter and son-in-law, Percy and Ruth Legett Jones. Before the month ended, J. B. Clack died at his farm near Hylton. With his brother, M. M., Clack had moved into Taylor County in 1873, hunted buffalo, and engaged in several clashes with bands of Comanches before they moved into the area.

Legett mourned his losses but seemed doggedly determined to remain active and interested in Abilene's welfare. In early March, 1926, he joined friends of Simmons University and helped to design a campus beautification program. The group planted fifty pecan trees along the south side of the campus and numerous cedars and shrubs around the library building and the dormitories. In April he congratulated the city commission when it voted to build the long-awaited municipal auditorium at Fair Park. At approximately the same time he encouraged President J. D. Sandefer to begin a campaign to raise $400,000 for a new administration building at Simmons University. When in May he learned that the Methodist Men of Abilene sought a convenient place to hold their annual picnic, Legett, a lifelong Baptist, hosted the Methodist group on June 2 at his home.

The following day, June 3, Legett attended Simmons University commencement exercises at the First Baptist Church and watched President Sandefer award the university's first master of arts degree to Mrs. P. E. Shotwell.

---

[14] Ibid., November 9, 1924. At a similar celebration in 1925, the following friends attended: H. A. Tillett, J. M. Wagstaff, Dr. J. C. Sandefer, C. C. Compere, R. W. Haynie, Henry James, Mack L. Wyatt, D. D. Parramore, Lee Signor, Sam Young, T. P. Davidson, Dr. L. W. Hollis, H. O. Wooten, W. J. Behrens, J. M. Radford, John Bowyer, R. L. Over, Morgan Jones, W. E. Kauffman, George L. Paxton, W. J. Bryan, Bernard Bryan, Dr. L. J. Pickard, Kade Legett, and Percy Jones (*Abilene Reporter*, November 8, 1925).

Judge Legett's children planned another buffet dinner at the mansion for the following evening to honor his son Kade, his daughter-in-law Annie Maude, and his older daughter Julia Legett Pickard, all of whom celebrated their birthday on June 4. Heavy rains and strong winds forced a postponement until Saturday. On the evening of June 5, consequently, Kade, Julia, and Ruth and their families arrived. They were soon followed by Lora Legett's sister, Mrs. Sam Young, and Mr. Young, and Lora's brother, John Bryan, and his family.

As the family gathered about the dinner table, Julia and Ruth were pleased to notice that Legett's spirits were high; he had seemed particularly depressed earlier in the day. During the course of the meal Judge commented upon the recent graduation exercises at Simmons, expressed pleasure that Abilene would soon build a municipal auditorium worthy of the city, and commented humorously about the Texas guberatorial race between Governor Miriam ("Ma") Ferguson and Attorney General Dan Moody. As the laughter around the table subsided, Legett's dessert spoon fell with a clatter to his plate. "What's the matter with Judge?" someone asked. Dr. L. J. Pickard, Legett's son-in-law, rushed to assist him but Judge had died instantly and without a murmur.[15]

An eight-column headline in the *Abilene Reporter* announced Judge Legett's death to shocked readers the following morning:

JUDGE K. K. LEGETT DIES SUDDENLY
Cerebral Hemorrhage
Brings End to Pioneer
Lawyer and Capitalist

The Reverend Dr. Millard A. Jenkens, pastor of the First Baptist Church, and the Reverend Dr. J. C. Burkett, pastor of the South Side Baptist Church, conducted funeral services at the Legett home at 5:00 P.M. the following day. A lengthy article in the *Dallas Morning News* announced the "passing of a political power in West Texas."[16]

Local editor Frank Grimes eulogized "one of the makers of West Texas." He praised Legett's contributions in "the huge task of estab-

---

[15] Kade B. Legett to Dr. Lee Scarborough, June 24, 1926, Legett Family Records, file 4, paper 13.
[16] *Dallas Morning News,* June 6, 1926.

lishing law and order 'West of 98.' " Grimes noted that Legett had
come to West Texas "in the 80s—that formative period in the life of
West Texas when real men and women were required. Here he became a political power and an influential civic leader."[17] In his editorial Grimes summarized Legett's numerous personal achievements
and enumerated his varied contributions to the development of West
Texas.

Two decades earlier, on April 7, 1906, Legett had written to his
friend Andy Adams: "This is not a land of legend and story . . . and
yet its history is not sterile and barren." By 1926, K. K. Legett's rich
and productive life had proved the truth of his statement.

[17] *Abilene Reporter*, June 6, 1926; see also *West Texas Historical Association
Year Book* 2 (June, 1926): 91–93.

# Bibliography

## Interviews

Clack, Bobbie. Abilene, Texas, May 1, 1970.
Clack, Tommie. Abilene, Texas, May 1, 1970.
Duff, Katharyn. Abilene, Texas, May 1, 1970, and July 15, 1973.
Gay, Ruth Bradfield. Abilene, Texas, July 15, 1973.
Jones, Ruth Legett. Abilene, Texas, July 16, 1973.
Pickard, Julia Legett. Abilene, Texas, July 17, 1973.

## Newspapers

*Abilene Daily Reporter,* 1904, 1905, 1907–1909, 1911–1913, 1915, 1919,
    1921, 1922, 1924.
*Abilene Reporter,* 1882, 1883, 1888–1900, 1913–1918, 1920–1923.
*Abilene Reporter-News,* 1956, 1971.
*Albany* (Texas) *News,* 1917.
*Buffalo Gap News,* 1880.
*Chicago Herald Examiner,* 1925.
*Dallas Morning News,* 1926.
*Dallas News,* 1905.
*Denison Gazetteer,* 1884.
*Haskell* (Texas) *Free Press,* 1909.
*Mobile* (Alabama) *Register,* 1893, 1894.
*Palestine* (Texas) *Daily Visitor,* 1905.
*Stamford* (Texas) *Tribune,* 1908.
*St. Louis Republic,* 1897.
*Taylor County News,* 1885–1899.
*Weekly Reporter* (Bryan, Texas), 1908.
*Western Weekly* (Abilene, Texas), 1925.
*Wichita* (Kansas) *Eagle,* 1897.

## Unpublished Sources

Agricultural and Mechanical College of Texas. Minutes of the Board of Directors. Vol. 1 (May 31, 1886, through September 8, 1905).
———. Board Minutes of the A&M College. Vol. 2 (June 12, 1906, through December 15, 1911).
Bowyer, John. Personal reminiscence. Abilene, Texas, [n.d.], Abilene Reporter-News Building, Abilene, Texas.
Bryan, W. J. Papers. Hardin-Simmons University, Abilene, Texas.
Corley, D. B. Personal reminiscence. Abilene, Texas, July–August, 1891. Abilene Reporter-News Building, Abilene, Texas.
Crane, R. C. Papers. Hardin-Simmons University, Abilene, Texas.
Doscher, J. Henry, Jr., Abilene, Texas. Letter to author, March 8, 1973.
Duff, Katharyn. Papers. Abilene Reporter-News Building, Abilene, Texas.
———. Abilene, Texas. Letters to author, 1970–1976.
Hailey, C. L. Personal reminiscence. Abilene, Texas, December 13, 1971, and March 25, 1972. In possession of author.
———. Abilene, Texas. Letters to author, December 13, 1971, and March 25, 1972.
Harris, William A. Staunton, Virginia. Letter to W. C. Bryan, April 14, 1883. In possession of Mrs. Ruth Legett Jones, Abilene, Texas.
Jones, Mrs. Percy (Ruth Legett). Abilene, Texas. Letters to author, 1970–1976.
Kincaid, Naomi Hatton. "The *Abilene Reporter-News* and its Contribution to the Development of the Abilene Country." M.A. thesis, Hardin-Simmons University, 1945.
Landers, Emmett M. "A Short History of Taylor County." M.A. thesis, Simmons University, 1929.
Langford, Ernest. College Station, Texas. Letters to author, March 23, 1970, April 13, 1970, and April 16, 1970.
Legett, K. K. Letter Book. In possession of Mrs. Ruth Legett Jones, Abilene, Texas.
Legett, K. K. Papers. In possession of Mrs. Julia Legett Pickard, Abilene, Texas.
Legett Family Records. Includes genealogies, letters, and diaries collected through the years by Judge Legett's three children, Ruth Legett Jones, Julia Legett Pickard, and the late Kade Bryan Legett. Additional materials have been contributed by other Legett/Leggett branches of the family throughout the United States and Canada. These records are located at 508 First National Ely Building, Abilene, Texas, in the custody of Mrs. Ruth Legett Jones.

Legett (Leggett) Genealogical Papers:
  Annie H. Legett, Port Lavaca, Texas.
  Earl P. Legett, Orlando, Florida, and Newark, New Jersey.
  Kade B. Legett, in possession of Mrs. Percy Jones, Abilene, Texas.
  James Watson Leggett, Smithville, Ontario, Canada.
  Lander L. Leggett, Corpus Christi, Texas.
  W. R. Nettles, Tishomingo, Mississippi.
  Mrs. M. J. Skinner, Bebe, Texas.
Looney, R. H. Personal reminiscence. Abilene, Texas, October 20, 1909. Abilene Reporter-News Building, Abilene, Texas.
Menn, Alfred E. "The Abilene Story." Manuscript in possession of Katharyn Duff, Abilene, Texas, n.d.
Miller, R. W. Personal reminiscence. Abilene, Texas, October 26, 1913. Abilene Reporter-News Building, Abilene, Texas.
Ribble, William Carnace. "The Development and Marketing of Agricultural Products in the Abilene Trade Territory." M.A. thesis, University of Texas, 1931.
Richardson, Rupert N. Abilene, Texas. Letters to author, 1970–1976.
Robertson, Samuel Luther, Jr. "The Life Story of William John Bryan, 1859–1948." M.A. thesis, Hardin-Simmons University, 1973.
Schreiner, Charles III. Mountain Home, Texas. Letter to W. B. Trammell, March 29, 1971.
Simmons, Robert S. Papers. Hardin-Simmons University.
Simmons College. Minutes of Board of Trustees. Vol. 1 (1891–1902). Abilene, Texas.
Simmons University. Minutes of Board of Trustees. Vol. 1 (1914). Abilene, Texas.
———. Minutes of Board of Trustees. Vol. 2 (1916) and Addendum No. 1: Resolution of Appreciation. Abilene, Texas.
Skiles, Elwin L. Abilene, Texas. Letter to Mrs. Percy Jones, September 4, 1970. In possession of author.
Slaughter, William. Personal reminiscence. Abilene, Texas, March 28, 1905. Abilene Reporter-News Building, Abilene, Texas.
Stephenson, John L. Abilene, Texas, April 1, 1908. Abilene Reporter-News Building, Abilene, Texas.
Stewart, Irene. "James A. Lowery and the *Taylor County News*." M.A. thesis, Hardin-Simmons University, 1951.
Taylor County, Texas, Records. Taylor County Courthouse, Abilene, Texas.
United States District Court Records: Bankruptcy Dockets. Federal Archives and Records Center, General Services Administration, Fort Worth, Texas.

Wiese, Vincent L. Fort Worth, Texas. Letter to author, May 5, 1973.
Wright, Sam P. Waco, Texas. Letter to W. C. Bryan, February 3, 1882. In possession of Mrs. Percy Jones.


*Published Sources*

Abilene, City of. *Street Directory.* Abilene: Fish Publishing Company, 1927.
Agricultural and Mechanical College of Texas. *Biennial Report of the Board of Directors of the Agricultural and Mechanical College of Texas, 1901–1912.* Austin: Von Boeckmann, Schutze, & Co.
Baker, Ray Stannard. "The Great Southwest." *Century Magazine* 64 (May, 1902): 5–15.
Benedict, Murray R. *Farm Policies of the United States, 1790–1950: A Study of their Origins and Development.* New York: Octagon Books, 1966.
Bonine, Michael. "Buffalo Gap, the Living Ghost Town." *The Junior Historian* 20 (September, 1959): 1–5.
Buck, Solon. *The Granger Movement.* Cambridge: Harvard University Press, 1913.
Buffalo Gap College. *Buffalo Gap College,* 1900, 1901. Buffalo Gap, Texas.
Burges, Austin E. *A Local History of A&M College, 1876–1915.* [n.p., n.d.].
Carrow, Catherine Ikard. "Amusements for Men and Women in Texas in the 1880's." *West Texas Historical Association Year Book* 23 (October, 1947): 77–106.
Casey, Clifford B. *A Baker's Dozen: The Caseys of Tuscola, Taylor County, Texas.* Seagraves, Texas: Pioneer Book Publishers, Inc., 1974.
Churchill, Frances M. "Notes on the Native Grassland of West Central Texas Since 1854." *West Texas Historical Association Year Book* 31 (October, 1955): 54–64.
Clack, Mary Hampton. *Early Days in West Texas* [n.p.], The Texas Series, 1932.
Clack, Tommie. "Buffalo Gap College." *West Texas Historical Association Year Book* 35 (October, 1959): 132–141.
Cofer, David Brooks. *Early History of the Texas A and M College through Letters and Papers.* [n.p., n.d.].
———. *First Five Administrations of Texas A and M College, 1876–1890.* [n.p., n.d.].
Connor, Seymour V., ed. *Builders of the Southwest.* Lubbock: Texas Technological College Press, 1959.

———. *Texas: A History.* New York: Thomas Y. Crowell, 1971.

———. "Early Land Speculation in West Texas." *Southwestern Social Science Quarterly* 42 (March, 1962): 354–362.

Cosby, Hugh E., ed. *History of Abilene.* Abilene: Hugh E. Cosby Co., 1955.

Cox, James. *Historical and Biographical Record of the Cattle Industry and the Cattlemen of Texas and Adjacent Territory.* St. Louis: Woodward and Tiernan Printing Co., 1895.

Crane, R. C. "The Beginning of Hardin-Simmons University." *West Texas Historical Association Year Book* 16 (October, 1940): 61–74.

———. "Ghost Towns of West Texas." *West Texas Historical Association Year Book* 17 (October, 1941): 3–10.

———. "Some Aspects of the History of West and Northwest Texas Since 1845." *Southwest Historical Quarterly* 26 (July, 1922): 30–43.

———. "When West Texas Was in the Making." *West Texas Historical Association Year Book* 23 (October, 1947): 46–61.

Dale, Edward Everett. *The Range Cattle Industry.* 2d ed. Norman: University of Oklahoma Press, 1960.

Dethloff, Henry C. *A Centennial History of Texas A&M University, 1876–1976.* College Station: Texas A&M University Press, 1975.

Douthit, Ellis. "Some Experiences of a West Texas Lawyer." *West Texas Historical Association Year Book* 18 (October, 1942): 33–46.

Duff, Katharyn. *Abilene . . . On Catclaw Creek: A Profile of a West Texas Town.* Abilene: Reporter Publishing Co., 1969.

———. "Yesterday and Today." *The Abilenian* 2 (Fall, 1972): 16–17.

Dunn, Roy Sylvan. "Drought in West Texas, 1890–1894." *West Texas Historical Association Year Book* 37 (October, 1961): 121–136.

Dykstra, Robert R. *The Cattle Towns.* New York: Alfred A. Knopf, 1968.

Fite, Gilbert C. *The Farmers' Frontier, 1865–1900.* Histories of the American Frontier, edited by Ray Allen Billington. New York: Holt, Rinehart & Winston, 1966.

Frantz, Joe B. *The Driskill Hotel.* Austin: Encino Press, 1973.

Gard, Wayne. "The Fence-Cutters." *Southwestern Historical Quarterly* 51 (July, 1947): 1–15.

———. *The Great Buffalo Hunt.* Lincoln: University of Nebraska Press, 1968.

———. "The Impact of the Cattle Trails." *Southwestern Historical Quarterly* 71 (July, 1967): 1–6.

Gates, Paul W. "The Role of the Land Speculator in Western Development." *The Pennsylvania Magazine of History and Biography* 66 (July, 1942): 314–333.

Gould, Lewis L. "Progressives and Prohibitionists: Texas Democratic Politics, 1911–1921." *Southwestern Historical Quarterly* 75 (July, 1971): 5–18.

Grimes, Frank. "Pioneers Laid to Rest." *West Texas Historical Association Year Book* 2 (June, 1926): 91–93.

Haley, J. Evetts, and William Curry Holden. *The Flamboyant Judge, James D. Hamlin: A Biography*. Canyon, Texas: Palo Duro Press, 1972.

Hammond, C. M. "How the Railroads Peopled Texas." *Frontier Times* 10 (October, 1932): 378–381.

Havins, T. R. "Sheepmen-Cattlemen Antagonisms on the Texas Frontier." *West Texas Historical Association Year Book* 18 (October, 1942): 10–23.

Hazel, Sybal. "Prohibition Campaign of 1911." *West Texas Historical Association Year Book* 18 (October, 1942): 92–115.

Holden, William Curry. *Alkali Trails, or Social and Economic Movements of the Texas Frontier: 1846–1900*. Dallas: Southwest Press, 1930.

Holden, W. C. "The Development of Agriculture in West Texas." In *Readings in Texas History*, edited by Eugene C. Barker. Dallas: Southwest Press, 1929.

————. "Frontier Journalism in West Texas." *Southwestern Historical Quarterly* 32 (January, 1929): 206–221.

————. "Immigration and Settlement in West Texas." *West Texas Historical Association Year Book* 5 (June, 1929): 66–86.

————. "Law and Lawlessness on the Texas Frontier, 1875–1900." *Southwestern Historical Quarterly* 44 (October, 1940): 188–203.

————. "West Texas Droughts." *Southwestern Historical Quarterly* 32 (October, 1928): 103–123.

Holt, R. D. "The Introduction of Barbed Wire into Texas and the Fence Cutting War." *West Texas Historical Association Year Book* 6 (June, 1930): 65–79.

————. "School Land Rushes in West Texas." *West Texas Historical Association Yearbook* 10 (1934): 42–57.

Hoppe, Eleanor Sellers, and Dorothy Parramore Sellers. *The Parramore Sketches: Scenes and Stories of Early West Texas*. El Paso: Texas Western Press, 1975.

Hough, Emerson. *North of 36*. New York: McKinley, Stone & Mackenzie, 1923.

Jackson, Clyde L., and Grace Jackson. *Quanah Parker: Last Chief of the Comanches*. New York: Exposition Press, 1963.

Jordan, Philip D. *Frontier Law and Order: Ten Essays.* Lincoln: University of Nebraska Press, 1970.

Jordan, Terry G. "Pioneer Evaluation of Vegetation in Frontier Texas." *Southwestern Historical Quarterly* 76 (January, 1973): 233–254.

Kerr, Homer L. "Migration into Texas, 1860–1880." *Southwestern Historical Quarterly* 70 (October, 1966): 185–216.

Kincaid, Naomi. "The Founding of Abilene, the 'Future Great' of the Texas and Pacific Railway." *West Texas Historical Association Year Book* 22 (October, 1946): 15–26.

Knight, Oliver. *Fort Worth: Outpost on the Trinity.* Norman: University of Oklahoma Press, 1953.

————. "Toward an Understanding of the Western Town." *Western Historical Quarterly* 4 (January, 1973): 27–42.

Lang, A. S. "Financial History of the Public Lands in Texas." *Baylor University Bulletin* 25 (1932).

Langston, Rosalind. "The Life of Colonel R. T. Milner." *Southwestern Historical Quarterly* 45 (April, 1941): 407–451 and 46 (July, 1941): 24–71.

McConnell, Joseph Carroll. *The West Texas Frontier.* Vol. 2 of *A Descriptive History of Early Times in Western Texas.* Palo Pinto, Texas: Texas Legal Bank & Book Co., 1939.

McKay, S. S. "Economic Conditions in Texas in the 1870s." *West Texas Historical Association Year Book* 15 (October, 1939): 81–127.

Martin, Robert L. *The City Moves West: Economic and Industrial Growth in Central West Texas.* Austin: University of Texas Press, 1969.

Mason, Zane Allen. *Frontiersmen of the Faith: A History of Baptist Pioneer Work in Texas, 1865–1885.* San Antonio: Naylor Co., 1970.

Merchant, Lawrence. *The San Simon.* Carlsbad, New Mexico: Nichols Printing, 1975.

North, Douglas C. *The Economic Growth of the United States, 1790–1860.* New York: W. W. Norton & Co., 1966.

*Our Homes and Country Illustrated.* Abilene, Texas: Chambers & Anderson, n.d.

Ousley, Clarence. "History of the Agricultural and Mechanical College of Texas." *Bulletin of the Agricultural and Mechanical College of Texas* 4th ser. 6, no. 8 (December, 1935).

Payne, John. "David F. Houston's Presidency of Texas A. and M." *Southwestern Historical Quarterly* 58 (July, 1954): 22–35.

Perry, George Sessions. *The Story of Texas A and M.* New York: McGraw-Hill Book Co., 1951.

Pollock, Norman. *The Populist Response to Industrial America: Midwestern Populist Thought*. New York: W. W. Norton & Co., 1962.

Richardson, Rupert Norval. *The Comanche Barrier to South Plains Settlement*. Glendale, California: Arthur H. Clark Co., 1933.

———. *Famous Are Thy Halls: Hardin Simmons University as I Have Known It*. Abilene, Texas: Abilene Printing & Stationery Co., 1964.

———. *The Frontier of Northwest Texas, 1846–1876*. Glendale, California: Arthur H. Clark Co., 1963.

———. *Texas: The Lone Star State*. 1st ed. Englewood Cliffs, N.J.: Prentice-Hall, 1943; 2d ed. Englewood Cliffs, N.J.: Prentice-Hall, Inc., 1958.

———, and Carl Coke Rister. *The Greater Southwest*. Glendale, California: Arthur H. Clark Co., 1935.

Robbins, Roy M. *Our Landed Heritage: The Public Domain, 1776–1936*. Lincoln: University of Nebraska Press, 1962.

Rollins, T. S. *Taylor County: An Early History of Pioneer Settlers*. Taylor County, Texas: Taylor County Old Settlers Association, 1923.

Sandefer, Inez Woodward. *Jefferson Davis Sandefer: Christian Educator*. Nashville: Broadman Press, n.d.

Scruggs, Guy A. "Abilene Christian College." *West Texas Historical Association Year Book* 21 (October, 1945): 3–19.

Shannon, Fred A. *The Farmers' Last Frontier: Agriculture, 1860–1897*. Economic History of the United States, edited by Henry David, et al., vol. 5. New York: Holt, Rinehart & Winston, 1945.

Simmons College. *Bulletin Simmons College*, 1920. Abilene, Texas.

———. *Catalogue of Simmons College*, 1892–1915. Abilene, Texas.

Smith, Henry Nash. *Virgin Land: The American West as Symbol and Myth*. Cambridge: Harvard University Press, 1950.

Smith, Ralph. "The Farmers' Alliance in Texas, 1875–1900." *Southwestern Historical Quarterly* 48 (January, 1945): 347–369.

———. "The Grange Movement in Texas, 1873–1900." *Southwestern Historical Quarterly* 42 (April, 1939): 297–315.

Spence, Vernon Gladden. *Colonel Morgan Jones: Grand Old Man of Texas Railroading*. Norman: University of Oklahoma Press, 1971.

Spratt, John S. *The Road to Spindletop: Economic Change in Texas, 1875–1901*. Dallas: Southern Methodist University Press, 1955.

Stelter, Gilbert. "The City and Westward Expansion: A Western Case Study." *Western Historical Quarterly* 4 (April, 1973): 187–202.

Stevens, Walter B. *Through Texas: A Series of Interesting Letters*. St. Louis: St. Louis Globe-Democrat, 1892.

*Texas Almanac and State Industrial Guide for 1970–1971.* Galveston, A. H. Belo Corporation, 1969.

Wallace, Ernest. *Texas in Turmoil, 1849–1875.* Saga of Texas Series, edited by Seymour V. Connor, vol. 4. Austin: Steck-Vaughn Company, 1965.

Walsh, W. C. "Memories of a Land Commissioner." *Southwestern Historical Quarterly* 44 (April, 1941): 481–497.

Webb, Walter Prescott. *The Great Plains.* Dallas: Ginn & Company, 1931.

———, and H. Bailey Carroll, eds. *The Handbook of Texas.* 2 vols. Austin: Texas State Historical Association, 1952.

Williams, J. W. "Robson's Journey through West Texas in 1879." *West Texas Historical Association Year Book* 20 (October, 1944): 109–124.

Wootton, Ralph T. "The Panorama of Oscar Henry Cooper with Emphasis on His West Texas Career." *West Texas Historical Association Year Book* 35 (October, 1959): 142–155.

# Index